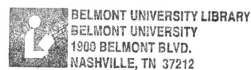

D0966849

CREATING THE SELF
IN THE CONTEMPORARY
AMERICAN THEATRE

CREATING THE SELF
IN THE CONTEMPORARY
AMERICAN THEATRE

Robert J. Andreach

Southern Illinois University Press

Carbondale and Edwardsville

Library of Congress Cataloging-in-Publication Data

Andreach, Robert J.
Creating the self in the contemporary American theatre / Robert J. Andreach.
        p.   cm.
Includes bibliographical references (p.   ) and index.
1. American drama—20th century—History and criticism.
2. Drama—Psychological aspects. 3. Self in literature. I. Title.
PS352.A53   1998
812' .5409353—dc21   97-36106
ISBN 0-8093-2178-5 (alk. paper)   CIP

The paper used in this publication meets the minimum requirements
of American Natinal Standard for Information Sciences—Permanence
of Paper for Printed Library Materials, ANSI Z39.48-1984. ∞

For my sons, Kevin and Jason,
and my daughter-in-law, Thelma

Contents

Preface
ix

1
Women's Theatre
1

2
Other Minority Theatres
31

3
Exemplary Selves in History
47

4
Exemplary Selves in Hell
82

5
Interactive Selves
102

6
Experimental Selves
131

Contents

7

Reconciling Selves

159

8

On the Eve of the Millennium

189

Conclusion:
Engaging the Spectator in the Creating

219

Notes

225

Index

235

Preface

In the mid-1980s, I was twice given the opportunity to review theatre for a New Jersey newspaper. Interested in contemporary theatre ever since my graduate-school days in English at New York University, when I discovered Off-Off-Broadway and the works of such European innovators as Samuel Beckett and Eugène Ionesco, Bertolt Brecht and Jean Genet, I welcomed each opportunity despite not having taught the subject. I always taught other courses, and twentieth-century drama in any English department of which I was a member was thought of as modern, not contemporary, which meant plays by Shaw, Ibsen, Chekhov, and other playwrights born in the nineteenth century. Although on the East and West coasts one could see plays by Maria Irene Fornes and Sam Shepard, for example, inside academe their names were known only to those who went to the theatre and only to avant-garde or experimental, as opposed to commercial, theatre.

As it turned out, not having taught the subject was an advantage. With the exception of O'Neill, I had not written on any American playwrights, and I had been able to maintain interest by never being far from New York City and other theatre centers. I was teaching at the University of Rhode Island, for instance, when the Trinity Repertory Company was establishing itself in Providence. By not having taught the subject, I did not seek confirmation for theories I entertained but took the assignments because I enjoyed going to the theatre.

Gradually I became aware of the contemporary American theatre as a distinct experience, the creation of which is the subject of this book.

The artists creating the experience are culturally more diverse than the artists of the first half of the twentieth century. I am not suggesting that the earlier period was culturally monolithic, but with the exception of Lillian Hellman, the principal American playwrights were white males. Karen Finley—a discussion of whose work opens this book—is a woman who performs, not acts in, her original theatre pieces, not plays, that attack the exclusive culture whose sole deity is "one male god." Now consider these names, so different from Arthur Miller, Clifford Odets, William Inge, Eugene O'Neill, Tennessee

Williams, and the other playwrights who reigned at mid-century: José Rivera and Spiderwoman, Suzan-Lori Parks and Philip Kan Gotanda. Or consider these names: The Ridiculous Theatrical Company, Split Britches, and El Teatro Campesino.

In 1950 they probably would not have been able to get their works staged. In the 1990s they are minority voices but so impacting on theatre that they are changing it. In making the journey from their old-world cultures to the new world of the "one male god," who is white and privileged, they have to decide what to take with them. Renewing their heritages, they make the new world multicultural.

Between Worlds, the title of an anthology of contemporary Asian-American plays, also could apply to plays by theatre artists within the dominant culture, men and women with names that, had women been mainstream then, would have fit right in with the reigning names of 1950: A. R. Gurney Jr. and Richard Nelson, Beth Henley and Tina Howe. Their works respond to the breakup of an old order, and their characters are voyagers, each of whom must decide what to leave behind in the old world and what to take to the new world, where one's experience is the minority voyager's experience. It is the creation of a new-world self. The creation should remind the reader of the American Dream, and much of the book has to do with the hope of self-realization in the new world. But I do not want to pursue the Dream until the second chapter, which gives a minority definition of the ideal, and the third chapter, which opens with a satire on the majority definition of it.

The second difference is that the forms in which artists create today are more diverse. I am not suggesting that the first half-century of American theatre was dramaturgically monolithic, but given the contemporary diversity in cultural content, a diversity of forms in which the content is actualized would seem inevitable. Monologues and performance, dance and movement, and recursive, rather than linear, action are obvious examples. Minority voices are on record rejecting Eurocentric drama.

Then, too, technology has a tremendous impact on theatre. Anna Deavere Smith's *Twilight: Los Angeles, 1992* utilizes video of the 1991 Rodney King beating and the 1992 rioting that followed the verdict in the trial of the police officers accused of the beating. A posted sign on the outside wall of the theatre space, one of many in the Joseph Papp Public Theater, alerted the audience for Rivera's *Marisol* to expect strobe lights and gun shots. The set of a Wooster Group deconstruction or that of a John Jesurun work usually contains television monitors. Performers of recent Richard Foreman works have worn body mikes.

For Jerzy Grotowski of the Polish Laboratory Theatre, theatre "cannot exist without the actor-spectator relationship of perceptual, direct, 'live' communion."[1] I want to add that theatre is a social experience. Spectators become aware of both perceiving and perceiving in a group. They become aware that their perception is affected by the interaction not only within the performance but also between the performance and the audience of which they are members.

Diversity of content and form interact to create multiple selves in theatre as in society, making theatre and society multicultural, each reflecting the other. Yet this book's approach to the theatre experience is not comprehensive in that it does not try to account for all contemporary American theatre art; not every artist who has earned recognition is represented. Neither is the approach chronological. Since this is not a history of the contemporary American stage, a discussion of an artist's work in one chapter does not preclude its reappearance in another chapter. Chapters 1 and 2 discuss theatre created by artists who identify themselves as members of minorities. But their creations are not restricted to the first two chapters. They are discussed throughout and especially in the closing chapters, for today's minority experiences may be the twenty-first century's majority experiences.

Nor does the approach dutifully address the relevant scholarship. Though the book is sprinkled with titles for topics that one might want to investigate, analytical studies of individual works rarely are cited and then only to remind the reader that scholars write about drama and theatre and that their critical positions in books, articles, and newspapers provoke thought. Only the work of one artist, Sam Shepard, receives multiple citations, and they are included only for the reader who might like to explore a body of critical judgments. At no point is criticism introduced for the sake of disputation. The book also avoids, until the penultimate chapter, the term "postmodern." Since the term is elusive, the reader might be tempted to try to fit individual works into a definition, should one be ventured at the outset. It is better to wait until we have looked at a variety of works. The preferred term, "contemporary," refers to theatre creations from the 1960s on.

In addition to teachers and students of theatre and drama, the book is written for general theatregoers, the audience without whom the creations could not take place. I teach at a school that draws students from all over the United States. Many of them would like to experience the contemporary theatre, providing someone gives them direction on what to expect. I like to think of the approach that follows as offering a direction.

The book's thesis is that the contemporary American theatre creates multiple selves in that they give voices to multicultural communities within the society, but they are fragmented and enclaved, exemplary and appropriated. Thus a countermovement is born, one that seeks through interaction to heal the divisions within selves and between and among them.

The created self is not simply a personal one. Each movement begins with the personal self, a self that expands almost immediately to theatrical and national selves. To attempt therefore to separate the selves would erect artificial barriers to the development being studied. Two examples must suffice for the moment. As Finley is reclaiming the female self from the dominant male culture, she is simultaneously creating the theatrical self denied a grant by the dominant male government. In Nelson's trilogy, which opens chapter 3, the creating self cannot curb its insatiable appetite until it is America.

The book does not stop the expanding self before it becomes theatrical and national. The argument, however, is not that the collective experience replaces the individual one. The argument is that the experiences—the creations—are interrelated.

The first two chapters examine plays and performance art created by women and by ethnic-racial minorities. Chapters 3 and 4 examine comparable works created within the dominant culture, works that reflect the breakup of an old order or old world. By the end of chapter 4, we will have reached the end of the descent through isolated selves and will be ready for the ascent to the healing process. Let us wait until we get there, though, before setting up the second half of this journey.

I wish to thank Hofstra University for permission to include material in chapter 5 that originally appeared in "Tally's *Terra Nova*: From Historical Journals to Existential Journey," *Twentieth Century Literature* 35.1 (1989); and the University of Mississippi for permission to include material in chapter 3 that originally appeared in "Creating a Self, Personal and National, in Richard Nelson's Trilogy," *The University of Mississippi Studies in English* ns 11–12 (1993–1995).

I also wish to thank Evie Peluso for the initial preparation of the manuscript and John K. Wilson of Southern Illinois University Press for taking the manuscript through the production process.

CREATING THE SELF
IN THE CONTEMPORARY
AMERICAN THEATRE

1

Women's Theatre

In the summer of 1990, Karen Finley became a cause célèbre in the world of performance art when she was denied an NEA grant for which a peer panel had recommended her. But that fact alone, interesting though it is for the light it sheds on the process and politics of government support of the arts in America, does not warrant the space accorded Finley in this book. Her solo piece, *We Keep Our Victims Ready*, does because the obscenity her detractors see in it supposedly was the reason for the denial. A victim is a living being sacrificed to a deity, the sacrifice being the ritual that actualizes the deity's myth. Since myth and ritual imply traditional narrative and prescribed form, Finley's performing the piece establishes the deity, or ruling culture, that exacts the sacrifice. Since the performance is allegedly obscene, it also establishes her irreverent, or nontraditional, attitude toward the dominant culture.

In the imaginative world of *We Keep Our Victims Ready*, there are many voices but only one body. The voices are those of the disembodied victims of a dominant culture that disfranchises minority selves by confiscating their bodies. And where the ruling culture does not break the spirit but dispossesses it, the master pursues the fugitive, allowing it no sanctuary. "Whenever I see a rainbow in the sky," the performance artist rages in the solo piece, "I only see an angel being raped."[1]

The dispersed selves, or spirits, speak through Finley, who becomes their medium in a performance that recovers their sanctity by purging her body of the masculine culture's depredation. By offering her body, by sacrificing it in the ritual, she returns to a time that approximates the present, a time in the beginning of Western theatre when women playwrights, denied access to power, empowered themselves:

The first women playwrights created in the medium their cultures allowed them—the language of the body. These were the women mimes who performed in the market places, the streets and before the theatres in classical Greece and Rome. Their theatre tradition was a silent one, consisting of physical dramatic invention. Their bodies were the sites of their texts. They were denied the permanency of the written text, along with its privileged association with theatre buildings, state revenues and pools of professional performers, all of which were available to men. Yet their performances were central enough in the culture for them to be included in the texts of theatre history. . . .

What kinds of plays were these women making and what is their contribution to theatre history? Scholars suggest that the mimes included satires on local personalities and current events as well as popular versions of the myths.[2]

Finley is a contemporary performance artist who writes her own material, which she realizes in performance; it is this theatre persona that she presents to the audience.[3] Although she has a voice that she uses to great effect, her body, like those of the playwrights described in the quoted excerpt, is the site of her text. Her plays, or performance pieces, also are like those of the first women playwrights in that they contain satires on local personalities and current events as well as popular versions of myths. The contemporary performer and the classical mimes share something else too: Both were denied state revenues.

In June 1990 a story broke in the newspapers about political censorship of art. Artists annually apply to the National Endowment for the Arts (NEA) for financial support of their projects. The evaluation process typically involves a juried decision by a peer panel in each category. The panel presents the names of those it recommends to the NEA's governing board, which normally accepts its judgment. Yet in the story as carried by the *New York Times*, the endowment's chairman was reported to have said that not everyone recommended would be awarded a grant. He gave as the reason "certain political realities." It was subsequently learned that Finley's application was one of four theatre recommendations the NEA rejected. Apparently the political reality was an objection made by critics of the NEA that its policy supports works they consider obscene. Cited as an example was *We Keep Our Victims Ready*.

The objection to Finley's solo piece was part of a national campaign by religious fundamentalists and conservative congressmen against the use of public funds to support material they judge obscene. She in turn made the current events with the personalities involved, notably Reverend Donald Wildmon and Senator Jesse Helms, the basis of the act-1 satire as she performed the piece in New York in the summer and fall of 1990.

Within weeks of seeing the performance, I purchased a copy of a collection of her monologues to compare the performed text with the published text. In print, *We Keep Our Victims Ready* opens with a monologue, "I Was Not Expected To Be Talented." Its voice is that of a working mother whose body has been so depleted by the strain of bearing three sons that she cannot have the daughter to whom she had hoped to give the opportunities denied to her by a government that by denying pregnancy leaves and maternity leaves to waitresses "wants to make it impossible for women to have a fair share along with men" (105). In its anger and bitterness for having had her body appropriated to perpetuate the ruling masculine culture, the monologue is consistent with the piece's other monologues, but "I Was Not Expected To Be Talented" did not open the piece when I saw it performed. The monologue that did, "It's Only Art," is included in the published collection as part of another piece, *Modern Prayers*.[4]

Nevertheless, I intend to discuss the piece as performed. I want to retain the feeling of a live performance rather than a reading of a printed text. The collection, *Shock Treatment*, contains no sense of how the monologues are to be performed.

We Keep Our Victims Ready consists of three acts played without intermission. Finley enters a stage with a bed on one side, a table and lectern in the center, and a chair on the other side. Wearing what appears to be a robe or housedress, she sits in the chair that is the set for the first act, takes a drink of water, and starts creating a persona. In act 1 she is not yet the medium through whom other voices speak, but she never lets the audience forget that she is performing and not at home. Speaking in her own voice, sometimes she reads from the text of "It's Only Art"; sometimes she shields her eyes from the lights to read the faces in the darkened rows. She not only interrupts her delivery to speak to the spectators, she makes them self-conscious by questioning their motivation for being there looking at her. Her sardonic laugh further disconcerts as she suggests that her viewers have been lured from customary nocturnal debaucheries such as watching television or drinking in bars on the expectation that her performance really is obscene.

Art is the subject of the first act, beginning with the national attack on art, which Finley mocks. Without mentioning the artists' names, she links two events that led to the campaign to change the present system of government support for the arts. The two were exhibits. The first, of Andres Serrano's work, contained a photograph of a crucifix standing in the artist's urine. About the same time that the religious right spearheaded by Reverend Wildmon was sending a reproduction of the Serrano photograph to every member of Congress with a call to action, the second event took place. The late Robert Mapplethorpe's work, which contained photographs depicting homosexual and sadomasochistic acts, was on exhibit in Cincinnati's Contemporary Arts Center. The gallery and its director were charged with displaying obscenity and brought to trial in the fall of 1990. While they were being acquitted, both the House of Representatives and the Senate passed endowment reauthorization bills in which each House stated its disapproval of obscenity in art but left the definition to the courts.[5]

By linking the two events, act 1 becomes a denunciation of a government that confiscates art depicting natural processes. Finley describes a museum in which all the art has been removed and all the toilets locked because "people might think someone peeing is art" and the government is determined to foster the illusion that "no one thinks that you ever piss or shit." To a list of individual artists banned from the museum—Michelangelo, for example, for being homosexual and Mary Cassatt for painting nude children—she adds the following: "All ceramicists were banned because working with clay was too much like playing with your own shit" and "All glassblowing became extinct because it was too much like giving a blow job" (69–70).

The result of the denial of expression rooted in nature is a stifling of creative energy, which withers or dispossesses the spirit and leaves the body lifeless—a hollow image to be exhibited in sanitized museums. Even critics are bored, for they have nothing to condemn. Into the wasteland come European visitors, guests of Senator Jesse Helms. Since they want to see art and since there is none in America, the Senator leads his guests, the Europeans joined by his conservative and fundamentalist friends, in self-expression. "Everyone started making pictures of houses on fire, of monsters and trees becoming penises, pictures of making love with someone of the same sex, of being naked on street corners, of pain and dirty words and things you never admitted in real life" (73–74). Inevitably, though, the Confiscation Police arrive and arrest everyone, including Helms, who as ringleader is tried for treason and executed.

Although the closing line of "It's Only Art" brings a howl of laughter and applause from a liberal audience knowledgeable of the Senator's voting record, the act's focus is not limited to the national campaign against the art in the two publicized events; it extends the campaign to include an attack on feminist performance art. In act 1, while Finley is linking national events to satirize them, she is linking herself to the events, for her body, the site of the solo piece's act 2, was rejected by the NEA for the same reason that the government bans self-expression from the museum. Because her body, like the works confiscated from the museum, is rooted in nature, it can be perceived two ways: as art or obscenity, depending on the perspective. She herself introduces the dual possibility because she inhabits the two perspectives. She is both within nature and outside it, evaluating it. At one point during her act-1 delivery, she stops, looks down at her lap, and questions, "Did I just get my period?" She walks offstage and returns moments later. Sitting, she tosses off "Nah, I'm okay," takes a drink of water, and resumes.

She dramatizes the dual perspective in act 2 by presenting herself as artist and exhibitionist, her body as art and obscenity, as she continues to play to the audience's sophistication while mocking it. When she leaves the chair to come to the table and lectern at centerstage, act 2 commences. She removes her robe to stand before the audience wearing only brassiere and panties. Turning around, she snaps the elasticized panty legs, which do not cover her buttocks. Facing front, she points to the pubic hair that the panties do not cover. "Is this what you came to see?" she asks. "Is this obscene enough for you?"

Her hope is that she will awaken the dual perspective of the spectators so that they will see the design in the seeming capitulation, the art in the degradation. On the evening I saw her, she was dissatisfied at one point with her delivery in act 2. She stepped aside to admit a misplaced stress, stepped back into the persona to repeat the passage, and then went on. It is a risk that she takes, undressed on a stage in front of eyes that see in theatre, no matter how avant-garde, only what conventional sensibilities can accommodate. But it is a risk that she must take because the performance will not work without risks.

The body that act 1 introduces is revealed in act 2. Since its exhibit without art is a flesh show, Finley, stripped of her art by the government, is exposed as an obscenity. Of course, that does not mean that she does not have a function. To the controlling government, base nature without redeeming artistic value is an object to be appropriated to serve the prevailing culture. A carnal creature, woman can be a lewd performer. Obliging, Finley stuffs gelatin into her bra and tosses candy to the audience. Not only does she sing for her supper, she is the main dish, an image the import of which only gradually dawns on the audience.

The motif of violation is introduced in "It's Only Art." When the guests at Senator Helms's party are asked to express themselves, a child crayons a picture of "her father hitting her. Then a picture of her alone and bruised" (73). The purpose of the violation is to begin at the earliest age training the female to accept the values of the controlling government, which is masculine. The sole deity in the pantheon, masculinity is monolithic and absolute: "All art from cultures that didn't believe in one male god was banned for being blasphemous" (70). Abstracted from nature, it is enthroned in the mind, from which lofty pinnacle it compartmentalizes life. In one of the monologues in act 2, "God is bureaucracy / God is statistics / God is what you make and not what you feel" (110). Woman's compartment is sexual.

This is woman's dilemma. If she worships at the male shrine, she can be included in his museum but as his hollow image of her as sex object. And to worship, she must violate her nature and her feelings. She must bear his sons and not the daughters she wants, and she must attend to his constructs while subordinating her life. To be true to herself, therefore, she must rebel against the confiscation, but by so doing, she is guilty of blasphemy and excluded with the other minorities from the museum. But exclusion does not guarantee that she will be left alone to cultivate herself. She can still be raped, just as the woman whose spirit flees while her body submits to the confiscation has her spirit pursued and raped in the rainbow.

Women are not alone as victims because the meaning of government changes from act 1 to act 2 as the theatre piece changes from social satire to interior drama. In act 1 the government is a political body in an everyday sense; it is a body of elected officials exercising authority to control and direct the making and administration of policy that impacts on public affairs. The government is predominantly white to reflect the racial composition of the electorate. Reflecting the gender of those elected, it is external to women, excluding them from the authority to control and direct the functions of the political unit.

When Finley moves to centerstage and removes her robe to begin act 2, she exposes her body, which houses the solo piece's second meaning of government. It is the myth of the "one male god," which we can call Eurocentric because the god is Caucasian. In addition to excluding women, the myth excludes from partnership all nonwhite, nonprivileged, nonaggressively masculine males. And because they lack a power base from which to force a change in the government as external political body, minorities lack autonomy. Their bodies are confiscated or discarded to languish on streets and in subways.

No longer external to its victims, this meaning of government is within society's members. No longer an elected political body, it is the culturally implanted and reinforced idea, or myth, that controls and directs society's values, specifically the belief that the power to succeed in public affairs is masculine. Sanctioned by religion, the power is deified as white and masculine because white males achieve success to a greater degree than do minorities and should continue to do so. Minorities, who are not privileged, are self-evidently defective when they measure themselves against the ruling government's standard. But they have their functions to serve as confiscated bodies. Refusal to serve is blasphemous; it denies the "one male god." In this sense of government, the feeling of inferiority is a self-inflicted wound, although it is reinforced by an NEA rejection of a grant application.

Another reason for calling this monolithic myth Eurocentric is that the narrative form that expresses it is Eurocentric. Taught in school as the form of Western drama, the action is linearly plotted to rise and fall from exposition through climax and resolution. Finley herself uses the form when she speaks in single voice in "It's Only Art," but she turns it against her detractors by having Senator Helms arrested and executed. When she speaks in many voices in act 2, she drops the form. She becomes the medium for multicultural females and males, changing voices for their monologues and within the monologues themselves, and she narrates the personal histories of violation in recursive, incantatory rhythms rather than in linear progression. The one encompassing violation that unites all voices is the inculcation in their bodies of a myth, as unnatural to them as the linear narrative expressing it, that dispossesses their spirits. The first speaker of "I Was Not Expected To Be Talented," who reveals that her body is so exhausted from carrying three sons that she cannot have a daughter, is but one of the victims. She identifies with victims: "the collapsed, the broken, the inebriated, the helpless and the poor—'CAUSE THEY LOOK LIKE WHAT I FEEL INSIDE!" (107).

The "We" of We Keep Our Victims Ready refers to all members of society who conspire to keep minorities in a victim frame of mind by having them worship a deity-myth-standard foreign to their needs. Minorities themselves are guilty. Women, for example, are accomplices by acquiescing in a dehumanization that reduces them to sexual objects.

In act 2 Finley takes the risk that has made the solo piece the talk of the theatrical town. Removing her bra, she smears her body with a chocolate-colored adhesive to symbolize the excrement that woman is in the dominant culture's value system. She will subsequently cover the chocolate with alfalfa shoots to symbolize the sperm men ejaculate into women's bodies, and then cover the shoots with tinsel to symbolize the ornamented object that is woman's proper role in an androcratic society.

She seems to be acquiescing. Through act 1 she has not surrendered her sense of her worth to the government as external political body. On the contrary, she has been blasphemous, mocking governmental restriction on artistic expression. Yet with the introduction in act 2 of the meaning of government as implanted myth, her courage seems to fail and she appears to justify the NEA's removal of her from the museum of grant recipients, for as she smears her exposed body, she transforms herself from defiant woman to vulgar sex symbol: both the male government's perception of woman and the defeated woman's self-perception as inculcated by the male myth. Tarred and feathered for public ridicule, she becomes a victim to be confiscated with other objects judged obscene.

Finley humiliates herself but not to honor the "one male god" whose myth demands minority sacrifice. She sacrifices herself for another reason. Preparing her body is the theatre piece's ritual. The smearing, which is done in stages throughout act 2, seems to say, "I'll be the disgusting pig of a sex object that men would have me be," but Finley is actually duplicating the confiscated body from which sacrificed minorities were dispossessed so that it can be the place of reentry for them. With each layer she sacrifices more of her self-esteem until she is selfless. Surrendering her autonomy, she becomes a medium through whom dispossessed minorities can return to life. Surrendering her self-control, she loses self-consciousness and goes into an autohypnotic state.

She becomes a shaman, one of whose functions in archaic societies is to "pursue the wandering soul of the sick person, capture it and bring it back into the body."[6] Everyone who sees the performance remarks on the performer's amazing ability to imitate speaking in tongues. Not every reviewer notes the shamanism, but the glossolalia goes hand in hand with mediation with the spirit world. Simulating a trance, Finley stands at the lectern and while rapidly changing pitch goes from anger to rage to jubilation. The anger and rage are the multicultural voices, male and female, of oppressed spirits whose monologues comprise act 2. They are repetitive expulsions of pain, each gaining narrative texture only as the shaman captures the spirit and brings it back into her body. The jubilation is hers, for by the end of act 2, she regains her "personhood" (132).

While Finley seems to be preparing her body to be a sex symbol, she really is purging it of the usurping myth's influence by returning it to nature. Smearing is covering the body with nature, burying it in an initiatory death as a prerequisite for rebirth, which is imaged in the act's and the piece's climax. A photograph of it highlights the theatre program and newspaper reviews and could be said to be the performer's logo. With surging emotion bursting open mouth and eyes and separating and extending fingers on arms flung skyward, Finley is the image of a woman reunited with herself. The gathering voices never materialize in their persons, but they manifest their presence in her, for by recovering herself, she recovers her dispossessed heritage. Recovering the dispossessed spirits, she recovers herself; recovering herself, she recovers them. No matter which way we say it, the experience is the same because the reborn feminine self is the goddess in whom and through whom all life is renewed.

Referring to a woman coated with chocolate as a goddess may seem to be a contradiction, but only if the word implies to the reader a pantheon of "beauties—'Venuses,' brides of the sky-gods." That conception, found in primers on Indo-European mythology, is not what is meant here or in the scholarship of archaeologist Marija Gimbutas, whence the quotation is taken. Her study of the symbolic artifacts for the religion of the Old European Great Goddess amasses a wealth of material to support her thesis that the "main theme of Goddess symbolism is the mystery of birth and death and the renewal of life, not only human but all life on earth and indeed in the whole cosmos."[7]

It is not necessary to quote authorities, however. All that one has to do is look at the performer. She is triumphant because she has actualized a feminine myth with its multicultural values. Divinity is within her, the source and center of life, requiring only that she be in control of her "personhood." By purifying herself of the unnatural masculine myth, then, she reclaims the goddess's mystical body in whom society's disfranchised are recovered, and they are brought back into life through a living body—a body in nature—rather than a sterile museum that bans nature.

Since nature includes death, act 3 moves to the stage's other side, where Finley, robed again, positions herself beside an empty bed and delivers a threnody for the departed who cannot be brought back. Separated by the death-and-rebirth experience of act 2, act 3 is played off against act 1, with the empty bed paralleling the empty museum. Both are emptied by the controlling government as ruling political body and inculcated myth. On the one side, it reduces life to objects for display in a sterile museum and where the life rebels, removes it. On the other side, it removes unacceptable life by ignoring social ills such as AIDS, poverty, and homelessness that decimate minority communities. Furthermore, the implication is that the government's racism and sexism contribute to the social ills by barring minorities from full participation in public affairs.

The voice is that of Finley, filled with pain and anger but now also grief and resolution to be herself. In the piece's concluding poem, she is no longer a lamb to be slaughtered to a "GOD" who "IS DEATH" (136) but a black sheep who will minister to the sick and dying but also to the living. If for being different, minorities are rejected by their families and denied partnership in the dominant culture, they can form their own family, their own community.

Finley shows the outcast the way to self-discovery. Her ritual is an initiation. Descending into death, the performer rises, arms flung skyward and mouth burst open, to commit herself to death's reality and life's renewal, to acceptance of difference, and to sharing of the life that she discovers gathering in her body.

The risk that Finley takes in imaging herself as a shaman is that she will validate the male perception of woman as an unconscious creature of nature requiring his conscious control. The risk that she takes in imaging herself as an obscene sex object is that she will substantiate the right-wing condemnation of her performance. She succeeds in winning over the audience because by herself on a denuded stage she realizes life and thereby creates a new self.

The life is in the performance—the very reason for the NEA rejection of her project, which rejection becomes the solo piece's metaphor. The white, male government denies feminine performance art because it does not conform to the white, male notions of art as exhibited in culturally sanctioned museums. Dispossessing herself of this factitious culture with a form of expression unnatural to a woman, Finley repossesses herself. By performing the dispossession and repossession, she creates a new self, for herself but also for the theatre. She restores to centerstage an old-world tradition marginalized by the culturally sanctioned Eurocentric drama.

She is but one artist in the restoration movement. Laurie Carlos, who had been in the Broadway production of Shange's *For Colored Girls*, wanted to discover herself in her world as the lady she played in the choreopoem does in hers. In an interview, she recalls how difficult it was for her and her collaborators to find a place in which to create because of the prevailing theatre's rules for theatre:

> There were no venues for what it was we wanted to do. None. None in any black world, in an Asian world, there were none in a white world. Performance art was the one place where there were so few definitions. The way that we have conversations, what occurs across time zones, what memory is, what color is, how music affects movement and memory and the texture of breath has nothing whatsoever to do with the Eurocentric playwriting form.

In a performance piece collected in the same volume with Carlos's interview, Fiona Templeton relates her struggle with the "masculine," Eurocentric form of narration that "starts somewhere" and continues until it is "concluded, perfected, finished, over."[8]

Taking an approach to the contemporary American theatre that is not chronological, the book opens with Finley because by reviving, with others, an art that is not "concluded, perfected, finished, over," she reminds the audience that not only do different cultures have different traditions but the old world and the new world have different meanings to different questers between worlds. For though first, she is not alone in discovering a self with stories to tell and myths to actualize that reveal a divinity as worthy as the "one male god."

Ntozake Shange's *For Colored Girls Who Have Considered Suicide When the Rainbow Is Enuf* received such popular and critical acclaim during its Off-Broadway and Broadway runs in the mid-1970s that it does not require an in-depth analysis. Yet I do not want to bypass it because later in the chapter its closing image will illuminate a scene in Wasserstein's *The Heidi Chronicles*.

In Shange's choreopoem seven performers wearing wraparound skirts over leotards, similar except for the colors, interact in one another's choreographed song. When at choreopoem's end they image a rainbow, emphasized are the colors; when they image a circle, emphasized is woman herself, beneath the different hues. Each woman retains the hue that life's joys and sorrows have given her, yet all are able to unite because they share the same life; and sharing, they understand one another. They are seven individuals, symbolized by the seven colors, who discover a common experience and heritage, symbolized by the circle that manifests itself as a rainbow. The two images are the same image, retracted or extended. In closing the performance, the ladies either retract into a circle or extend into a rainbow because the goddess, the feminine self, is both communal and individual, cultural and personal.

No one climactic image transforms the stage in Marlane Meyer's *Etta Jenks*. The transformations develop from the enactment of nineteen scenes in which characters appear and disappear as the play voyages from the entrance in Hollywood to the goddess's kingdom in Mexico and back, from the upper world to the underworld and back, and from life to death and rebirth in a new self.

The play opens in the Los Angeles train terminal with the arrival of Etta Jenks, a woman in her early thirties. Befriended by two brothers, she decides on a career in films, but with limited funds and no acting background, accepts work in pornographic flicks produced by a man named Ben. Believing that his interest in her is personal, she goes with him to Mexico, the capital of the porno industry, specializing in flicks in which the female is executed. Her stay is short. She returns to the States, where she gets a job in a dance hall. Meanwhile, her friend Sheri, lured by the prospect of a fast thousand dollars and drugs, goes to Mexico with her boyfriend, trusting that he will protect her. When she disappears, Etta hires a professional killer and his partner and with them makes a second Mexican journey. Once she introduces them to Ben as vendors, she leaves, again for the States; they proceed to kill the producer. *Etta Jenks* ends with Etta's disappearing by train, just as she appeared in the first of the nineteen scenes.

The play's repetitive action dramatizes the recursive pattern of an ancient myth: that of Persephone in the underworld. *Homeric Hymn II (To Demeter)* tells the tale of Hades' abduction of Persephone, daughter of fertility goddess Demeter; the mother's sorrow; and the reunion of mother and daughter, who will enjoy each other until the latter must once again disappear into the earth, for Hades, when commanded by Zeus to return his bride to her mother, tricks her into spending part of each year as queen with him in his underground kingdom of the dead. Yet each death holds the promise of rebirth, for Persephone will return each spring on a land Demeter makes fertile. As the hymn ends, the fertility goddess fulfills her pledge to the men of Eleusis, who built a temple to her, by initiating them into her mysteries, the Eleusinian mysteries. Honoring the reunion, they became ancient Greece's most famous religious rites.

An exhaustive study of the relationship between the ancient tale and the contemporary play would be inappropriate, but I will give highlights. The incest in Etta's family parallels that of the Zeus-Demeter-Persephone constellation. Etta remembers her father-grandfather as a "great big red-faced man"[9] who would cloak himself with a blanket and chase her around the house, prompting her mother to move with her away from him. "Red-faced" would not be an inaccurate description of Zeus, whose name is translated as "bright" or "shining" and who, according to one version of the myth, in one of his many guises fathers Dionysus with daughter Persephone by his sister Demeter.

Etta is befriended by twin brothers, one deaf and one blind. Burt and Sherman are guardians of the gateway to the underworld, Hollywood, which terminates in the underworld filmmaking industry in Mexico. Burt introduces her to Ben, the porno producer, who is described as "ugly" (167); having "many moles" (137) on his body, which would darken his complexion; and "primordial ooze" (128). When he kisses, he leaves a "taste of dirt" (159) in the woman's mouth. Like Hades, whose helmet renders him invisible, the porno king is elusive, although he is "too slimy not to leave a trail" (143).

To young women drawn to Hollywood's glamour, Ben offers a chance to break into films by building credits in pornographic flicks. After the aspiring actress makes a few in Los Angeles, he takes her to Mexico, where unknown to her, she will star in a snuff film, a flick in which she will be snuffed out. On her second Mexican trip, Etta asks him about her friend Sheri. She vanished while making a movie, he explains. "I kept waiting for her to come back. But she never did. And then I noticed this smell, like gardenias, overpowering . . . it seemed to hang in the air for hours." Gardenias are his "favorite flower" (165), he concludes. It is not a narcissus, the flower Hades uses to ensnare Persephone in *Homeric Hymn II*, but the gardenia does have highly fragrant, showy blossoms.

Ben's underworld is the kingdom of the dead not only because performers are snuffed out but also because pornography is the death of the spirit. In a production note playwright Meyer equates bestiality and death when she indicates that all the characters except Etta, Burt, and Sherman should "*be possessed of a certain animal quality . . .*" (116). Once the play begins, Ben "*looks like a man mutating into a wolf*" (122). When Sheri's boyfriend tells her, Sheri, that she can make a thousand dollars in Mexico, she wonders whether she will have to perform with a donkey. Ben enjoys coupling children and dogs. In the flick he watches in scene 6, the girl is in a doghouse.

Etta Jenks is a descent into the death of the body to release the spirit. Meyer's play is a variation on Finley's performance piece in that Ben confiscates women's bodies for pornography, but he does not think that he dispossesses the spirit because he does not believe that a woman has a spirit. His kingdom is the ultimate denial of the human mystery, the reduction of feminine sexuality to pornographically framed images so that once shot on film, the performer, having revealed everything about herself, is no longer needed and is executed. She is replaced by another female, or body, which is the same thing to the producer, who trains aspiring actresses in Los Angeles for the Mexican trip by having them wear animal skins. Even if the play's title were not her name, Etta would be the heroine. Her refusal to don the costume in scene 7 prepares for the play's first reversal. In scene 10 she has returned alive from Mexico, a feat accomplished by reversing Ben's conception of the female's role. She earned money to get out of Mexico by tying a client with his necktie, stepping on him, and calling "him dog. Dog" (139).

The Persephone myth informs the contemporary play, giving a context to otherwise gratuitous images. In scene 10 Etta works in a dance hall, where a customer approaches her with an invitation to go to his house. "I'd like to show you our collection of porcelain figurines" is the inducement. "There's one that looks just like you" (141). Figurines are pervasive in reconstructing the Great Goddess religion. According to Gimbutas, the miniature sculptures that were used in rituals are "found in quantity in almost every Neolithic settlement and cemetery."[10] In the next scene, when Etta remarks, "I feel like somebody slipped the bones out of my body" (147), the reference is to excarnation, the process of burying a person's bones in a tomb shaped to resemble the womb because the goddess as Earth Mother was worshiped for her regenerative powers. Finally, on Etta's second Mexican trip, Sheri's snake tattoo is described as "shedding skin" (164). This dynamic detail of renewing itself by sloughing off its old skin identifies the serpent as a symbol of the life-giving, death-wielding, self-renewing goddess.[11]

The most convincing parallel between the two works is not verbal but visual. The women appear and disappear so that their absence is as pregnant as their presence because when they reappear they are transformed. Meyer's contemporary reworking of the ancient myth is to have women release their spirits into new bodies as their way of challenging the male reduction of them to animals. Women in the play talk about dematerialization. Sheri practices it in Los Angeles. In Mexico she dematerializes into spirit, but the question of whether or not she is murdered the play leaves unresolved, for a scene subsequent to her disappearance implies that she is alive. By being ambiguous, the playwright restores the mystery to feminine sexuality, demystified in this play by a secular, commercial culture metaphored in pornography.

By dematerializing themselves, women renew themselves. They transform themselves through the three stages of femininity: Kore the Maiden, Persephone the Nymph, and Hecate the Crone subsumed under the Great Goddess Demeter. When Etta as Persephone returns from Mexico in the play's first reversal, she is reunited not with a biological parent but with a parenting culture that revered women as aspects of the Great, or Triple, Goddess before a patriarchal culture supplanted it.[12] Almost miraculously she becomes a mother. In scene 13 the audience learns that she has a daughter being reared by a couple who can give her the family life that she, Etta, could not provide.

After the excarnation referred to in scene 10—the death of the old self—Etta creates a new self. When she arrives in Los Angeles, she is Kore the Maiden. Physiologically she is not a virgin, but in terms of experience that affords insight into herself, she is. Lost in the big city, dependent upon men for securing a livelihood, she does not know who she is or what she wants. She becomes Persephone the Nymph when she goes to Mexico, when she descends to the depths of male sexuality that by exploiting female sexuality degrades a woman to an object. When she returns to the States, in scene 10, she becomes Demeter not as Corn Goddess but as Nurturing Goddess sorrowing for the missing Sheri, who, by disappearing in Mexico, becomes Persephone. When Ben's ex-partner tells her that he cannot understand why she would go to Mexico a second time to have the producer executed for the sake of Sheri and the other women who performed in his flicks because they were no better than degenerates, her answer resonates throughout the play and all of contemporary feminist literature: "I am other women" (170).

Etta's repeated disappearance from the old self and reappearance in the new self are the transformations that the spectator sees in the 19 scenes. But Meyer also transforms the ancient myth in the reworking of it. The old-world death becomes new-world pornography. Women challenge male confiscation of their bodies by taking the journey into this hell to dematerialize. Neither Etta nor Sheri is raped; each performs in pornographic flicks initially hoping to break into straight films and then for the money. Neither woman is abducted;

each goes to Mexico of her own volition. Both disappear from the underworld capital, Etta twice.

By making the chthonian journey that which must be taken, Meyer not only returns control of her destiny to the woman by having her take responsibility for her body but returns to her guardianship of the Eleusinian mysteries of life and death. I do not know how else to understand the play's closing scene. If Mexico is annihilating death, legally Etta probably is an accessory to murder and morally she is a monster.

In this scene an aspiring actress named Shelly approaches Etta, who is vacating her talent-coordinating office, for assistance in breaking into films. At first the older woman takes the position that the office is closed for business, but as Shelly tells her that a mutual friend who conducts dematerializing seminars recommended her, the ex talent coordinator identifies with her. She is eighteen, a girl whose virginity was taken by her "stepdad" when she was twelve and who has no objection to appearing in porno flicks such as "whip movies" because she has been cast as a "dominant" in her other job, a role that allows her to vent her hatred of men. She confides that she sometimes thinks herself capable of killing them (172–73).

Recognizing a teenager who should be entering the Persephone phase of her life, Etta as Triple Goddess-Great Mother writes a note on a business card and hands it to Shelly, who leaves. Presumably it will introduce her to people who will acquaint her with opportunities in Mexico, where she can suffer the initiatory death that is a prerequisite for growth. The *"stage lights go to black"* as Etta herself then *"seems to vanish"* (174), I assume into the female self's next phase of becoming.

In this chapter, the next phase of becoming is Wendy Wasserstein's *The Heidi Chronicles*, the most contemporary work so far. Since women participate in America's corporate life, they participate in an ongoing breakup of traditional values.

We Keep Our Victims Ready begins with the assumption that the male has confiscated the female's self. Wasserstein's play does not begin with that assumption. The male would like to confiscate the woman—as a wife to satisfy his domestic needs and as a wife or mistress to satisfy his sexual needs—so that with those needs attended to he can concentrate on furthering his career, but he is not always successful. While some women accept the arrangement if the payoff is big enough, some are not interested regardless of the promised payoff, and others challenge the very notion of such an arrangement. Yet even though women in Wasserstein's imaginative world are liberated, they lack a female self and myth. The play's dominant culture, like that of Finley's performance piece, is male.

The Heidi Chronicles is a series of episodes tracing the development, from mid-teens to early forties, of Heidi Holland and her yuppie peer group as they discover their careers, their relationships, and themselves. In act 1's second scene, at a 1968 New Hampshire dance for presidential candidate Eugene McCarthy, college student Heidi meets college dropout, newspaper editor Scoop Rosenbaum, the man who will become a law student, magazine publisher, and her lover, remaining her friend after his marriage. Irritating her by his aggressiveness while trying to pick her up, he realizes that she is "thinking something," to which she replies, "I was wondering what mothers teach their sons that they never bother to tell their daughters. . . . I mean, why the fuck are you so confident?"[13] In the next scene, a few years later at a consciousness-raising meeting to which a friend brings her, one of the members explains not what parents teach their sons but what they teach their daughters that makes them lack confidence. "Heidi, every woman in this room has been taught that the desires and dreams of her husband, her son, or her boss are much more important than her own" (181).

For women to gain confidence, they must be taught that their desires and dreams are equally important; they must have their culture taught. First, though, they must agree on the values that make up their culture. As the woman just quoted continues, referring to the prevailing masculine culture, "And the only way to turn that around is for us, right here, to try to make what *we* want, what *we* desire to be, as vital as it would undoubtedly be to any man. And then we can go out there and really make a difference!" To determine which values are vital to them, the women must "really start talking to each other" (181). At this stage in the play's action and in Heidi's life—she is twenty-one and a graduate student in art history—*The Heidi Chronicles* seems to duplicate the view of *For Colored Girls*. By sharing their experiences, women can establish a culture of shared values and forms, and from that a community of moral and political force to ensure that the culture is respected.

In Shange's performance piece, the audience sees and hears the culture and the community developing. Wearing similar wraparounds colored differently, the interacting women retract into a circle to emphasize their shared life and extend into a rainbow to emphasize their individual experiences that emanate from that life.

In the comparable scene in the play, the consciousness-raising meeting, the audience sees and hears the difficulty in developing a culture and a community. Wasserstein's women also image a circle at this scene's end but with a difference. Their clothing so clashes that the dissimilarity is emphasized. The three youngest, who can share dating patterns, are separated from the other two by marital status and sexual orientation, and the distance separating them is symbolized by the difference between the blue jeans worn by the three and the immaculate whale turtleneck and pleated skirt worn by the mother of four daughters and the army fatigues worn by the lesbian.

Within each subgroup, there is variance that exceeds the distinctive joys and sorrows that color a woman's life with its own hue. Claiming that she is "just visiting" (177), Heidi is reluctant to discuss her personal life with the others until the lesbian goads her into revealing that she allows Scoop to determine how she feels about herself. And at scene's end, when they form a circle to sing a "favorite camp song" (183) that the mother sings with her four daughters, the lesbian breaks the ring to put an Aretha Franklin record on the turntable.

Their clothing signals their liberation not only from traditional stereotypes but also from the traditional values that bound them together as a community. The feminist movement has liberated them to wear blue jeans and army fatigues, but they do not know what their new values are supposed to be because they do not know who they are. They lack a new identity to correspond to their new freedom.

In their desire to test their new freedom, the women in the play so extend themselves that they lose the coherence of the community. In what amounts to a meditation on the feminist movement's failure to achieve its high ideals, Heidi analyzes her sense of betrayal at a meeting of her high school alumnae association. The essence of the betrayal is that she feels "stranded" by a movement the appeal of which is its solidarity. "I thought," she concludes, "the point was we were all in this together" (232).

Extending themselves across life's surface, they also lose their individuality. Susan, Heidi's friend from high school, does not seem to stop moving. When the audience first meets her in act 1's opening scene, she is rolling up her skirt so that the boys at the dance will notice her. By act 1's closing scene, she is waltzing with a girlfriend from Montana that she brings to Scoop's wedding.

In between the two scenes, she joins a consciousness-raising group in Ann Arbor, Michigan; turns down the idea of starting a law journal devoted to women's legal issues to work on behalf of women within the establishment; with Scoop clerks for the Supreme Court; and becomes a radical shepherdess-counselor at a women's health and legal collective in Montana. That years have passed and she has not discovered herself she admits in act 2. When Heidi suggests to her friend, now a television vice president, that trying to be every person prevents her from being one person, Susan replies, "I'm sorry, honey, but you're too deep for me. By now I've been so many people, I don't know who I am. And I don't care" (224).

Wasserstein's play chronicles the coming of age of the post–World War II baby boomers in an age that spoiled: the decades of revolution in everything from civil rights to musical styles to sexual behavior until codes of conduct dissolved into existential values and societal mores into personal gratification. During this period of dizzying sociological dislocations and technological advances, yuppies made fortunes overnight in the investment and information services, real estate, communications, and entertainment. Younger women were especially vulnerable. Liberated by the feminist movement and spurred on by the lure of seemingly unlimited career opportunities and earning potential, they were urged to fulfill themselves as their mothers could not and as victims in Finley's monologues cannot.

In the play, women like Susan are liberated from stereotypical roles, but without a new unifying identity they cannot establish a culture. Without their own culture, they accept the values that define the dominant culture. They imitate male behavior. At the alumnae meeting, just before she confesses that she feels stranded, Heidi sums up her attitude toward her peers who have used the feminist movement for their personal aggrandizement. The image, traditionally masculine in its crudest form, fixes the violation of their feminine nature and the betrayal of the values for which the liberation was fought. "I'm sure the hotshots have screwed a lot of thirty-five-year-old women, my classmates even, out of jobs, raises, and husbands" (231).

For these women, surface appearance is everything, or in the play's terms, form is content. Not so for Heidi. She is committed to traditional feminine values, disqualifying herself from the discussion of lesbian rights, for example. Only when she is sure that she can support an issue does she become engaged. She takes up the banner for women artists outside the Chicago Art

Institute not because she belongs to a movement but because equality of men and women is the belief on which her values are built and the basis of relationships. The man to whom she offers herself as an equal partner in a loving relationship rejects her, however. Threatened by equality, which for him means competition, Scoop marries another woman.

Heidi realizes that Scoop is incapable of sharing with her, except sexually and only when he needs her, just as she realizes that the confidence to which she is drawn masks the shallowness of a man accustomed to having his way. Yet she wavers. By coming to his wedding, she puts the idea in his head that she will be his mistress, despite her protestation that she came only because Peter, a gay friend from her Chicago days, and Susan, who clerked at the Supreme Court with him, wanted to. To salvage her self-respect, she fabricates an editor she is "sort of living with" (198), but the lie is unconvincing to him, for whom form is content. Her form at his wedding implies a willingness to resume their relationship after he settles into marriage.

The stress of trying to retain her traditional values while creating a self for the contemporary world is too much for her. The self that began to develop at the consciousness-raising meeting and the art institute demonstration begins to disintegrate. Act 1 ends with Heidi's head shaking *no* to Scoop's profession of love while her body yields to his embrace as they dance at the reception in New York's Pierre Hotel. That she does not surrender reveals her strength of character. Surface appearance is not her sole reality, but she would not be real were it not seductive.

For baby boomers in the audience, *The Heidi Chronicles* must have been awarded the 1989 Pulitzer Prize for Drama and the 1989 Tony for Best Play for realistically chronicling the heroine's deepening disillusionment with the movement that was expected to unite women in a common cause: their self-determination. I doubt, however, that many realized that there are two Heidis in the play. We are, in other words, at the point where we must examine the play's structure, which progressively adds art to the chronicling and depth to the surface until the heroine creates a self and a myth.

Each of the acts of *The Heidi Chronicles* has a prologue in which Heidi, a Columbia University art historian, gives a lecture, with slides, on paintings by women artists who deserve to be in the canon, despite their omission from the textbooks that students purchase for art courses. The two prologues take place in 1989, but it is impossible to say precisely how much time intervenes between them—not much, though. Since Heidi in the act-2 prologue compares a painting in that prologue with one in the first, the second may even be the end of a lecture that begins in the first. In any event, each prologue shifts to a scene from an earlier time in the art historian's life, which is then carried forward through the episodes comprising the act. Act 1's closing scene, the wedding reception, is set in 1977; act 2's, and the play's, closing scene is set in 1989. Yet we must remember that chronologically the final scene is followed by the two scenes in the Columbia University lecture hall: the two prologues, which establish a framework for the episodes.

In each prologue, Heidi analyzes for the class a few paintings whose subjects are women and then from the images extracts a summary generalization, which we can call a definition of femaleness. Since a painting in the first prologue reminds her of a girl at a high school dance, "hang[ing] around, a fading rose in an exquisitely detailed dress, waiting to see what might happen" (161), the first generalization applies to a girl passing into womanhood. The prologue over, the scene shifts to Heidi and Susan, age sixteen, at a high school dance in 1965. The younger Heidi illustrates the definition by hanging around not only in this scene to see what might happen after Susan rolls up her skirt to attract boys but also at the consciousness-raising meeting to see what might happen with the movement that claims to speak for women of her generation.

The episodes, arranged and enacted under art historian Heidi's direction, are in effect animated slides, and the lecturer-director is in effect a surrogate playwright who structures them so that the audience can see the self develop in Heidi's earlier incarnation until it begins to disintegrate when confronting the man from whose eyes and lips she took the measure of her worth at that time. The common experience that the women in the Ann Arbor church basement discover that enables them to form a circle at meeting's end is the recognition that men determine their sense of their worth. As Heidi that day in 1970 finally admits about Scoop, "I allow him to make me feel valuable. And the bottom line is, I know that's wrong" (182). Seven years later, still dependent upon Scoop, she does not make the admission in the New York hotel. She does not have to. It would be too humiliating—after all, he just married someone else—and, besides, the structure makes the admission for her. Act 1 closes with her disintegration.

The fact that Heidi the lecturer-director allows the audience to see Scoop's incredulous reaction to the younger Heidi's fabrication of a live-in lover means that she has been able to distance herself from her younger self. By the time of the prologues, Heidi has matured so that she can present the entire work as a dramatization. It is a dramaturgically structured staging with which to draw the audience, addressed as Columbia University students or alumnae association members, into the theatre experience to witness first the self's disintegration and then its integration, or creation of a new self.

Act 2's prologue hints at the discovery that matures. After analyzing paintings, art historian Heidi compares one in the second prologue with one in the first. "There is something uniquely female about these paintings. . . . What strikes me is that both ladies seem slightly removed from the occasions at hand. They appear to watch closely and ease the way for the others to join in" (206). Act 1's passivity becomes act 2's activity. Because act 2's subject is not act 1's girl passing into womanhood but a woman, femaleness is not waiting around for experience to happen, but neither is it masculine aggressiveness. Femaleness as the mature female self is actively drawing others, audience included, into experience; it is love of life that integrates.

The discovery of the self occurs on two levels, within history and within the heroine herself. With the dissolution of the peer feminine community, Wasserstein's heroine turns for guidance to women painters whose works the dominant masculine culture suppresses by excluding from galleries and textbooks used in art classes.

When Heidi meets Scoop at the New Hampshire dance, she tells him that she is planning to be an art historian. "I'm interested," she goes on, "in the individual expression of the human soul. Content over form" (171). By taking her stand on content, or the soul's expression, she comes down on the side of substance in the conflict between substance and surface, or style, found throughout contemporary life and theatre and given its most brilliantly inventive images in the shoot-out between Hoss and Crow in Shepard's *The Tooth of Crime*.

Scoop's stand is diametrically opposed to hers: "But I thought the point of contemporary art is that the form becomes the content" (171). His life is the triumph of form, or style, over content, or substance. He marries because the image of a man whose star is rising requires a family, but he has no intention of honoring the marriage vow, so that Heidi is not surprised when he tells her that he sold the magazine to run for Congress. He will be as trendy in politics as he was in publishing.

The heroine's declaration of a career occurs in 1968. At the consciousness-raising meeting two years later, she declares that the particular expression of the feminine soul she is pursuing in her Art History Graduate Program at Yale is "images of women from the Renaissance Madonna to the present" (180). The exhibition in the prologues of paintings that image feminine values before the dislocations of the social revolutions gives a symbolic dimension to the play's primarily realistic mode of presentation, a dimension that deepens as the action progresses. The paintings are real—the theatre playbill identifies them—but the presenter must delve below the art world's officially sanctioned surface to recover her suppressed heritage, which she presents not as relics to be worshiped but as proof that values once did exist and can again. Thus the images are guides to the discovery, also below the play's realistic surface, of the source and center of the culture that in 1970 the lesbian in army fatigues insists must be taught to girls so that they can grow up feeling as vital as men.

Heidi's strategy as Wasserstein's surrogate playwright of shifting from recovered historical image to contemporary episode prepares the stage for the manifestation of the second discovery: the bringing forth of a contemporary image of femaleness by play's end. In the second prologue she includes herself in the definition of femaleness that emerges from an analysis of the paintings when she tells the audience as art class that women "appear to watch closely and ease the way for the others to join in. I suppose it's really not unlike being an art historian" (206). The prologue then shifts to episodes dramatizing the heroine's search for herself, a search that climaxes in her confession at the alumnae meeting of feeling stranded.

When director Heidi presents the stranded Heidi going to her long-time friend, Peter, in the following episode, she dramatizes an alliance of women and gays, who in Finley's *We Keep Our Victims Ready* join forces to strengthen their subservient roles and marginalized voices. She has always been attracted to Peter, who shares her values, the principal one of which is love. Unfortunately for her, he cannot share it in its sexual form, for he is gay. Yet his sexual experience enables him to provide her the inspiration to resolve her predicament. Since he is different from the heterosexual males whose culture prevails in society, he must discover who he is; he must go inside himself. Only after he knows himself can he search for fulfillment in the minority culture to which he is drawn. Thus in this scene, which enables Heidi to reverse her descent into isolation and return to life, he reminds her that there are alternative families to those sanctioned by the dominant culture if one is true to himself. As he is. Peter is not superficial. His tears, brought on by the impending death of his lover through AIDS, bring to the surface the depth of his emotional life.

Having shown woman's past in the recovered paintings, Heidi shows her present and her future in the episode she fashions as the resolution to the quest. It is a luminous composition set in a room empty of furniture, except for a rocker, with the walls freshly painted white and sunlight streaming through the window. Her artistry is so convincing that the spectators forget that chronologically the prologues come last. Their theatre experience closes with the union of mother and daughter.

That Judy is adopted is significant on two counts. Had Heidi brought forth the girl from her womb, feminists could accuse Wasserstein of reverting to the pre-feminist stereotype of woman as producer of babies, an implication that Heidi thinks she hears in one of Scoop's comments and that she lashes out against. Secondly, by adopting a baby, she restores the mystery eroded by women who behave as if they were men, but Wasserstein does not mean anything "lovely . . . delicate . . . [or with] overall charm" (206), definitions of femininity the art historian rejects in the second prologue. Femininity is love actualized, and love is divinity actualized. The image of a woman in a rocker cradling her adopted daughter is a variation on the image of divine birth. It is a contemporary Madonna, the heroine's contribution to the expression of the feminine soul that she has been studying since the 1960s.

Surrogate-playwright Heidi counterposes act 2's closing scene against act 1's closing scene. In the first scene, the self disintegrates when the younger Heidi attends Scoop's wedding at the Pierre Hotel. In the second scene, he visits her in her new apartment, symbolic of her new self, where she does not have to invent a live-in editor because she dates a real one. Scoop, who sang the lyrics to Sam Cooke's "You Send Me" to her at the reception, and his wife have a son. She has a daughter, to whom she sings the same lyrics. Pictorially the first scene is tense, ultimately driven by Scoop; the second is one of repose with Heidi and Judy forefronted. Scoop leaves before the scene is completed.

In the play's closing scene, Wasserstein creates a myth to reveal rather than an episode to chronicle.[14] Exemplary myth is a natural creation for the surrogate playwright, an art historian. It also is appropriate for a skeptical audience since it illustrates rather than explains. In an age of dislocation and dissolution, it integrates experience. Finally, unlike the failure of love that the play depicts in the quickie date and the temporary relationship, the love given birth in the rocker is both timeless and time bound. The revelation that the audience witnesses is the birth that comes from within the female soul and from which all feminine values flow.

But it is a contemporary myth for a contemporary age. The women in the works by Finley, Shange, and Meyer discover an old-world goddess, hidden but retrievable, who sustains them in their quest for identity by giving them living myths with communal rituals in which they can create Finley's "personhood." Parturient and parthenogenetic, the goddess empowers her discoverer to procreate a new life and create a new life by creating herself anew.

When Heidi attempts to create a self rooted in tradition, the self is so fragile that it disintegrates under Scoop's pressure at a ritual so broken off from tradition that it mocks the notion of community. She has paintings excluded from men's museums, but though they are valuable guides to the female self in previous centuries, they do not come alive or lead her to porcelain figurines. Neither does she have women's stories against which to compare her experience. Theirs sound like men's stories. The implication of *The Heidi Chronicles* is that the world is so broken and by women themselves that the stranded heroine cannot hope to discover a living old-world goddess. Heidi must create a new self and a new sustaining myth from within herself.

She does, combining the best of both worlds. She has an editor lover with whom she can be parturient should she choose to, although since he is not a presence in the play, that is unlikely. She has an ex-publisher who wants to be her lover. And she is parthenogenetic. By making space in her heart and home for a stranded child, she becomes a mother. Together they are the nucleus of a new community and culture nurtured in love.

Like Heidi, I have been selecting images to illustrate, but having finished with Wasserstein, I am finished with the triumphant goddess. Once Finley established "one male god" as the metaphor for the dominant culture, I wanted the reader to see that minorities dissent because they feel that the dominant culture applies a discriminatory standard to exclude them from full participation in political and theatrical life. Their theatre works, then, not only affirm their contribution to America but their right to contribute because they possess a power equal to that of the "one male god."

Discovery of the goddess—or for other minorities, other empowering gods—

is the discovery of the power to create one's own life rather than have it created for one. The performance of the Split Britches Company's *Split Britches* in 1981, which depicts the lives of three women creating themselves in rural Virginia, brought prominence to founders Deborah Margolin, Peggy Shaw, and Lois Weaver. The three are versatile and not averse to directing their sense of humor on themselves. In 1992 Shaw and Weaver performed Margolin's script, *Lesbians Who Kill*.[15]

I do not want to conclude the chapter with performance art because the chapter opened with it, and I do not want to create the impression that women playwrights' contribution occurs primarily in performance art. I also want to correct what might appear to be an imbalance of goddess discovery. Consequently the chapter closes with an examination of a play by a woman whose theatre we will have occasion to return to, just as we will examine the theatres of other women artists in subsequent chapters. But we turn to Maria Irene Fornes now because the play ends in tragedy and not in reconciliation.

The 1983 play, *Mud*, depicts the primeval state in which neither time nor place is specified, a state in which human beings and animals, constructed shelter and natural landscape are only incipiently differentiated. Everything about the play is elemental. Two, and then three, characters share a wooden structure *"which sits on an earth promontory."*[16] The original two characters are a young man and woman in mid-twenties who mate "like animals" (28) until Lloyd becomes ill with an infection that renders him impotent, although he disputes Mae's charge that he "can't get it up" (17) by pointing to a mark on the wall as the height of his ejaculation the previous day. Later he changes the account of the orgasm from masturbation to fornicating with the pig.

Neither account shocks Mae, for they communicate on a rudimentary level. When she, ironing clothes, complains that the combination of laziness and illness prevents him from working in the field picking corn, she exaggerates ironing to drive her point home. "I work. See, I work. I'm working . . ." (19). Aspiring to a better life, she also goes to school but lacks confidence in herself because rather than stimulate her to achieve, school reinforces her experience of failure. Illiterate and ill, Lloyd does not stimulate her either.

The third character does stimulate her. Possessor of a larger vocabulary than she, Henry is better integrated than she with the environment to which she aspires, so that even though he is some thirty years older, she is in love with him. "I want your mind," she proposes to him as they kiss. "Did you feel my mind?"

he asks her. "Yes. I did," she replies, kissing him again. "I did. I want you here" (25). His acceptance means that in the bedroom he replaces Lloyd, who must now sleep on the floor in the other room.

Mae is not lying to Henry about what she feels. In the scene immediately following the one in which he moves into the wooden structure, they have a conversation at the dinner table that sums up the function of education in Fornes's imaginative world. After she admits that she cannot pass the tests at school because she has difficulty retaining the lessons taught, he counters by arguing that knowledge is vital, not to pass scholastic tests, but life's tests. "What would be the use of knowing things if they don't serve you, if they don't help you shape your life" (26), Henry asks rhetorically. In Fornes's theatre, education liberates because it enables the woman to imagine herself in new roles into which she can grow. But education can empower only if pedagogy, education's instrument, awakens the senses so that the woman can experience what she is learning.

Lloyd speaks only to Mae's body. In scene 1 she tries to explain to him that arithmetic, one of the subjects she studies in school, is more than adding and subtracting single digits, but he cannot grasp the concept beyond that level. Exasperated when she mentions multiplication, he calls her to the chair where he is sitting, grabs her hand, and presses it against his crotch. Angered, she pulls her hand away and returns to ironing.

Henry speaks to her whole being not only in his position on the function of knowledge but also in his thanksgiving to the Lord for filling the soul. When at her request he repeats grace, she cries, for she feels that he understands the hunger she has to fill her soul with knowledge. In scene 6 she sits at the table reading a passage in a primer about a starfish. She has to follow the "*written words with the fingers of both hands*," but "*her reading is inspired*" (27) as she discovers a new world. When a frustrated Lloyd, angered that she can do something he cannot, slaps the textbook from the table, she slaps him.

Act 1 ends with Mae again at the table reading, this time about a hermit crab, but her greater facility reveals a greater assimilation of primitive life and therefore movement toward higher life. The more of the latter that she absorbs, the more empowered her self becomes, as the scene's closing image reveals. The men are present, Lloyd on the floor listening and Henry in a chair reading a newspaper. When Lloyd lifts himself to mouth a curse at Henry for encouraging her to improve herself, Mae, seated centerstage, senses the tension. She looks from the one man to the other, and though she does not speak, Henry feels the look and returns it.

In between the two reading scenes, the audience sees and hears her growth in two other scenes. In scene 7, to the man who has become her husband, she defends Lloyd's right to continue living where he has lived ever since her father befriended him as a homeless boy. To defuse Henry's jealousy, she confesses that she and Lloyd used to mate like animals but assures him not since his arrival because she is no longer an animal. He has brought "heaven" to "this place" (28), she tells him. Henry brings something else too, a present that speaks to her feminine soul as lovingly as does the dinner-table thanksgiving. In scene 8 he gives her lipstick and a mirror. She does not pull back from him as she did from Lloyd. After applying the lipstick, she puckers her lips, and he kisses her. By scene's end the feminine soul and the masculine environment are reconciled through the senses.

Scenes in a Fornes play are like the epiphanies that Stephen, James Joyce's artist as a young man in *Stephen Hero*, considers collecting and that Joyce himself did collect. An epiphany is a sudden manifestation of the latent spirituality in an everyday scene or object that transforms it from trivial to charged. Its soul shows forth for the subject, who apprehends in its radiance its metaphysical nature. If theatregoers think of the scenes as imagist poems after the movement that flourished in the 1920s, their author becomes an imagist poet of the theatre. Imagism sought to free poetry from nineteenth-century conventions and sentimentality, grounding it in concrete sensory impressions: sharp, clear, distinct images that create a single effect.

Each scene in act 1 of *Mud* is a revelatory image with everything extraneous burnt away by the showing forth of the image's soul, which is Mae's soul. Each image incrementally clarifies her to herself and the audience. Sensuously united with Henry's masculine environment in scene 8 following her separation from Lloyd's masculine environment in scene 4, she is moving from the darkness of mud toward the light of self-realization.

Act 2 should accelerate the movement, but it does not for the reason just given: There are two male environments. Fornes's theatre typically involves the heroine with two men, one significantly older. The two men come from different cultural environments, each with an attitude toward women. Each man batters the woman differently. In the one environment, battering can be metaphoric with the man an insistent suitor for her affection. In the other environment, the man batters physically. The dictatorial husband in the 1985 play, *The Conduct of Life*, applies physical torture.

We should not conclude, however, that for the Cuban-born playwright, the old-world man is automatically crueler than his younger new-world counterpart, who is automatically more sensitive to a woman's psychology. Fornes is neither simplistic nor predictable. Both men can be loving and abusive, their battering metaphoric and physical. Nor does the man's age identify his attitude. Whereas the older man in *Mud* is new world, the older one in the triangle in the 1987 *Abingdon Square* is old world.

Furthermore, though the Fornes heroine discovers the goddess within her, she is no angel. As she grows in the new world, she can become materialistic, perverting the American Dream herself, and she can be cruel. An ugly scene in act 2 of *Mud* has Mae unleashing a verbal attack on the stricken Henry that drives him from the chair to the floor, where she kneels next to him, mercilessly condemning him for taking her money.

Because of the triangle in a typical Fornes play, the heroine's journey to self-realization causes conflict between the two men. Act 1 of *Mud* ends with a scene in which Mae, reading about a hermit crab, sits centerstage, flanked by the two men. Compositionally she balances the two antagonists, for although she has chosen Henry's environment, she is sympathetic to the man from whose environment her soul evolved. She not only neutralizes their hostility but also mediates between them to reconcile them. Act 2, however, opens with a scene in which she is not present, the first such scene in the play. Compositionally the men, each seated to one side, balance each other. Neither is ready yet to claim centerstage, but the tension between them does, for it stretches across the stage, filling it. Barely able to tolerate Lloyd's interrupting his concentration by talking about his visit to the clinic, Henry silences him by ordering him to have the prescription he was given filled.

The play's clarity shifts in act 2's early scenes, with each scene a revelatory image of the masculine self. As she begins to discover herself, Mae affects the men's self-images and their attitudes toward her and each other. Lloyd, for example, awakens. He wants to learn how to read, and one scene, 14, images his halting attempt with the textbook passage on starfish that Mae read with inspiration in act 1. He gets no sympathy or encouragement from Henry, though, who is convulsed with laughter as he mimics the attempt. But even before the reading exercise, Lloyd moves to preempt centerstage. By scene 12 he alternates performing cartwheels and holding body-building poses as he touts his adolescent masculine self.

So long as Mae is a spiritual and moral force, she maintains a balance between the two, but something happens in act 2 that tips the balance. Henry suffers a paralyzing accident, which puts him at the mercy of Lloyd, from whom he extracted a confession of theft of his money to pay for the prescription. Lloyd tries to follow Mae's instructions and feed him, but the stricken man does not cooperate, spitting out his food. To make matters worse, he mocks the illiterate's attempt to read and then remains silent after stealing Mae's money, leaving her no choice but to blame the younger man, who has already confessed to theft. After all, she reasons, her husband could not have taken the money, since he cannot walk.

Alone with his wife, whose silence spells disaffection, Henry attempts a sensuous reunion in scene 15. He unzips his fly, but he does not ask Mae to come to him as Lloyd did in scene 1. To prove his ability to satisfy her even though crippled, he pulls himself to a standing position by holding onto the table and slides toward her. He pleads that he loves her and needs her love, as he moves his pelvis against her body, impassive to his desire and his pain. When he ejaculates, he loses what little muscular control he has and crashes to the floor. "You can walk, Henry. You took my money" (37), she accuses as she stands over him.

Their weight pulling her back into the mud—into the ugly scene 16, where she kneels next to Henry—Mae announces her intention in scene 17 to find a "job. And a room to live in. Far away" (39) from the two men. Lloyd will not tolerate her leaving. With Henry powerless to stop him, the younger man kills her. Identifying with the starfish, which lives in the dark, she dies longing for the light.

Mae's dying words should remind the theatregoer of the discovery of the goddess in the sun image toward the end of *For Colored Girls*. In *Mud*, however, there is no savior, male or female. There is only the recognition that the journey to self-realization must continue, even though the quester, male or female, feels the ambivalence of a divided existence in a broken world, one part going back into the past of history and myth to recover the heritage and another part voyaging forward in the hope of creating a new, integrated, self.

2

Other Minority Theatres

The ambivalence toward the journey is apparent moments into the first episode of a play by an Irishman set in the old world just prior to the voyager's departure for the new world. Brian Friel's *Philadelphia, Here I Come!* takes place between seven in the evening and the following morning, a few hours before Gareth O'Donnell is to leave Ireland for a new life in America. Two actors play the role because, although Gar knows that he has no future in the village of Ballybeg in County Donegal, the decision to leave has divided him into two selves, a Public and a Private. The play is a dialogue between the two as the young man prepares for the journey, with the cast maintaining the illusion that only Public can hear his alter ego to converse with him and that no one, not even Public, can see him.

Two images summarize Gar's reasons for emigrating. During the course of the evening, three fellows that he palled with since school days stop by to say goodbye. After a few awkward minutes, they leave, professing excitement at the prospect of drinking at the hotel and picking up two English ladies there. Private, who knows better, reminds Public of the nights Gar went with them. In the disparity between an Irishman's boasting about his sexual prowess and the truth of his standing in the raw wind outside a hotel and furtively peeping at two women within who will not look up from their knitting, Friel captures the reality of life for a people tormented by the disparity between their country's glorious past and shrunken present.

The second image comes from within the O'Donnell family. Widowed three days after Gar's birth, father and son have so drifted apart over the years that they have nothing to say to each other beyond the daily operation of the former's dry goods store, where the latter works. Middle-aged when he married a much younger bride, the father has some forty years on his son. In the play's most poignant moment, speaking to his housekeeper, he wonders why he and Gar cannot communicate, particularly on the eve of his departure. "Maybe, Madge, maybe it's because I could have been his grandfather, eh?"[1]

In the father's age, Friel symbolizes the culture of Gar's past, just as in Madge's answer he points toward the culture of Gar's future. "I don't know," the housekeeper answers. "They're a new race—a new world" (97). *Philadelphia, Here I Come!* does not tilt toward the new world. Early in the play, Private asks Public if he is fully aware that he is leaving the land of his birth for a "profane, irreligious, pagan country of gross materialism" (32). Since Gar must leave, the issue is not whether he should go but what of his old-world culture he should take with him.

He takes the images of his last hours in Ballybeg, "distilled of all . . . coarseness" (77), to be stored in the memory and played as a film "over and over again" (99) in his new home in Philadelphia. Absorbed images of his native culture are the heritage this voyager takes with him to sustain him until he is assimilated into his adopted culture, at which time his hope is that his self, divided between the worlds, will have integrated the cultures. He will have created a new, whole, self.

Not every voyager takes his old-world heritage with him. In the second scene of act 1 of David Henry Hwang's *FOB*, one of the play's three characters, Grace, recounts her identity crisis. At age ten she arrived in southern California from Taiwan. Ignored by Chinese American girls born in the States, she tried to pass as a Native American by bleaching her hair and hanging out on the beaches where the white kids congregated. It was not until senior year in high school that she was able to accept herself. The scene is dramatically important because it explains Grace's motivation as the play's pivotal character between the other two.

The play opens with the entrance of a well-dressed young man through the rear door of Grace's family's restaurant, where she sits in the back room. A new arrival, speaking Chinese, Steve wants to know whether the restaurant serves a particular item of Chinese cuisine. When she tells him to check the menu, he becomes imperious. Speaking English, he identifies himself as Gwan Gung, god of warriors.

Since Steve is scrawny, the identification is funny, but only partly so. Having suffered through her own identity crisis, Grace sympathizes with the plight of the foreigner who, no matter how well-off financially, must cloak himself in a guise that gives him strength and dignity in an unknown environment. Unfortunately, Steve takes the role too seriously. He is a Chinese variation of the "one male god" who expects others to serve him.

Able to see the insecure immigrant beneath the mask, Grace orchestrates the play's action. She invites to the restaurant, not yet open for business, the third character, her cousin Dale, a second-generation American of Chinese descent, who in a monologue comparable to Grace's, confesses his pride in "making it in America."[2] But he will not help Steve adjust to the new environment. Resenting his imperiousness, he mocks the Hong Kong money that sent to America another FOB: another fresh-off-the-boat gook.

When it becomes clear to Grace that the two young men cannot get along, she becomes Fa Mu Lan, the woman warrior who takes her father's place in battle. Striking two pots together, she initiates the ritual that she and Steve enact in the second half of act 2. "You are in a new land, Gwan Gung" (47), she tells him. Finally understanding, he allows the woman warrior to slay the god who, dying honorably, frees the young man to be himself. Now when he asks her to go dancing with him, Grace accepts because he is learning how to act in his new home. They leave the stage to Dale, who was able to participate in the ritual's commencement but not its conclusion.

As the two leave, Steve offers Dale his hand, but Grace's cousin rejects the offer because he does not want to belong to their society. The self he created does not integrate cultures but denies the old-world heritage. In the monologue quoted from above, he explains that he has overcome the "Chinese-ness" of his parents. "So, I've had to work real hard—real hard—to be myself. To not be a Chinese, a yellow, a slant, a gook" (32). He knows the names of Gwan Gung and Fa Mu Lan, of course, but he cannot participate in the second half of the ritual because he cannot bring them to life in the new world. For him they have no place in America.

For Dale the American Dream is shedding the past in order to be assimilated into the dominant culture. The play opens and closes with him alone onstage stereotyping new immigrants in verbal images that do not change: "Clumsy, ugly, greasy FOB . . ." (6, 50). His attack reveals his fear. By appealing to a common origin and heritage, to a bond that links them ethnically and spiritually, Steve, the newest voyager from the old world, threatens his, Dale's, self-image as someone who has overcome the stigma of a minority identity.

Grace presents another perspective on the American Dream. She has entered American culture but not by denying her Asian culture. She brings it with her, and she renews it by studying Chinese American history at UCLA, just as she renews American culture by inviting newcomers to enter it. Respecting the myths and legends of her old-world heritage, she can incarnate them in the new world, bringing Fa Mu Lan to life to assist Steve in navigating the journey between worlds. He dies as Gwan Gung in America, but the myth lives in him too. Not by abandoning the old-world heritage for the new-world self, as Dale does, but by accepting the heritage as a shaping force on the selves they were when they arrived, individually and collectively Grace and Steve can continue to create themselves and their society. The culture they have assimilated will expand and enrich American culture as they become assimilated.

With Grace's mediation, Steve seems to be headed toward realizing Gar's hope of a new, whole, self in a new, constantly expanding, society enriched by multicultural infusions. The destination, however, lies in the future. In the introduction to the collection of plays that includes *FOB*, Hwang defines the social experiment that distinguishes the new world from the old. "Though it is often observed in the breach, America—at least in principle—subscribes to the notion that whoever takes residence on these shores may call them home." The experiment is the American Dream of social equality, the context in which Hwang places his plays and himself while he was composing them. Each play in the volume he introduces he relates to the phase of self-identity he was in at the time of writing it—assimilationist or isolationist-nationalist, for example—for even though the definition expresses the Dream as a social promise, the self cannot be understood apart from the society that is expected to accept it.

Ideally, the new-world experience should create through interaction of old and new a new, whole, self because the assimilation should incorporate into the social body the voyager who arrives with the old-world images absorbed in his old-world self. Yet the ambivalence persists. Hwang does not use the familiar melting-pot metaphor for the experiment but does use a term between ethnocentrism and assimilation: "multicultural." The latter term he spells out toward the introduction's end when he writes that "over the next decades, as Caucasians become increasingly a plurality rather than a majority in this country, we will struggle to evolve a truly progressive nation, one in which different ethnic, political, and social groups co-exist in a state of equality." The closing line hints at a unity beyond co-existence of ethnic groups: "In both my life and my work I will continue to grapple with an American dream for the future."[3] But the reality is that assimilation as society's goal, imaged in the melting-pot metaphor of the twentieth century's opening decades, has been replaced in the century's closing decades by multiculturalism, imaged as separate but equal, hyphenated mini-nations within the nation.

The increase in the number of theatres performing gender, ethnic, and racial experiences reflects multiculturalism's rise. "'We are not Africans, but African-Americans,'" Suzan-Lori Parks is quoted as stating about her culture. "'We have to make beauty out of what we're stuck with.'"[4]

More musical theatre than play, *The Death of the Last Black Man in the Whole Entire World* reprises the black race's history from its origins in antiquity to its transplantation in the new world, where the black man in his fictional and mythological embodiments is killed again and again, only to be born again and again. Parks makes beauty by dropping the European "d" that "ended things ended."[5] Making the world "roun," or whole, again, she celebrates an African-American experience in an African-American idiom. Theatrically, the dropping of the closing "d" means the dropping of the Eurocentric form of narration that moves linearly through rising and falling action to closure. In its place she recovers an older form rooted in nature in which movement is endlessly cyclical unless broken by factitious intervention. The final recitative is that of the Black Woman With Fried Drumstick. "Thuh black man he move. He move. He hans" (276). His "hans" connect to his arms, which connect to his trunk. Like nature, he has come "roun" in his body again, re-membering an old-world life in new-world images and thereby creating a new, whole, self within his hyphenated culture.

August Wilson's plays have characters who have not come "roun" when they make their first appearance, who are dismembered from their community because they cannot let go of the "d" affixed to them by the white man. Herald Loomis in *Joe Turner's Come and Gone* has died once, but that once was not enough, although when he eventually tells his story, it is a tale of impressed labor for Joe Turner, a seven-year bondage that separated him from his wife and daughter, an illegal slavery that broke his heart.

Even before the audience hears his story, it sees the death imaged in his person. The time of the play is August of 1911; the place is a Pittsburgh boardinghouse. Despite the summer heat, Loomis enters the house wearing a hat and a long wool coat, which he does not remove. He cannot unburden his soul when he arrives, eating by himself and resisting the overtures the others make to him. Just as he wears one symbol of his encumbrance, he holds another. Following his release from impressed labor, he went searching for his family. He found his daughter at her grandmother's house and took her with him. That he accepts his responsibility for her makes him a man of conscience, yet by squeezing her hand, by not letting her out of his sight despite the fact that she is a growing girl, he cannot face the future. He is searching for his connection with the past in the person of his wife Martha.

He is not the only one searching. The play reflects a diaspora of the twentieth century's opening decades when, as Wilson writes in the play's preface, "from the deep and the near South the sons and daughters of newly freed African slaves wander into the city." Dispersed, "isolated" from their heritage, they come to the house searching for lost mates and relatives, the ones in whom they found their identity in the past. For them to discover their "new identity as free men of definite and sincere worth," they must "reconnect" with life.[6] One of the tenants, Mattie, must realize, for example, that she cannot have the man who left her after their two babies died but must find another man.

The boardinghouse, owned by Seth, a Northerner born of free parents, and his wife Bertha, is the gateway to resurrection. Here before the new arrival can wrap himself in fresh sheets, he must scrub himself clean of the grime from the journey—a baptismal rite. One tenant, Bynum, a conjure man, performs his magic ritual over slain pigeons in the backyard, where a boy will claim to have seen the risen Miss Mabel, Seth's dead mother. In the house, Bertha performs her magic ritual *"to which she is connected by the muscles of her heart and the blood's memory"* (87).

Here the old self must die—like Steve as Gwan Gung in *FOB*—but not by denying the past. The voyager must embrace it as his heritage. Seth and Bertha function as Grace does in Hwang's play. They keep the heritage vital in the house's communal activities such as the juba, Wilson's African equivalent to Hwang's Asian ritual. The stage directions describe it as *"reminiscent of the Ring Shouts of the African slaves. It is a call and response dance"* (52). All except Loomis participate because of all the characters he is the most shackled to the past, which is multilayered in Wilson's theatre.

Loomis is shackled to Martha. Separated for ten years, he feels that he cannot recommence living until he sees her again, if only to say goodbye to that part of his life and self he bonded to her. He is shackled to his hatred of Christianity for what he feels is its betrayal of him. He was a deacon performing his pastoral duty when Turner's men took him prisoner. Hence he pictures Christ as a white slave driver. He is shackled to a past he suppresses. He admits that he is searching for his wife, and he reveals his attitude toward Christianity as soon as he hears the juba performers call upon the Holy Ghost. He does not, however, bring to the surface the suppressed past until midway through act 2.

The juba participants' near-frenzied clapping of hands while calling upon the Holy Ghost drives Loomis into a rage, provoking the act-1 climax. Collapsing, with Bynum on the floor next to him drawing him out, he relates the vision that fills him with dread. He sees bones walking across the water, sinking to the bottom, and being washed up onto the land but with flesh on them.

Consistent with multilayered characters searching for themselves through a multilayered past, Wilson's imagery is multilayered. An image of rebirth, the risen bones hark back to the biblical tale of Jonah in the whale. Loomis himself refers to the tale later in a play that contains numerous biblical allusions. An image of death, the sunken bones are those of his ancestors, slaves transported across the ocean. Yet it is the rebirth that terrifies him, that in one of the contemporary theatre's most harrowing of images keeps him writhing on the floor as he tries to rise at act's end, for it calls to him to stand as a free man on his own two feet. To rise from the depths where he lies between worlds, he must unburden his encumbered soul. He must die again to be reborn.

Telling his story is his death. He must admit that in the eyes of white society as represented by Turner, brother of the governor of Tennessee, he could be enslaved without anyone's concern because he was no more than a "worthless" nigger (73). From the time of his arrival at the boardinghouse, he has acknowledged his American past—marriage and ministry—but not his African heritage, the reason for which is hinted at in his becoming a Christian deacon. He makes no speech comparable to Dale's rejection of his racial heritage in *FOB*, but he felt that being a deacon invested him with worth. That explains his feeling of betrayal. As a result, even though his experience recapitulates his race's experience in the new world, he is isolated, estranged from himself and sustaining rituals.

Singing his song is his rebirth. Wilson is a weaver of monologues, a creator of songs. For Bynum, every person must sing his/her song; it is the self's expression. A person has to find the right song before he/she can sing it, however, for although many search down long roads for it, it is not found without but within the person. Turner confiscated his body and, as Bynum explains to him, would have confiscated his song, or self, had he, Loomis, not hidden it from him. But in hiding it in the degradation of slavery, he has become so private a person that he has hidden it from himself, a truth the audience sees dramatized when he tries to touch Mattie but does not know how because he has not touched a woman since the days when he wanted to touch only his wife.

Telling his story, in act 2 to Bynum and Seth, releases his buried past and self. He begins to find his voice and begins to reconnect with a world outside his private person, that of his African-American community, the members of which share his heritage: its suffering and its joy. No longer encumbered, he returns their daughter to her mother, and, making peace with the latter as she made peace with his memory years earlier, he smears himself with his blood, ending his displacement. *"Having found his song, the song of self-sufficiency"* (93), and with Mattie following him, he leaves the house for a new future in the new world. In Parks's metaphor he has come "roun."

The ending is comparable to the ending of *FOB*. Loomis says goodbye to Martha and Zonia, to his hatred of Christianity, and to Joe Turner, who has come and gone.[7] He does not obliterate the past from his consciousness, which would be impossible to do anyway, and he expects to see his daughter again. Recovering his African heritage, he integrates it with his American experience to become a whole African-American in an African-American community, a community with its own culture, one that is different from white culture.[8]

Herald Loomis has become symbolic, as the play has been in the process of becoming since its naturalistic opening. As he passes through the gateway, *"free to soar above the environs that weighed and pushed his spirit into terrifying contractions"* (94), Loomis becomes the Shiny Man of Bynum's vision, the "One Who Goes Before and Shows the Way" (10). He becomes the herald of a new life in which an African-American can create a new self whose song is worth singing partly because it is nourished by a song tradition rooted in an African past.

The song tradition is strongest in Wilson's *The Piano Lesson*, in which a brother and a sister are separated in their attitudes toward their heritage as symbolized by a piano. The play is set in Pittsburgh in the 1930s in the home of Doaker Charles; his niece, Berniece; and her daughter, the same age as Loomis's daughter. The play opens with the arrival of his nephew, Boy Willie, with a friend, Lymon, from the South with a truckload of watermelons, the sale of which will give the nephew one-third of the money he needs to purchase land in Mississippi, owned by the Sutter family, the white family that once owned his family on that land. One-third of the money he already has, and the remaining third he expects to realize from the sale of the piano, in Doaker's parlor, that he and his sister own. On it are carved scenes and faces from the family's history.

Boy Willie intends no disrespect for the family's history by wanting to sell the piano. For him the piano is valuable in that it can be sold for land, which is alive and therefore renewable. With land he can plant, harvest, and plant again. He can nurture and grow crops that support and renew life. On the land, he will keep the heritage alive because it is a tradition alive in his own person.

In *Joe Turner's Come and Gone*, the audience sees Loomis's attitude toward the past imaged in his person, isolated and dressed in black. In *The Piano Lesson*, the audience hears Boy Willie's attitude in his person. He bursts into the house glad to see his uncle and asking about the other uncle, Wining Boy. Exuberant, he wants his sister and niece to wake up and come downstairs so that he can tell them of his plan to buy the land.

This is what makes Wilson the master he is of the contemporary stage. Boy Willie does not articulate his position to his uncles about the living tradition that is his family's heritage. Their verbal and aural images are the tradition kept alive by them in their folk songs about women and marriage, gambling and working on the railroad, and in their monologues about the crafting of the piano when the family was enslaved; the taking of it from the Sutter family by the father of Boy Willie and Berniece and his two brothers, the uncles Doaker and Wining Boy; and the deaths of the father and the hobos that were caught with him on a train boxcar set afire. Folk songs beget folk songs in a communal activity comparable to the juba. At one point the men stamp their feet and clap their hands as they harmonize. Monologues beget monologues as each man contributes to the telling of the family story.

The men are so exuberant in so exuberant a play that Wilson's artistry threatens to defeat his theatre. Boy Willie and the storytelling that bursts into communal song command the stage. They should, for as the men pass the monologues from one to another, repeating and embellishing the rhythms until the story becomes not only the family's history but also the race's heritage, they sing the songs that express the African-American experience.

Berniece, however, also should command the stage. Yet since she neither wears a stark outfit nor has a brooding presence, her role can be minimized as a woman's role not equal to the men's roles.

Berniece is the play's Herald Loomis. The signs are all there. In act 1 she absents herself from the house's communal activities, at most making an appearance before retiring to her room, where she lives as single parent with her daughter. She severs continuity with the past by shutting the top of the piano when her mother dies. She disconnects herself from life, withholding herself from Avery, the preacher who wants to marry her. "You too young a woman to close up,"[9] he tells her. She denies closing up, yet her ordering Boy Willie's female companion from the house when she catches them fooling around on the couch supports Avery's insight that she is repressed.

With Boy Willie and the other men, she embodies a truth at the heart of Wilson's theatre: how one feels about himself/herself and how one feels about his/her culture are interdependent. For Berniece the piano is an inert heirloom and must remain that way even if she has to use a gun to stop her brother from moving it. She is not ashamed of her family's history. She is so embittered by the violence the men are capable of and the suffering the women have had to endure that she wants to forget the history. When she was a girl and playing the piano, the mother "could hear my daddy talking to her," she tells Avery. "I used to think them pictures came alive and walked through the house" (70). She stops playing when her mother dies because she does not want the spirits walking again. For that reason, although she allows her daughter to play the piano, she does not want her to know the history associated with it. "I ain't gonna burden her . . ." (70) is her attitude.

The history of the piano and the race is not a burden to Boy Willie; it is a cause for "celebration," which if his niece knew it, he argues, "She could walk around here with her head held high" (91). For him, being black does not put him at the bottom of society, where the mother teaches the girl that they are, but at the top of life. His words do not persuade his sister. Berniece blames their father's taking the piano, which led to his death, for their mother's sorrow and loneliness, and she blames her brother for the death of her husband, killed while taking wood with him and Lymon. For her, black history is a heritage of tears.

But like Loomis, she begins to respond to the activity in the house—to Lymon, who puts perfume behind her ear one night and kisses her neck. Buried with the past, life beckons to her, and as the men have been trying to make her see, she is too much of a woman to waste herself. Although I think the play would work without the scene, apparently Wilson wants to emphasize the relationship between self-repression and cultural intimidation.

A few weeks before Boy Willie arrives in Pittsburgh and just after he died, the ghost of the man, Sutter, who killed his and Berniece's father, arrived to haunt Doaker's house. Why? The obvious answer is to prevent the son from selling the piano that the Sutters, by owning the Charles family when the work was crafted, believe is theirs. A less obvious answer is to prevent the movement of the history crafted on the piano into the public world, where it would be admired. The Sutters with Joe Turner represent the one male god whose culture suppresses other cultures' songs, stories, paintings—myths—by denying them space in museums, textbooks, and the like.

When Boy Willie fights the ghost, Berniece finally realizes what she must do, in a thrilling finale to a rousing play. Sitting at the piano, she finds her song, which is an *"exorcism and a dressing for battle"* (106). She calls upon her ancestors' spirits to aid her brother, and it is not difficult to imagine the figures coming to life on the piano and mounting the stairs to do battle for the right to their sustaining tradition.

With Sutter's ghost exorcised, Boy Willie can leave to get money for the land elsewhere. Having brought the tradition to life in her song, Berniece will renew it by teaching it to her daughter on the piano.

Each August Wilson play sums up the African-American experience for the decade in which it takes place. Perhaps because *Two Trains Running* takes place in Pittsburgh in 1969 and should therefore sum up the experience for the turbulent civil rights decade, it does not seem to meet expectations. Yet the play is as powerful as the two already examined.

Like the boardinghouse and the family home in the other two plays, the restaurant in which *Two Trains Running* is set houses the communal experience. The set, more a diner than a restaurant, is the place of congregation for a variety of characters, each of whom in response to external or internal stimulus spins his/her story. The stories are less focused on an experience that brings them to the diner or on an object in the diner than they are in the other two plays because the characters neither live under the same roof nor are connected by blood and because they are focused more on the world outside the diner. Nevertheless their stories, the monologues that create Wilson's theatre, share a common thread.

The characters want what they believe is their due in life. They do not, however, agree on what that is beyond knowing that it will give them their identities, their self-worth. When one of the characters, a numbers runner, comes into the diner, he comments on the crowd in the street, to which the play's philosopher replies with an observation that applies to the diner's habitués as well. "The people out there looking for opportunity. Whatever's out there in the way of opportunity, sooner or later it's got to pass through. You can't find out what's out there sitting at home."[10]

Searching for opportunity, they are searching for themselves in the avenues open to them: entrepreneurship; gambling; religion, self-styled and orthodox; and the community's elders and savants. Here too they disagree on the best avenue. One man's formula for success is another man's folly.

Not only can they not agree among themselves on what they want, with the exception of two, the characters are not certain that what they want will satisfy their individual need to be worthy of respect. Even the most convinced, Memphis, the restaurant owner who demands that the city meet his price for the property it must acquire for its renovation project, dreams of reclaiming the property confiscated from him in the South from which he was forced to flee in the 1930s. The least convinced is Sterling, recently released from the penitentiary. All that he knows is that he wants to be somebody, as he tries to explain to West, the funeral-parlor owner:

> I'm gonna get me two or three Cadillacs like you. Get Risa to be my woman and I'll be alright. That's all a man need is a pocketful of money, a Cadillac, and a good woman. That's all he need on the surface. I ain't gonna talk about that other part of satisfaction. But I got sense enough to know it's there. I know if you get the surface it don't mean nothing unless you got the other. I know that, Mr. West. Sometimes I think I'll just take the woman part. And then sometimes that don't seem like it's enough. (93–94)

Between the times of the two earlier plays, 1911 and the 1930s, and the time of this play, the African-American community lost the heritage contained in a house and piano. Having lost it, Pittsburgh's blacks mill about the street looking for opportunity or dream of winning a pocketful of money in a crap game. *Two Trains Running* is focused but in a way different from that of the plays set in earlier decades or that of *The Heidi Chronicles*, for Wilson's drama and Wasserstein's drama are comparable, with each predicated on a midcentury breakup of values.

Wilson's play does not have an articulate spokesman such as a distinguished graduate to express to an alumnae association bitterness over the failure of the movement that was expected to unite them. It does not have someone like the lesbian in army fatigues to plead unity to her sisters at a consciousness-raising meeting. It does have, however, the anger of Wasserstein's play toward those members of the community who have turned against one another to make it in America. "Cheating and fooling the people" (7 and 12) are the numbers runner's and Memphis's castigations of the community's two wealthiest members: the self-styled prophet of his own church and the funeral parlor owner.

Wilson's play has a spokesman, but he is not articulate beyond the two sentences he repeats: "He gonna give me my ham. I want my ham" (14).[11] As the other characters explain to newcomer Sterling, nine and a half years ago, Hambone agreed to paint the fence by the meat market owned by a white man, Lutz, for a chicken, with the condition that he would receive a ham should he do a good job. Hambone believes that he did a good job, but since Lutz does not, he told him to take a chicken. Refusing, the black man has every day for nine and a half years, Sundays included, posted himself by the meat market to speak the only words remaining in his vocabulary.

Hambone preserves the core of the African-American heritage, the reason for a community. Nothing less than his due in life will satisfy him, and he knows exactly what it is and who owes it to him. He demands justice from the white man.

He is one of the two characters that I excluded above. The other is Risa, the diner waitress who scarred her attractive legs with a razor to force men to perceive her, according to the stage directions, *"in terms other than her genitalia"* (3). She and Hambone are linked throughout the play. Whenever someone tired of listening to his one note tries to make him leave, she defends him. She feeds him and sees to it that he has warm clothing in cold weather. When he dies, West discovers that his body is scarred all over, but no one knows whether the wounds were self-inflicted or not because he lived alone and dies alone. His death is as symbolic as his life. Whereas people line the streets for blocks to view the prophet of the future laid out with his jewelry and hundred-dollar bills, only a few pay their respects to the workman of the past who demanded justice.

By setting the play in 1969, Wilson eliminates the two historical figures, both mentioned in the play, whom a multiracial audience would recognize as spokesmen in the 1960s for African-American aspirations. By 1969 Martin Luther King and Malcolm X were dead. By eliminating a spokesman, the playwright is faithful to the dual perspective that I think he wishes to maintain. *Two Trains Running* has no single-minded spokesman because between 1911 and the late 1960s, the community in the Pittsburgh of *Joe Turner's Come and Gone* ceased being single minded. By the time of the later play, the community has diversified in income, religion, politics, attitudes, and aspirations. With the exception of Hambone and Risa, all of the characters are entrepreneurs, from painting houses to owning a funeral parlor, or want to be. They worship differently and recreate themselves differently. Some have lasting relationships, and some do not.

Diversity is one of the play's realities that can be explained sociologically. The other reality, in the midst of diversity, defies explanation. Hambone's single-mindedness is admirable but mad, so mad that Wilson himself describes him as *"self-contained and in a world of his own. His mental condition has deteriorated to such a point that he can only say two phrases, and he repeats them idiotically over and over"* (14). Despite succumbing to the lure of material possessions, the others in the diner continue the culture's oral tradition. Their songs, rich in history and lore, are the myths told to newcomers like Sterling. Hambone has no following. Arrested in the past, he is the one about whom followers should create myths were they not gawking at Prophet Samuel.

Is the audience supposed to empathize with a man so dedicated to his vision that life passed him by or with the diner habitués, fed up with nine and a half years of his two repeated sentences, who want to get on with their lives? The audience can empathize with both because by maintaining the dual perspective, the play is ambiguous. Hambone's behavior is abnormal. Risa's identifying with him brings him back into the group. The complication, though, is that her behavior is abnormal. The men cannot understand why a woman would disfigure herself to make a statement about herself.

If there is a clue to Wilson's attitude toward Hambone, it comes at play's end in his death and in the responses his death elicits. He died "real peaceful" (90), the philosopher reports. Though some of his people sought to exclude him from the diner's communal life, he had the tradition in which he believed to sustain him. He did not perceive himself or his craft as inferior.

Of the lives he touched, Risa wishes that she could afford a good casket so that he would not have to be buried in a welfare casket. Some of the diner people go to the funeral parlor. Not only does Memphis contribute fifty dollars for flowers, the death galvanizes the diner owner. With the money awarded him by the city, he vows to return to Tennessee and fight the battle he had put aside years earlier. And in the play's closing image, a bleeding Sterling bursts into the diner with a ham that he took from the meat market and that he gives to West to put into the casket with the dead man.

The ending does not lessen the ambiguity but passes it to Sterling because the audience does not know whether the act is a personal statement or the assumption of Hambone's role as keeper of the reason for the civil rights movement. The image he creates is that of a bleeding Loomis, the man who recapitulates his race's new-world experience, but whether he is the herald of a new life or is remanded to his old self in the penitentiary, we do not know. And we may never know, yet in the series of plays, we have a masterful telling of twentieth-century African-American myths.

Before concluding this chapter, I want to correct what might appear to be an imbalance of self-discovery occurring, not within a gender enclave as in the previous chapter, but within a racial or ethnic one. Eduardo Ivan Lopez's *A Silent Thunder* is a two-character play. Joe feels alienated in the States because he is perceived as Hispanic and in Puerto Rico because he is perceived as mainland American. Only his U.S. Marine uniform gives him an identity. Stationed in 1966 on Okinawa, he meets Kimiyo, who feels alienated from her island culture because she wants to go to Tokyo, where the opportunities are more numerous, and from the mainland culture because she is perceived as provincial Okinawan. Together the two discover themselves.

Lanford Wilson's *Redwood Curtain* is a three-character play. Teenager Geri is the daughter of a Vietnamese mother, who sold her to an American couple within a month of her birth, and an American father, for whom she searches. Unable to reconcile his Southeast-Asian experience with the America to which he returned, Lyman, an ex-serviceman, has retreated behind a redwood curtain in northern California. Geneva, Geri's aunt, feels uprooted now that a logging company will deforest the land on which her family has lived for decades. Together the three discover themselves.

The first two chapters of this book are devoted to minorities because, by voyaging between cultures, they highlight the quest that every person who would be a citizen of the new world must undertake. The terms have been expanding and will continue to expand as we encounter theatre created within the dominant culture, the subject of chapters 3 and 4. The old-world culture may be European or Chinese, African or Vietnamese, but it may also be native to a region of America—the agrarian, rural South, for example—that the voyager must leave for another region—the industrialized, urban North. Not only does the uprooting not have to involve transoceanic travel or border crossing, the geographic change may be no more than the address within a city. The quester may be leaving one socioeconomic class for another, for every group has its upwardly mobile, whether called yuppies or the talented tenth.

Every group has those who cannot make the journey, who cling to the old-world values that sustain them. Every group has those who will shed anything and everything of the old culture for membership in the new culture. Every group has those divided between the two worlds.

The next two chapters examine plays in which the breakup of dominant, unitary standards causes their adherents to do what many of the minorities do. They fragment, form enclaves, become exemplary, and appropriate selves. Two plays illustrate the point. One of them, by a black author, has a black character who passes for white at work because he perceives white culture as dominant. The other, by a white author, has a white character who practices speaking a black idiom because he perceives black culture as supplanting white culture. And lest we forget, Wasserstein's Heidi accuses her sisters of acting like men to get ahead.

One reason for concluding this chapter with *A Silent Thunder* and *Redwood Curtain* is to show that the quest for identity is universal. It is so for Jessica Hagedorn. Born and raised in Manila, the Philippines, she came to San Francisco while an adolescent. "I don't care whether you're an immigrant or native-born," the artist comments on her writing, "you're discovering who and what and where you are all the time."[12]

Characters in the dominant culture also recover their heritage and reconnect to it. They create self and society anew. They assimilate. But the book's second half is the healing process for majority and minority cultures.

Another difference is readily apparent. Chapters 1 and 2 begin with the personal self, which expands to the theatrical self, with the national self developing more slowly. Chapters 3 and 4 begin with the personal self, which expands to the national self, with the theatrical self developing more slowly.

3

Exemplary Selves in History

Scholar and critic Roger Shattuck puts in historical perspective the quest for identity that follows from the breakup of an old order. In *The Innocent Eye*, he explores some of the developments that followed from the shifts, occurring in the seventeenth and eighteenth centuries, away from the belief that birth determined a person's station in life. Asking one sweeping question raised by the revolution in attitude—"How then were citizens to find their place in the world? their role in life?"—he offers a tentative answer: "Citizens of the modern world have sought not so much a station as a *self*, a personal identity or individuality, a self which also gradually displaced the earlier term, *soul*."[1]

In this context, for members of majority and minority cultures alike, the old world is the world in which one's place in the community establishes one's identity and the new world is the world in which one creates an identity, or self. The context is not very different from that of the preceding chapter in which the old world is the community held together by tradition and shared values and the new world is the problematical Pittsburgh of August Wilson's *Two Trains Running*, with people milling about the street on the lookout for opportunity.

Following the passage that I quoted, Shattuck goes on to suggest four directions the search for self-discovery has taken in the past two centuries. For citizens of the modern theatre, the two most interesting are the third and fourth, undertaking to create a self from subjective processes and in the histrionic sensibility. They offer more possibilities for the theatre than the other two, making money and pursuing amorous adventures, because the third enacts an experimental, non-naturalistic drama and the fourth requires an audience to validate the creation.

The two directions shape a group of three plays by Richard Nelson, writing from within mainstream America in the sense that his characters do not represent minorities. Whether or not they were conceived as a trilogy, they can be thought of as forming one. They share the same metaphors and imagery. Furthermore, the three plays were produced in New York in a ten-month period from March 1978 to January 1979. Two had been produced before, yet the fact remains that their author was to some degree involved in the staging of the three within months of one another, a fact that prompts André Bishop, then Playwrights Horizons' artistic director, to link them in the introduction to the volume in which the second is anthologized: "*Jungle Coup* was the second of three plays (after *Conjuring an Event* and before *The Vienna Notes*) in which Richard explored his obsession with the written word and with the possibilities of remaking history when the writing or reporting of it all but obliterates the truth."[2]

I, too, see the plays as linked, but by the creation of a self, the condition for membership in the modern world. The trilogy defines the issues attendant upon the condition so clearly that we can relate them to the issues of the preceding chapters, particularly the issue of what the voyager takes with him on the journey from the old world to the new, from station to self, from community of tradition and shared values to the quest for a new sustaining center. The first play dramatizes the creation of the self; the second, the challenge to the creation from the depths of the jungle (Shattuck's third direction: subjective processes); the third, the challenge from the heights of civilization (Shattuck's fourth direction: the histrionic sensibility).

Conjuring an Event opens in the Pen and Pencil Club. Of the four characters seated at the large wooden table, the first to speak is Charlie, the play's protagonist. From the table he lifts the plate over which his face with blindfolded eyes has been hovering and smashes it while yelling, "*Why can't I smell this!!*"[3] None of the other three characters at the table reacts, although a fifth character, seated apart from the group, looks up from the newspaper he has been reading.

Charlie's soliloquies supply the exposition. Having proven himself as a reporter of sporting events, having exhausted the thrill of accounting for them, he wants to conjure one. Instead of in-depth reporting, he wants to "press unrestrained into absolute depth-reporting!" Instead of being outside an event looking at it after it happened, he wants to be "*inside looking out*" (140) as it is happening. That is, he wants to be so sensitive to breaking news that he can cross the boundary separating the reporter from the event he reports by summoning the energy at life's core into an event. His purpose is not to summon the energy outside of himself into an event that he then can objectively report in a news story—by starting a fire, for example—but to summon the energy within himself so that he can report its flowing as an event.

Because the human being perceives events through the senses, Charlie primes his "to touch, taste, smell" the story out of himself. "To flush it out!" (140). He has his eyes blindfolded and his girlfriend seated next to him to ensure that he has a selection of plates, each of which contains an everyday item like salt, which by sniffing he tries to identify. That no one at the table reacts to the plate-smashing indicates that his companions are inured to his lack of success and frustration. Not only can he not conjure, he cannot report either.

The two modes of experiencing life are the play's two poles because they are two metaphors for two activities of the human mind. Conjuring, which is intuiting the world, is rooted in imagination. Reporting, which is analyzing the world, is rooted in apprehension. The play locates the first activity in the undifferentiating unconscious, which collects images, and the second activity in consciousness, which differentiates images into events and composes them into reports. They are two poles because the development of consciousness from the unconscious has separated the mind into two halves, each forming a self and thereby separating the human being into a divided self.

Yet the division is not irreconcilable. In a reminiscence that recalls passages in O'Neill's *The Hairy Ape* and *Long Day's Journey into Night*, one of the four characters at the table, a publisher, deplores the passing of the time when a reporter was so in harmony with life that he was a medium through whom the universe's energy flowed. That was before he was lured away from reporting by Hollywood's glitter and money. Although he is opposed to priming the senses to conjure because it is an attempt to induce an experience that he believes should occur naturally, from his description of reporting's golden age as an age of "magic" (143–44), a term associated with conjuring, reporting and conjuring were the same experience.

Charlie is too ambitious to be satisfied with nostalgia. He wants to reunite the two activities, as he states emphatically in the first soliloquy. Although he wants to go beyond "just facts and figures" and "natural observation," he also wants to "compile beyond understanding" (140). The verb is an activity of the conscious mind; the prepositional phrase, a location in the subconscious mind. With his reputation as a reporter of sporting events secure, he feels that he can give the "total involvement" (148) required to summon one, despite the danger. The publisher, who bolts from the room when he realizes that the reporter is priming to conjure, explains. Other reporters have attempted the feat, but invariably they came too close to the energy and either were singed by the surge of current and are no longer effective reporters or were burned and driven mad.

Charlie is well aware of the risk. To flush the story out of himself, he must activate his divided psyche, which means activating energy in a surge that could upset the psyche's equilibrium and thereby threaten his sanity. The audience hears the division from the moment the play begins. "Listen to the prep, Charlie" (139), begins the first of the play's many soliloquies in which the protagonist talks to himself as if he were two separate persons. In a sense he is because his personality is split between an ego determined to expand consciousness and an unknown nature hidden in the silent recesses of his being. So absorbed in his soliloquies that he unlocks his unconscious, he releases his hidden self, whose appearance is prefigured in the fifth character in the room, who leaves his seat apart from the group to confront the vacillating reporter as act 1 ends and who returns in act 2 in the guises of old reporter and coach to appeal to his ego to continue pressing.

He does continue until the audience hears and sees the division healed in act 2. The actor playing Charlie must be able to alternate voices and mannerisms to enact, as if in a boxing ring, the protagonist's two selves as they contest for dominance of him. As his conscious mind, or self, falls asleep, his flushed-out subconscious mind, or self, takes possession of him and conjures with the repeated invocation, "Shapes arise!" (169). In the dialectics of the internal conflict externalized as a boxing match, his awakened consciousness takes possession of him with the repeated declaration, "I consume" (171), followed by a list of the shapes he incorporates into his story, his report of the event.

Even though the surge of the unconscious bloodies his mouth, consciousness wins the match. Before the unconscious can overwhelm the mind, driving Charlie mad by surging unchecked, consciousness assimilates its energy, as symbolized by the imagery of consuming. In the language of psychological growth, in the individual's process of creating a self, his ego-centered conscious personality acquires greater reality as it consumes contents of his unconscious.[4]

Act 2 is the creation, both of the new, whole self and the new, whole story. Charlie conjures an event in which he is the center looking out through his expanding consciousness. The first released shapes are rushing images of phases in the physical making of a newspaper, but as the new self takes control, he focuses the rising shapes as reported images of specific historical events, such as Sadat's visit to Israel and Ali's whipping of Foreman, until he reaches the crowning event: the creation of himself. An integrated self speaking in a new, assertive, voice, he transforms his energy into a story that merges conjuring and reporting. He begins his report by confessing to the audience that he always wanted to be a reporter, but as he assimilates conjured images to publish himself as a newspaper, he creates a new form: the news story as prose poem.

The new form manifests the new self creating it: an expanding "I" that is itself being created by an enormous ego that by turning inward for the newsworthy story activates the division in Charlie's psyche that the audience hears and sees. It is this enormous ego that opens the olfactory organ and releases the subconscious mind, surging in a *"flash powder explosion"* (164) into the protagonist's conscious mind. In the normal process of psychological growth, as consciousness assimilates contents of the unconscious, the individual's psychological center shifts from ego to created self. In *Conjuring an Event,* the surge is so powerful that assimilating consciousness cannot arrest the expansion. Ego creates a self that devours everything conjured in a Whitmanesque free verse that runs for pages in lines such as these: "I am the buyer, and I am the seller. The consumer and the consumed. I am the one and I am the many!!" (173).

Even if the new self wanted to curb the ego's appetite, the attempt would be thwarted by the audience's applause. Whenever Charlie wavers, the coach spurs him on by playing a tape of a cheering crowd and at one point by turning up the house lights so that he can see the spectators. Their presence activates in him a susceptibility as potentially dangerous as the susceptibility to his subjective processes. They activate the histrionic sensibility, further inflating his ego.

Creating a self can be, and frequently is, tragic. One must have an ego to want to create, yet the greater the ego the more monstrous the self created. In *Conjuring an Event,* however, the new self is described as only a *"bit monstrous"*

(173) as it begins to emerge because Nelson forgoes tragedy for satire in a tone set early by the absurdity of sniffing salt as a preparation for enhancing one's involvement in life. By act 2 the absurdity of comedy becomes the exaggeration of satire.

Voracious Charlie presses beyond the normal assimilating stage in the individual's development to assume national and epic proportions. The voice that begins the transformation scene as the autobiographical "I" of the reporter recounting his early experiences becomes the mythic "I" of the Whitmanesque seer whose *Song of Myself* is a celebration of the one in the many and the many in the one—a vision both personal and cosmic. However, there is a difference. The birth is a parody of the bard's discovery of his role as poet of an America that embraces all forms of life. Charlie's uncovered self conjures a catalogue of Americana to be consumed by the reporting self until the new self is hypertrophied but not imperial.

There is no dignity to this act of gluttony. In his desire to expand consciousness so that he can be the best reporter, Charlie assimilates every image that the undifferentiated unconscious releases until his consciousness becomes undifferentiated but only because it is indiscriminate. "I consume every shitful act imaginable," he boasts, "every act of true love believable and sift out the hits from the flops" (171). A satire of self-creation, *Conjuring an Event* ends with him, bouncing and dancing, victorious in the boxing ring. "*I said, Meeeeeeeeeeeeeeee!!!!!!!!!*" he chants, giving the "*all-familiar #1 sign*" (174) to an applauding audience as the coach snaps his photo.

In a book or even a chapter on Nelson, I would pursue the creation of mythic and national selves in such plays as *Rip Van Winkle, Some Americans Abroad*, and *Two Shakespearean Actors*, but that is impossible here. And anyway the trilogy takes us deeper into the creation of a personal self, the crucial event in Nelson's imaginative world, the event from which all other events follow, including the creation of a national self. I therefore will withhold introducing the issues that emerge from the trilogy until we complete the analysis of the second and third plays.

Jungle Coup, the second play, opens with the protagonist's priming, not for conjuring, but for reporting. The locale is a village in the African jungle. While his assistant, Mott, cranks the transmitter for his radio broadcast to editorial headquarters, the reporter, Hopper, paces about "*mentally . . . readying himself.*"[5] Within moments of broadcasting, though, he becomes unhappy with the report, an unhappiness aggravated by Mott's failure to have ready a tape of recorded screams to simulate panic in support of his analysis. When the assistant, in answer to his request for a critique after he slams off the transmitter, tells the broadcaster that he thought the story "pretty smooth," Hopper directs his disgust at him, reminding the radio operator that a story is not supposed to be smooth, but is "supposed to grab" the audience. The kind of story does not matter. What does is that it release the energy at life's core so that it can "combust and explode and rage out of control." Only this kind of story will, in one of the trilogy's iterative images, "burn" the audience. Knowing that his "stale . . . tired . . . emotionless hackneyed canned shit" was not burning anyone, he slammed off the transmitter (243–44). On Mott's advice he leaves to take a break by walking around the village.

When he returns, he gives the kind of news story he has just described, one that rages out of control. He smells the "stench of confusion" and tastes a "madness" as he conjures the chaos overrunning the village. "I no longer see any reason," he says as he reaches the climax in the image of unleashed energy burning everything in its path, "but an instinct, a gut without its shell, without skin, without clothes, bare AND BURNING ALIVE!!" Though his assistant plays the panic tape and he looks toward the village, Hopper, like Charlie in *Conjuring an Event*, is turned inward, feeling within himself "emotions running wild" and "foaming at the mouth" (250–51). No critique is necessary for this story because he felt the panic grab him.

Jungle Coup carries over from the earlier play the image of explosively surging energy and the tape of a cheering stadium crowd, which Mott comes across while searching for the panic tape. For the mind's two activities, the second play adds new terms to replace "report" and "conjure." When Hopper returns from the break, he explains to Mott what he did wrong in his first broadcast. "I was trying to *construct* the touch—not *present* one. I was plotting, not feeling. So nothing was coming off gut-level. Now I know better" (247–48).

By separating the two activities, Hopper reveals his divided self. In the first instance, he builds a structure; in the second, he feels the collapse of the structure. Addressed by him as distinct activities, the poles are manifested as separate experiences, each the subject of its own news story. When constructing, he composes verbal images to build a news story; recorded sound effects supply any needed emotional coloring. He does not integrate his verbal images with his feelings because they express separate realities. Intellectual reality, or activity, is expressed verbally as a report devoid of feeling. Emotional reality is expressed aurally as a conjuring of sounds from within himself devoid of composure.

Neither does he assimilate constructed verbal images or presented aural images with apprehended images from the sensory world. In his divided self, consciousness exerts control only in matters involving its own activity. When it attempts to structure other experiences—irrational emotional ones, for example—it inhibits their expression, and for the panic to be genuine, it must rage. The sensory world is excluded from conscious assimilation for the same reason. The broadcaster disregards apprehended reality for imagined reality because if he reported what he saw in the jungle, he would be out of a job. There is no revolution outside himself. He has, in effect, increased the surge of energy in *Conjuring an Event* by asking and answering in the affirmative the following questions: If one can conjure his unconscious with its repository of archetypal images that fit all situations, why bother with apprehended images of an event? Why not simply imagine the event, in this case a jungle coup?

Hopper is not mad when the play opens. He broadcasts the ongoing coverage because a revolution is hot copy, and he maintains the equilibrium in his psyche by alternating the currents. Yet by maintaining the division between the two activities, he allows each to expand unchecked by the dialectical corrective that merging them creates. And they continue to expand until they generate a check, not from an uncritical public, but from rival media companies. If his media company devotes ongoing coverage to a revolution because there is an audience for it, competing companies want their own coverage. The play's third character, Bellows, is a reporter sent by his editors into the African jungle to report back the story to them.

Bellows is the agent that sparks the play's action. When Hopper realizes that the rival reporter will expose the deception that he has been perpetrating, he moves the transmitting station to another village, a location he plans to establish as the coup's new front. Claiming that both his editors and the rival editors will believe him and not Bellows because they will want to believe him —because a revolution is more newsworthy than a nonrevolution—he sets off into the jungle to meet Mott, who will transport the supplies by jeep, at the new station.

Even though the electricity metaphor is developed comically, Charlie's ego alternates his conscious and subconscious currents until he can direct the flows into a unified flow—egomaniacal and gluttonous, but a sustained self nonetheless. Hopper alternates the currents within himself that build and collapse structures. He does not direct them into a unified flow that creates a sustained self; he transmits them. These currents, or activities of his conscious and subconscious minds, are the imagined stories that he broadcasts as ongoing coverage. Since in Nelson's trilogy the story created manifests the self that creates it, Hopper's can be called an imagined self. So long as his revolution is not challenged, he can continue transmitting it because it is ongoing within himself. Inevitably, however, as we have seen, the story will be challenged, and when that happens, he retreats into the jungle in search of a station from which to transmit unchallenged again.

The play's scenic design also reflects the self. The jungle into which Hopper flees is not an external station but a stage analogue to his psyche, where the threatening external reality cannot follow. The map proves unreliable as a guide through the uncharted landscape. His watch stops, leaving him in suspended time. And Bellows removes the transmitter battery, breaking off his communication with the outside world.

The pattern of psychological growth is the same throughout the trilogy. Before he can create a self, each protagonist must release the energy within himself with which to create. This discovery is the third of the four directions that Shattuck suggests modern humans have taken in their search for self-discovery. The direction is inward to the subjective processes, and the journey is perilous, for the quester can get lost in the interior. Charlie has a girlfriend, a brother, and finally a coach standing by him. Hopper has no one because he chooses to be alone. His sole connection with external reality is his assumption that there is an audience to whom he transmits his subjective processes, or alternating currents: the energy that is his imagined story and self. Once Bellows prevents transmission by removing the battery, he loses his one outlet, and the energy can only intensify within him. He is trapped in his imagination.

To stay "hot" (259) as he treks through the jungle, Hopper practices for his next broadcast. He constructs an account of a political assassination, with a description borrowed from the Kennedy motorcade assassination, and then presents panic, which for him is screaming. Neither verbal nor aural reality can sustain him, however. Without audience approval, he cannot be sure how the broadcast plays.

With the jungle sounds getting louder, he loses confidence in his judgment about what constitutes a good report, so that with each attempt he imagines a more sensational happening until he is broadcasting a massacre of civilians and a cannibalistic ceremony. Trapped, his energy so increases in alternating currents that one short-circuits the other. Never having been called upon to assimilate contents of the unconscious or apprehended images, his consciousness is inadequate to the task of seizing the rushing images, and his control breaks down.

He has fallen victim to the danger Charlie is warned about. Having released the irrational in himself, his imagined self unravels as the encroaching sounds become *"very much like gales of laughter"* (259). They are both a comment on his deteriorating mental state and his progressively fantastic reports, for he is lost. In a scene parodying Marlow's vision of the bonfire ceremony the night he wrestles with his and Kurtz's soul in *Heart of Darkness*, Hopper cannot tell whether or not he is imagining, and he jumps or falls from what he sees as a waterfall onto rocks below, where he imagines that in a gorge he is rescued by Mott and Bellows, who have been scouring the jungle for him.

Like the transformation scene in *Conjuring an Event*, this too could be the stuff of tragedy: a parable of the artist, who must pay a terrible price for mining his subconscious mind for his art. But Nelson is not writing tragedy. In fact, *Jungle Coup* goes beyond the satire of the first play, to become farce.

In the depths of the interior, Hopper turns and confronts the theatre audience, soliciting its help in regaining control of himself by communicating with him. Taking centerstage and shouting down the sounds of encroaching madness—"Go ahead you noisy fuckers! I'm ready for you!" (265)—he lists the events he can invoke, asking the audience to indicate its preference. His repertory is mad: interviews with Amelia Earheart,[6] the Lindbergh baby, Hitler in a secret bomb shelter, Jimmy Hoffa with Mary Jo Kopeckne; scenes from nature, spoiled or unspoiled; starving children, lepers, and so on. When his trump card, conjured panic, fails to excite the house, he is in despair until he imagines himself playing with children and hitting a home run. As he presents the event, the spectators go crazy, "dancing on their seats" until the "stands are vibrating!" (269). The scene ends as he, seated onstage, puts down the microphone in front of the seated audience.

Burned out, he quits broadcasting, leaving behind him the transmitting equipment for which he no longer has any use. In the play's closing scene, he tells an amazed Mott and Bellows that Hopper died of a football injury as sixty thousand silent spectators in the stadium watched. But, they ask, "If Hopper is dead, then who are you?" Unable to chant Charlie's victorious self-assertion, he answers as he exits, "Nobody. (Pause) Nobody important" (272). He has failed to create a sustained self.

The trilogy is most satirical when an audience is introduced. Bellows learns what Hopper knows: that editors want coverage of a revolution, whether it exists in the sensory world or in the mind. When the protagonist exits, his former rival picks up the microphone and while cranking the transmitter broadcasts the story that reporter Hopper has been found alive after being kidnapped and tortured by the rebels. It is fitting therefore that the trilogy's concluding play creates the self that Hopper fails to. This undertaking is the fourth of the four directions that Shattuck suggests modern humans have taken for self-discovery, in their histrionic sensibility.

When the protagonist of *The Vienna Notes* says in the play's opening scene, "See if it plays. . . . Get yourself ready. 'Cause this kinda thing you gotta get while it's hot,"[7] he sounds like reporters Charlie and Hopper. He does not look like them, though. Nor does he act like them. He is one of civilization's finest who write not for a newspaper but in a form reserved for the privileged. A U.S. senator who lost the presidential election in a close contest, he is in Vienna at the invitation of a committee to give a lecture. He is accompanied, as always, by his secretary, whose primary responsibility is to write, as he verbalizes, his memoirs. "Entry" (74) and "story" (77) are the play's terms for a unit of dictation.

Senator Stubbs, secretary Rivers, and a second woman, Georgia, the committee chairwoman, are in the hotel suite booked for him by the chairwoman, who becomes progressively more upset that neither he nor his secretary responds to the preparations she has gone through to make his stay in Vienna enjoyable. Just before leaving, she explodes, cursing his lack of courtesy and sensitivity. Once she leaves, Stubbs dictates the entry while Rivers records. He became aware of Georgia's presence when he felt the anger rising in her voice. Likening it to a spreading rash, he resigned himself to suffering through it because a senator is accustomed to intrusions wherever he goes, although he wanted to yell at her to shut up.

This first entry, which sets the pattern for all subsequent ones, reveals the memoirs' theme. Petty as it is, Georgia's outburst is nonetheless one more instance of the sudden surge of the irrational in life, transformed by the Senator revealed in the memoirs as a calm, deliberate man for whom the irrational is that which, intruding upon his consciousness, is brought under control by his consciousness. He apprehends images in the external world but as impressions and sensations that trigger feelings in him, feelings that he controls and transforms through his expression of them in his memoirs. His self is the measure of reality, and his expression, his verbal images, is the means of creating the self.

The opening scene functions as a prologue, and the closing scene as an epilogue. The six intervening scenes of *The Vienna Notes* take place at Georgia's farmhouse outside the city, to which the chairwoman invites Stubbs and Rivers for dinner. These six scenes should be thought of as the play proper. As scene 2 opens, the three characters enter the farmhouse. Stubbs dictates his impressions and sensations experienced during the car ride from the hotel, Rivers writes, and Georgia calls for her husband to come greet the guests. Within minutes the house is attacked by masked terrorists who have killed the husband. Rivers's firing of Georgia's handgun repulses them temporarily.

There is a logic to Hopper's journey in *Jungle Coup*. When he releases panic in himself to present to his audience, he initiates his fate. Since he relies on subjective processes as the sole source of reality, it is only just that he confront by himself the terror of the encroaching irrational. Stubbs, on the other hand, is attacked by the irrational in life in the persons of terrorists who in a phone call in scene 3 give their demand. They will allow Rivers and Georgia to leave unharmed if he surrenders to them, for they want him and not the women. In each subsequent scene the terror comes closer, climaxing in scene 7 with the blasting of the door off of its hinges. What the Senator does to withstand the siege is the play's plot.

The most civilized of Nelson's three protagonists dictates, except that is not the right term. *The Vienna Notes* does not add new specialized terms for the two activities. The terms most often used are "think" and "feel." Stubbs thinks before he verbalizes the entry, which is a series of impressions and sensations transformed into a story of an event, and he feels the event while verbalizing it. Although he uses the same process throughout, it is most clear at the opening of scene 3, where he is "*standing and thinking*: . . . Okay. Maybe. Then: door. Then: duck. Then: bang. Then: okay. Right." When he has the correct sequence of impressions and sensations set in his mind and "'*envisions*'" the scene in his imagination, he begins (82). If he feels the event, in this or any entry, as he did at the time of the experience, he is "*into*" it (74). The story is playing; grabbing him, it will "grab" the audience (79). Thus he neither reports-constructs as a separate activity nor conjures-presents as a separate activity; rather he integrates the two in his verbally expressed histrionic sensibility.

Acting or performing is the most accurate description of what Stubbs does. In an author's note appended to the text, which complements Shattuck's discussion of the histrionic sensibility, Nelson defends the Senator's acting as being consistent with man's instinctive need to express himself: "The dramatic, or the art of acting our feelings, is a civilized means of getting ourselves across, understood, and empathized with" (102).

In scene 3, Stubbs acts out for Rivers how Georgia should have revealed her discovery of her husband's body. He criticizes her sudden scream of panic (and, by implication, Hopper's screaming) because it lacks control. He does not use Hopper's term "construct," but he argues for structure in drama. If the series of impressions and sensations has a "built in thing" (79), it lends itself to story transformation. If not, he must build the structure into it in the transformation. "Where's the build in that?" (81) he criticizes Georgia's scream. At the same time, though he does not use Hopper's term "present," he faults structure at the expense of feeling. At one point, encouraging Rivers to express her feelings, he tells her to start again. "More . . . immediacy, I think. Know what I mean? It sounds like you have it all figured out" (93). In the same scene he snaps off Georgia's expression for "faking the emotion" (94).

The problem with the spontaneous scream of panic is that it lacks drama's transforming power. A dramatic event implies actors and an audience, and as we have seen in the trilogy, an audience expects appearance rather than raw reality—and the more conspicuous the better—for in a media-programmed society, power resides in the image rather than in the thing itself. The three characters lose their tempers during the siege, scream to relieve the tension, and even get physical with one another; but by performing control, they create the appearance of control, deterring the terror's advance.

Panic also lacks civilization's transforming power. Since Stubbs believes that rational people control their environment, creating a civilized self is the mission of every person in whom life's sudden attacks of irrational terror trigger uncontrollable emotions; one's civilized consciousness must disarm the incursions of the savage part of the unconscious—the id. To accomplish that, people must transform unleashed panic and encroaching madness by integrating reporting and conjuring, constructing and presenting, and thinking and feeling in their verbally expressed histrionic sensibility.

Of Nelson's three protagonists, Stubbs appears to be the most integrated; but in reality he is not. He too stands exposed by the satire. Scene 8 occurs two years after the blasting of the door off of its hinges. He and his secretary are again visiting Vienna, but the audience never learns what finally happened at the farmhouse. He does not want to talk about that day because he is tired of the story.

Nelson's third protagonist is not defeated, but his triumph is hollow, the consequence of his strategy of trivializing his encounter with the irrational by detaching himself from its power. The play's epilogue, scene 8, is a reading of the memoirs' entry in which the Senator on election night learned that the initial reporting of Ohio in his column was a mistake and that by losing the state, he had lost the presidency. But he would not break down and cry as others at campaign headquarters were doing. He would lose with dignity, a man in control of himself.

That is a description not of the protagonist but of the personality the protagonist's performances created for the memoirs. It is a persona: a stage or public self. Aware throughout of the strain caused by acting a role for posterity, Stubbs relaxes and asks Rivers to read the election night story, which he considers giving that night for his lecture. He will imagine himself among the listeners so that he can gauge audience reaction. About himself Charlie can say, "*I am!* . . . *Me!*" while about himself Hopper has to say that he is "Nobody." The trilogy closes with Stubbs's response to a self manifested apart from himself. "I really do feel for that man. And so will they. It will play. It will play. It will play" (101).

The author's note appended to the text contains a paragraph on the "notion of HISTORY" as it supplants the traditional "notion of HEAVEN." Though he uses the term "personality" rather than "self," he makes the same point that Shattuck makes in the passage quoted at the beginning of the chapter: In the modern world, personality, or self, displaces "soul." For Nelson writes that in an age that renders the soul and its struggle for immortality irrelevant, the citizen of the modern world achieves immortality with future generations by "attempting to create as good, exciting, and empathetic a personality as he can" (102). The trilogy's irony is that in the Senator's securing of a place in history, he may have to ignore history.

During the Astor Place riot that erupted in New York City in 1849, thirty-four people died and over a hundred more were injured. That historical event is the basis of Nelson's *Two Shakespearean Actors*. At the height of the riot, the playwright has the American actor, who is discussing the art of acting with his British counterpart, scream at the rioters, "I told you before, to just leave us alone!!!!!"[8]

Like the riot, the revolution in *The Vienna Notes* is real, but whether real or not, the end result is the same as in *Jungle Coup*, where the revolution is imagined. Though each play's protagonist is more susceptible to the stimulus flowing from one part of his nature than from the other—the artist to his subjective processes and the Senator to his histrionic sensibility—for both, internal impulses take precedence over external events. Now we can appreciate Nelson's forgoing tragedy for satire in creating a personal self. It is the American measure of reality.

The self as a measure of reality in American literature has been studied by Quentin Anderson, whose terms "imperial self" and "hypertrophied self" I used midway through the section on Nelson. Between the time I originally wrote the section as an article and the time I incorporated it into this book, Anderson published another book, which continues the study. He distinguishes between two opposing views that shape American thought and literature, which he calls the exemplary mode, or exemplary self, and the interactive mode, or the self interacting with society. In the first the self "is the sole judge of our experience." The second "entails a growth of our sense of things grounded in interplay with others."[9]

Emerson, Thoreau, and the others who write in the exemplary mode did so to counter America's rising materialism and commercialism, which fragmented society and the self. Charlie's gluttony, however, results from creating in the exemplary mode. Charlie puts himself in the center of the universe as the subject, not interacting with the world, but appropriating it as the proper object for him until the reporter as subject and the reporter as object become the same experience. He fuses contents of his unconscious with apprehended events until consciousness not only consumes all experience but also creates it to consume it, until there is no distinction between the reporter and the world. And since nothing is external to Charlie's personal self inflated into the national and universal self, Hopper and Stubbs, who follow him and also create in the exemplary mode, forgo history or society or anything else that really is external to the self.

Nelson gives no reason why Charlie wants to be exemplary beyond the desire to be. The implication is that dominant cultures devour; that is how they get to be dominant. The result is twofold. The devouring corroborates dissenters' perception that America's obsession with being number one is cultural imperialism, and it justifies minorities' wariness of assimilation.

There is another reason, however, for being an exemplary self, which is why the term had to be introduced at this juncture. The works dealt with in the previous two chapters are outside the dominant culture. With the exception of individuals such as Hwang's Grace and Steve, who are assimilating, and individuals who betray their values to get ahead, the groups are cultivating separate but equal enclaves within America. We could go back to chapters 1 and 2 and evaluate the enclaves as strongholds of exemplary selves—selves who create the world as an extension of themselves—were it not for the absence of the satire that pervades the plays in chapters 3 and 4.

The works in this and the next chapter are within the culture that was dominant. If it still is, it is so only temporarily, because it is under increasing attack from without and collapse from within. The characters who are exemplary are so because now they are being excluded, and creating the world as an extension of themselves is their way of clinging to the reality that sustains them, although the playwrights know that the reality is a dead past. The satire is directed against the hollow values and the clinging to them.

I have arranged the works so that as a general rule we can see the progression in disintegration and satire. As we descend through the crumbling landscape, the satire increases. We begin, therefore, with satire tempered by respect for the enclaved values, which are worthy, and sympathy for the enclaved characters. This playwright understands that a dominant culture breeds exemplary selves who when displaced into an enclave do not know how to be anything but exemplary.

Even before A. R. Gurney's *The Dining Room* begins, the description of the set, a room so lovely that it might be *"on display in some museum, many years from now,"*[10] reveals that tradition in the play's imaginative world has lost its vitality and suggests what might have happened to the piano in *The Piano Lesson* had family members in Gurney's play gained possession of the Charles household. Though Boy Willie in Wilson's play wants to sell the piano so that he can raise money to buy land in Mississippi, he and his sister Berniece do not argue about the money that the sale will realize but about the significance in each one's life of the tradition that it symbolizes. To them the piano is more than furniture. The comparable scene in Gurney's play takes place in the centerpiece of a house on the market and expensive because in the preceding scene a client is so intimidated by it that he does not make an offer to the real-estate agent. Although a middle-aged brother and sister have only one day in which to divide the house's contents, they defer choosing lots because neither wants to risk losing the room's contents. Neither says why, but the reason is obvious: The sale will command a good price. She accuses him of planning to sell the furniture, but he acts offended by the charge. To them the dining room is valuable for the valuable furniture it contains.

The structure of Gurney's play, which is kaleidoscopic rather than linear or recursive, also reveals tradition's death. The house passes through many families, but they transmit nothing from one to another except the deed. The dining room is not the repository of shared history and not the locus of communal activity. The culture that built the room with French doors opening upon a lovely garden with flowering crabs has vanished.

In *The Dining Room*, three actors and three actresses play a total of fifty-seven characters, of all ages from children to grandparents, from many families. Since they make no costume changes as scenes blend and overlap in the single set and since only one character appears in more than one scene, the six performers must rely on speech and gesture to convey the changing attitudes toward the room over time. Language denotes the era.

In one scene a father impresses upon his school-age son and daughter that they will be allowed to dine with the adults when they are mature enough to appreciate the ritual of dining in the most revered of rooms. In another scene a girl named Sarah gets the liquor for herself and friend Helen while the two wait for their dates, who are "bringing the pot." To Helen's request that they party in the dining room, Sarah replies, "I'd get all up tight in here," because having to eat dinner in the room on the rare occasions when both parents are home "sucks out loud" (333–34).

Gurney is both critic of what a character in the play designates, as an example of "vanishing cultures," the "Wasps" of "Northeastern United States" (338) and chronicler of their decline. In a scene in act 2, a mother with teenage son and daughter waits for the father to finish a phone conversation before signaling the maid to commence serving dinner. When he enters the room, he announces that he must leave immediately because his brother, the children's uncle, was insulted at the club, an insult to the family name that he must re-dress. The remarks had to do with Uncle Henry's personal relationships as a bachelor. "You mean Uncle Harry is a *fruit*?" the son lets slip out, to which the father retorts, "I WON'T HAVE THAT WORD IN THIS HOUSE!" (344).

WASPs of the northeastern United States exclude the vernacular and honor Finley's "one male god" about whose sexual orientation there can be no ques-tion. The exclusion from WASP institutions of personal choice in self-expression explains their decline, but Gurney also is critical of the superseding culture as manifested in the debased language of the two young women waiting for their dates. Thus his theatre is ambivalent. The old order is breaking up for what may be not a new order but disorder.

The scenes in *The Middle Ages* blend and overlap, but since they are pre-sented linearly, the play dramatizes the vanishing of the one culture and the superseding of it by another or others. The single set is the repository of shared history and the locus of communal activity but only for the privileged. It is the trophy room of an exclusive men's club, membership in which is by birth or invitation. Sometimes two, or three, or all four of the play's characters inter-act over a span of decades, during which time the club declines from its apogee as a bastion of selectivity to its sale and conversion to a center open to all.

The interaction reveals the differing attitudes. One of the characters, Charles, is the club president. He is in conflict with his son, Barney, who rebels against his father by rebelling against the selectivity. A place of father-son confrontation, the room is the place in which Barney is erotically involved with Eleanor, who with her mother, Myra, is a club guest. Though attracted to Barney's maverick behavior, Eleanor marries his brother for his standing in the society, yet not without reservations about club policy: not allowing women as members, for example.

As Charles ages and Barney matures, the one's culture supersedes the other's culture, which vanishes. Yet the power shift is not directly or simply from fa-ther to son. Myra, who marries Charles, and Eleanor become stronger, reflect-ing the post–World War II rise of feminism in America. Eleanor even flirts with the idea of an extramarital affair. And when Charles dies and Barney pur-chases the club, it is Eleanor who encourages him to convert it into a center open to all cultures.

As a realization of the American Dream, the play's ending is a fairy tale. Barney gets the girl of his dreams and gets to change the rules of the society that has always tried to make him conform. Eleanor, who is separated from his brother, gets the best of both worlds. With the brother she had security and lovely children; with Barney she will have excitement and the opportunity to practice her feminist principles.

With or without the ending, *The Middle Ages* plays very well. The WASP club's strength is its "closed universe,"[11] which promotes stability: One knows who he is and where he is in relation to it. Comprehensive, its rules become the code by which all behavior can be judged; transmittable, they become the tradition to which the elect swear fidelity. What the non-elect swear to is inconsequential because they are excluded from the group; they do not count. That is the club's weakness. A "closed universe" promotes inbreeding, which chokes off growth and life. Eventually the membership becomes attenuated from lack of oxygen, which is why Barney is forever opening windows in the room.

The strength of an open universe is that its new infusions promote growth and diversity. Its weakness is that democracy can promote debasement, and not merely in the language of two young women in a dining room but in Barney's pornography, an activity so pervasive, as in Meyer's *Etta Jenks*, that it has become a metaphor for the new, or modern, world.

The monastic club as repository of shared values is a metaphor for the old, or medieval, world, the period of Western history in which estates were solidified and conduct codified. If a work borders the tension between the two world views as Wasserstein's *The Heidi Chronicles* does, the old world is America when traditional values held the field, and the new world is post–World War II America after traditional standards have gone under and the landscape is devoid of guideposts.

Released from the old order by the breaking of traditions, the quester loses his identity. Barney has a fling at being bisexual and amasses the money to buy the club by producing pornographic films. His membership revoked by his father, he must disguise himself as a woman to gain access to Eleanor at the weekly Ladies Day that she sponsors in the club. He sheds the disguises, or false selves, only after he and Eleanor collaborate to create new selves.

As they leave the room, *"as if to their own wedding"* (60), the lights come down on an image that corrects the fairy-tale ending by showing how the American Dream can be realized. Just before leaving, Eleanor puts the deed to the club, which will now be open to all, in a silver cup that years earlier Barney referred to as the "Holy Grail" (26). In one version of the medieval legend, the Grail is the cup in which Joseph of Arimathea collected the blood of the Savior whose self-sacrifice is a model of spiritual perfection. Since the image unites the quest for the highest of medieval ideals with the quest for the highest of modern ideals, it suggests that an America that does not forgo the past but that weds the spiritual goal of the vanishing old-world culture with the social goal of the superseding new-world culture will realize the Dream of wholeness in the self and society.

In the closing scene of *The Dining Room*, one of the characters recounts her dream of a "perfect party" to which she has invited "all our favorite people" (351) from various walks of life. A decade after *The Middle Ages*, a character in another play attempts to actualize his conception of such a party. In *The Perfect Party*, Tony is a New England university professor who has given up teaching the history of civilization to put all his energy into hosting a perfect party. If the party is successful, he sees himself becoming a consultant on parties, perhaps one day a host of his own television show. His preparations include notifying metropolitan newspapers of the event in the hope of being reviewed. Lois is a stringer for a New York newspaper who hopes that writing a review that her editor notices will secure her a full-time position as reporter. Her preparation is coming to Tony's study, the play's one set, in advance of the event to acquaint herself with his preparations, such as guest list, which he displays in an elegant leather folder.

Of the three plays, this is the funniest, with the humor turned in on itself to a greater degree than in the other two. In keeping with their grand designs for the evening and themselves, the two characters speak in inflated rhetoric. Since the play's title is a metaphor for their conception of the American Dream, Lois concludes that "if the party succeeds, it will mean that America itself, as a social and political experiment, will have succeeded." Tony is only too eager to concur. "That's it."[12]

The party fails to meet their expectations for a reason best examined in the next chapter. We also have to look at the wife's expectations in an even later chapter.

Although Gurney's plays are ambivalent about the future, his characters must leave the past. The vehicle for navigating the voyage between worlds is the party. It is civilization's way of easing the entrenched out of the cloister through interaction with other questers, an interaction to which each quester brings his history and values.

Charles L. Mee Jr.'s *The Investigation of the Murder in El Salvador* is much more direct; its metaphor is revolution. When the murder occurs offstage, the audience thinks of Archbishop Romero, slain while celebrating mass in 1980 and memorialized in theatre and film, but the victim is not named. Neither is the murder consciously investigated by the six characters, the host and five guests, who gather with a bodyguard on the terrace of the host's home.

The six characters, some of whom are American, are portraits of estrangement, their viewpoint fixed in a world being blown apart. When one speaks, it is a monologue about playing cricket or shopping for silk wall hangings. The response, if there is one, is a laugh held too long by another, who feels the subsequent silence but does not know what to say. When not speaking, the character lapses into preoccupation. Alert, he eats and drinks from trays carried by a black butler until he drifts into another reminiscence, perhaps the description of a sybaritic pleasure such as engaging in sadomasochistic sex or preparing exotic dishes. Should he shift position in his chair, he lapses again, becoming animated only to indulge his jaded appetite or to argue about fashion.

Unlike the monologues in a Wilson play, the monologues in Mee's play do not coalesce into a shared history. Spoken reveries punctuated by silence or an awkward laugh, their effect is a disjointedness, epitomized in the character who does not speak until the play is well underway. A stroke victim, Howard is strapped into a wheelchair. As he regains consciousness, he raves incoherently about his contacts with the politically powerful until he slumps back into a comatose state, or until he too is murdered, for the six are estranged from the events enveloping them.

A scream is heard offstage at the beginning of the play. Questioned by the host as he serves, the butler says that he did not scream but that perhaps a maid did. Told to produce her, he does. When he and the black maid enter, both blood splattered, they admit to having seen a corpse, which has since disappeared. Excused, they resume serving because the host and guests do not want to have to confront anything that disrupts their leisured life.

Only an act of the will keeps the revolution in check and only temporarily, however. One source of tension is between the host and the servants. Another is within the guests, whose reminiscences and sybaritic indulgences are progressively swamped by images of revolution as they become aware of the blood and rising sound level. In the production that I saw, one of the women went into the downstairs room, closed the sliding door, and screamed into the microphone, but she could not shout down the noise outside the room or stop the images projected onto the wall. Neither can the other woman arrest the inevitable. The last vacuous speech is spoken by Lady Aitken just before the sounds of gunfire and explosions reach a deafening crescendo. "There are still people who do it every day but it isn't what it used to be. People are wearing the wrong jackets and don't even know the rules."[13]

The butler, on the other hand, has a speech in which he admits that he has suffered a loss of identity—"unhinged" is his word (85)—in the changes taking place around him. The journey between worlds is a test of the self, enabling the quester to create a new self. The butler should survive the revolution to discover himself. The host and his guests, all of whom cling to their old selves and dress codes, have their decadent days numbered for them.

The revolution has been completed before the next play opens. In Eric Overmyer's *Native Speech*, the protagonist, Hungry Mother, has to construct his underground radio station "from the detritus and debris of Western Civ. . . ."[14] A play of the early 1980s, it could take place after the urban riots of the 1960s or the Los Angeles riots of the early 1990s, with language the old order that is in rubble. Verbal images have become separated from their traditional referents to the extent that language no longer refers to the dominant culture's experiences and institutions but to the experiences of urban America with its guerrilla warfare in bombed out buildings. Native speech has become the verbal images of street and sex, drugs and music: codes known only to the initiated.

On this devastated, foreboding landscape whose darkened ruins conceal feral life, the protagonist is creating a self through an unlicensed radio station that broadcasts a few hours a day. A white man in a play whose characters are predominantly minorities, he calls himself Hungry Mother. Like the names of most of the characters, his name reflects his existential situation. He is hungry to survive and the inventor of himself. To be listened to in order to be accepted, he must verbalize the native speech when not playing his selection of hit recordings.

Overmyer's play is a variation on Nelson's trilogy. Modern humans create themselves by verbalizing the merging in their consciousness of contents of their unconscious and apprehended images. In one of the play's metaphors, Hungry Mother creates himself by transmitting the merged images, but in another of the metaphors, he is unlicensed. He is a white man trying to survive in a world in which minority cultures are on the rise so that the rushing images that his consciousness must assimilate are underground images symbol-ically and literally. They are not his tradition. As one of the black characters says to him, "The barbarians have smashed the plate glass window of West-ern Civ and are running amok in the bargain basement" (160).

In prefatory notes, Overmyer insists that the nonwhite characters, nine of the eleven live speaking roles, must be played by "Asian-American, Hispanic, or Native American actors" (155). Because he is an outsider, these characters listen to Hungry Mother as a barometer of what is happening on the street from an outsider's perspective and as a barometer of how well an outsider can assimilate native speech to become an insider.

Though he does assimilate to create images and himself, he also fabricates images and himself. In a flashback scene, he describes to his listening audience a striptease being performed by a studio guest, an African-American woman who calls herself Polish Vodka. The climax to the description could be screamed by Nelson's Hopper while broadcasting the jungle coup. "I ONLY WISH I COULD DESCRIBE IT TO YOU FULLY! WORDS FAIL ME! OH! OH! OH! . . . oh" (198).

The parallel between the two broadcasts is that in neither case is anything happening outside the speaker that corresponds to the speech. Polish Vodka is standing to the side listening to the description. In a contemporary scene with her, when she tells him where she lives, he switches from being white to black. "No, but I know the neighborhood. Intimately. *(Black again.)* Watchew dew down dere, woman?" (164).

The plot alternates monologues in which Hungry Mother creates an exem-plary self and interactive scenes that should correct the exemplary self. In an interactive scene with the character Belly Up, he learns that the patho-rock group, Native Americans who call themselves Hoover and the Navajos, whose music he champions on the air, really exists. He is surprised because in the atomized world they inhabit there is no guarantee that, for example, actual people make the music on the albums recording companies distribute.

But except for his learning pieces of information, the interactive scenes have little effect on him. *Native Speech* resembles Nathanael West's novel, *Miss Lonelyhearts,* in that despairing people write letters detailing their pain to a male newspaper columnist-radio broadcaster. Miss Lonelyhearts gets so in-volved in their personal tragedies that he begins to suffer for them until he be-comes a mad Christ figure. The difference between the two protagonists is that although Hungry Mother gives voice to his letter writers by reading their letters on the air, he does so for his own enjoyment, privately dismissing them as crazy. When he consents to meet with one, the play's other white character, she turns out to be a desperately lonely woman seeking human contact, but he callously tricks her into revealing her pain on the air. He does go to bed with her later in the play but rules out any intimacy between them. That is "out of fashion. . . . A blast from the past" (191), he tells her. She eventually commits suicide.

Unable to empathize, he moves away from an old-order communal experience. But he is creating a new self. His sound is carrying; an audience tunes into his broadcasts, though much of what he transmits is fabricated.

Nelson's Hopper goes mad. Overmyer's Hungry Mother gets in trouble with the African-American drug- and sex-lord, the Mook, who controls the local turf and who, to eliminate the competition that Hungry Mother generates, implicates him in drug trafficking. The underground broadcaster's defense is that he is fabricating, a defense he tries on Belly Up before he has to plead it to the police. "I made it happen. Made it all happen. Make it up—make it happen. I kept . . . talking about it . . . reporting it, you know? Fictional fact, a metaphor . . . sort of true, you know? . . ." Belly Up squashes the notion that by broadcasting the word, he causes its referent to become manifest, calling such a notion "paranoid schizophrenia" and "egocentric cosmology" (195–96). We should recognize the latter as a capsule description of the exemplary self.

Yet Hungry Mother is right. In Overmyer's theatre, language and imagination create the self and the world. When Hoover and the Navajos appear, they play the white man's stereotypical Indians to amuse themselves before making yowling sounds. They then wreck Hungry Mother's studio by smashing piles of his records. But that is patho-rock music! When the prostitute Polish Vodka decided to leave the Mook's stable, she renamed herself Free Lance, at which time she became her name.

In Overmyer's imaginative world, language is metaphor. By fusing disparates, the artist creates metaphors. By linking himself to something that he is literally not, he creates himself to be that, as in his opening monologue when the underground broadcaster introduces himself as an "argot astronaut" (157). Fabricating is creating new, fresh metaphors that become, if not absolutely true, to return to the defense he tries on Belly Up: "sort of true."

The fresher his metaphors—the more imaginative his grasp of the disintegrating world—the more empowered Hungry Mother's self becomes and the more threatening to the Mook, who has his goons mug him before turning him into the police for broadcasting without a license. Transforming reality, metaphors create reality. They integrate the ruins in new, fresh relationships. Minorities are in the ascendancy because their metaphors, bred in America's urban areas, control urban reality by creating its images. The African-American, coming into his own after centuries of domination by the "one male god," cannot allow a white man to take over his turf any more than he can allow one of his stable to go Free Lance on him, thereby setting a precedent that others might cite. When the ex-broadcaster rejects the ganglord's offer to work for him, the Mook leaves, his raucous laughter taunting the white man to keep practicing reverse assimilation. "Keep after them blackisms, boy! . . . You get to be a nigger yet" (205).

Hungry Mother sees himself as a "victim of history" (206). Since the white man's culture is in ruins, the survivor must assimilate the rushing images of underground cultures; to create a self in the world, he must transmit his metaphors. Yet the more creative he becomes, the greater the risk he runs of having his "mouthpiece shut down" (204). And if he is unable or unlicensed to broadcast the native speech that is becoming the dominant culture and has to revert to the native speech that once was dominant, his verbal images degenerate into clichés and he suffers the loss of self. Nelson's Hopper walks away from the transmitter because he cannot create metaphors to engage an audience. Overmyer's protagonist has his transmitter taken away from him because he can create them. *Native Speech* closes with Hungry Mother, in a studio with the sound shut down, speaking dead metaphors and wishing that he were black.

Since Hungry Mother connects with the past, he belongs in this chapter and not in the next chapter's gallery of disconnected characters. He is not totally exemplary either in that he attempts to merge his inner need with outer reality through metaphor-making, which is a joining of disparates (although he does not interact in his social life). He is a divided self with nowhere to go. With the old world ruined and the new world closed to him, his enclave is his self. It is all that he feels he has.

The next work has divided selves too, but it also has an exit from Hungry Mother's dead end. Before he became the director of *Jelly's Last Jam*, the producer of the New York Shakespeare Festival, and the director of *Angels in*

America, George C. Wolfe was a successful playwright, probably best known for a theatre work that had its world premiere at New Jersey's Crossroads Theatre in the spring of 1986 and from there moved to the New York Shakespeare Festival to become one of the hits of the 1986–87 Off-Broadway season. Theatre work is the most accurate term for *The Colored Museum,* which resembles a revue more than a play. It has musical numbers, and its mode is satire, of such uncompromising wit that Frank Rich, reviewing for the *New York Times,* hailed the author as the "kind of satirist, almost unheard of in today's timid theater, who takes no prisoners. . . ."[15]

Yet as trenchant as the wit is, it is the mode within each exhibit or scene, eleven of which make up the work. Satire does not account for the architectonics of the exhibits: the rationale for the order in which they appear, for their arrangement is not desultory. *The Colored Museum* has a design that is Dantean.

The first exhibit is entitled "Git on Board." An actress as airline stewardess comes onstage and, addressing the spectators, identifies the flight as "Celebrity Slaveship"[16] on a run from the Gold Coast to Savannah with a few stops in between. The satire is pronounced but good natured. The multicultural audience is instructed in the fastening of shackles and, because they breed rebellion, in the prohibitions against "call-and-response singing" (2) and drum playing.

The thrust of the exhibit is through verbal presentation and multimedia images to introduce the audience to the African-American's new-world experience. The non-African-American familiar with other African-American theatre should recognize some of the references. In Wilson's *Joe Turner's Come and Gone,* the boardinghouse through which the blacks who come to Pittsburgh pass as the gateway to the new life is the place of communal rituals such as the juba, "*reminiscent of the Ring Shouts of the African slaves. It is a call and response dance*" (52) with one of the men actually drumming on the table while the others move about it clapping their hands. It is this ritual that Herald Loomis not only cannot participate in but its near-frenzied clapping drives him into a rage, provoking the play's great act-1 climax.

Another recognizable reference occurs at the exhibit's end when the stewardess, Miss Pat, alerts the spectators-as-slaves to check the overhead before exiting. "Any baggage you don't claim," she completes the sentence, "we trash" (5). Though the metaphor is not uniquely African-American, it also is in Wilson's play. The sons and daughters of former slaves who come to Pittsburgh carry their baggage with them. In both works baggage is a metaphor for one's psychological scars, one's personal past, one's racial heritage.

"Git on Board" functions as a prologue. Although performers in subsequent exhibits address spectators, they always are addressed as spectators, not as participants in the action as they are in this opening exhibit. "Git on Board" is one of two exhibits that take place above ground level, the other being the eleventh and final exhibit, which interestingly closes with Miss Pat's voice once again telling passengers to check the overhead. Any unclaimed baggage, she reminds them, "we trash" (53).

We are ready to begin examining the Dantean design of Wolfe's satire. "Nel mezzo del cammin di nostra vita . . . ," translated "In the middle of the journey of our life . . . ,"[17] begins the *Inferno*, the first of the three divisions of Dante's *Commedia*. Awakening in a dark wood, Dante realizes that he must imitate Christ's death and resurrection to be restored to the grace from which he has fallen. The *Commedia* with its divisions of hell, purgatory, and paradise is the record of that journey to redemption, which covers the period from Good Friday through mid-week after Easter Sunday and which culminates in Dante's beatific vision, following which he returns to his mortal state dedicated to recreating the visionary experience in his poetic testament. What transpires, in other words, between the opening canto, or prologue, to the *Inferno* and the closing canto of the *Paradiso* is Dante the poet's vision of the depths of death and heights of life through which Dante the pilgrim journeys. With the exception of the final cantos of the *Commedia*, his guides are Virgil for hell and much of purgatory and Beatrice for the Earthly Garden on Mount Purgatory and the heavenly spheres.

Since the first and last exhibits of *The Colored Museum* close with the stewardess's reminder to passengers to check the overhead before exiting, the intervening exhibits may be said to occur as a visionary experience—in the twinkling of the eye, so to speak. That is one of two visionary experiences in the work, the second described in the final exhibit. The stewardess, Miss Pat, is the first of two guides, a turncoat in that she is herself black but a guide nonetheless, one who has made the flight many times before. The flight itself she refers to as "this middle passage" (2), which would be at best a strained echo of the opening line of the *Inferno*. I mention it, however, for a reason. Although there are places in *The Colored Museum* where the language can allude to the *Commedia*—The Bottomless Pit on the descent and the flight into infinity in the second visionary experience are examples—the argument is not that Wolfe's theatre art is verbally indebted to Dante's poem. The debt is to a design, a configuration that is Dantean.

"You can't stop history! You can't stop time!" (5), the Celebrity Slaveship's guide tries to shout down the rising drumming, which signals a burgeoning rebellion and interferes with the stewardess's invocation of the African-American's new-world history as the plane flies through a time warp that compresses the history from the slave's plantation servitude through the soldier's Vietnam service. The elements that unify his new-world experiences are pain and suffering. Not pointless suffering but transfiguring suffering, Miss Pat illustrates the presentation:

> All right, so you're gonna have to suffer for a few hundred years, but from your pain will come a culture so complex. *And,* with this little item here
> . . . *(She removes a basketball from the overhead compartment.)* . . . you'll become millionaires! (3)

The satire here is directed against blacks who connect with their past but only superficially. They have no commitment to their culture but find it useful. Thought of as soulful suffering, the culture is the cross that the frustrated and disappointed must bear, or it is the apprenticeship that the aspirant must serve before signing the professional contract.

Dante's hell is the place to which the impenitent go to spend eternal death. Conceived as funnel shaped, it descends from the earth's surface to its center in decreasing circles through which sinners fall until they reach the level appropriate to their sins. The greater the sin, the heavier the weight on the sinners' souls and the farther they fall. There is a magnificent justice to this eschatology, for hell is nothing more than unredeemed nature. Since the impenitent in life chose to reject God the Father, the Son, and the grace that Christ's action in man confers on him to redeem him, hell is being oneself for eternity; the sinner is forever what he was without redemption. Liars lie, thieves thieve, murderers murder on a landscape devoid of saving grace. Furthermore, the condemned know their punishment; they act in eternal pain and suffering. In terms of Wolfe's metaphor, the sinner is the self who never claimed his Christian baggage: the heritage of doctrine and teaching that, had he accepted it, would have saved him.

On each circle, Dante and Virgil encounter one or more sinners who identify themselves and tell the stories of their sins that dropped them into hell.

In the first exhibit following the one I consider the prologue to Wolfe's work, a black woman comes onstage, as all the exhibits will, on a revolve. She identifies herself as Aunt Ethel cooking up a batch of Negroes, the ingredients to whom are such superficial concerns as "PREOCCUPATION / WITH THE TEXTURE OF YOUR HAIR" and the characteristics of whom are that they "DISCARD AND DISOWN" (7–8). The exhibit is general. No Negroes appear to express any feelings.

The first to tell why they are an exhibit are a black couple in "The Photo Session," who discarded and disowned the "contradictions" of "existence" to be glamorous images in *Ebony* magazine. They naively thought that by renouncing life's pain they would not experience it again, except that with the onset of eternity, they are beginning to feel the "pain that comes from feeling no pain at all" (9–10). They are succeeded by Junie Robinson. He is a black soldier killed in combat who returned to his outfit to kill his buddies so as to spare them the suffering that inevitably awaits the black man upon his return to civilian life.

"The Gospel According to Miss Roj" is the first exhibit since "Git on Board" to have its locale given a name. "THE BOTTOMLESS PIT" (14) is a gay bar.

In canto 11 of the *Inferno*, Dante and Virgil come to the edge of a cliff below which lies lower hell. The pit is the city of Dis. Between the time that Virgil outlines the composition of lower hell to Dante and the time they descend into the abyss in canto 17, the pilgrim and his guide encounter, among other sinners, bands of sodomites who must run in endless circles in a desert of burning sand on which fall flakes of fire. In one band, Dante meets and converses with a compatriot from Florence, a prominent political leader and writer.

From the smoke and haze of The Bottomless Pit emerges Miss Roj, bizarrely dressed and every few moments ordering a drink from the waiter because presumably he is ravaged by thirst. His appearance marks a division between upper and lower hell in *The Colored Museum*. The couple in *Ebony* magazine and the soldier are frozen in image and pose on the revolve. They speak but do not act. They feel, but the feeling is stirring rather than goading, in the latter case because Junie Robinson is described as *"somewhat dim-witted"* (11). Miss Roj and subsequent exhibits also made a choice in life—which is why they are in hell—but with increasing gravity. They knowingly chose style over substance, appearance over reality, emotional distancing over engagement. Miss Roj explains that he learned to snap his fingers at the comments and looks his difference elicited from people and learning that, adopted it as his strategy for dealing with pain and suffering. "Snap for every time you walk past someone lying in the street, smelling like frozen piss and shit and you don't see it. Snap for every crazed bastard . . ." (17).

The Colored Museum is descending from the opening superficial connection to disconnection, comparable to Dale's shedding of his heritage in *FOB*. Accompanying the increasing gravity is an increasing depth of feeling. As the sinner tells his story of discarding and disowning pain and suffering, he feels the pain and suffering with increasing intensity, which causes him to distance himself through the strategy he adopted, which in turn fuels his guilt, driving him into a frenzy of guilt feeding pain and suffering. The torment increases until the exhibit revolves offstage, tracking the circle until it will reappear onstage for the sinner's eternal enactment of his sin and punishment. Just before Miss Roj disappears in a blast of smoke, he dances *"as if driven by his demons"* (18).

When the smoke clears, the audience encounters the next exhibit on the descent from airplane flight to street level. In "The Hairpiece," a woman must decide which of her two hairpieces, an Afro wig or a long, flowing wig, she should wear to lunch with her boyfriend. She has two because in life she changed her image whenever he changed his political ideology. Thus her strategy for disengaging herself from the pressing issues of her day was to fracture her psyche into a divided self, transferring to her hairpieces the conflict ravaging her. The exhibit may invoke Adrienne Kennedy's "Funnyhouse of a Negro," which takes place inside the madness of a black woman who, wishing to be white, wants to kill her African heritage. Hair loss is a motif in the one-act tragedy.

Wolfe never lets the audience forget that his theatre work is a satire. The two heads opposite each other on a vanity table yelling back and forth over which one the mistress should wear to lunch is a stage image that no amount of multimedia effects can duplicate. But the total exhibit is painful too because behind the talking heads the woman experiences the pattern of guilt that stokes suffering discussed in the preceding exhibit. Screaming in indecision, she pulls the two wigs from the table as the lights come down on three bald heads.

"The Last Mama-on-the-Couch Play" is a parody of *A Raisin in the Sun*. Less obvious perhaps is the allusion to Shange's *For Colored Girls*. Toward the end of the choreopoem, the Lady in Red tells the story of Crystal and Beau Willie. In this horrific story, Beau Willie is so filled with self-loathing for what he feels life has done to him that he drops the two children from the apartment window.

The comparable scene is enacted and not narrated in Wolfe's exhibit. Its enactment intensifies over the preceding exhibit the cycle of guilt feeding pain and suffering. After the Son drops the two black dolls, symbolic of his culture, his wife, the Lady in Plaid, suffers *"primal pain"* (27), terminated only when the Narrator takes the acting award from Mama and gives it to her. This exhibit is the cycle's fullest treatment in *The Colored Museum*. The characters act out the sin, experience guilt feeding pain and suffering to an excruciating degree, and then have the feelings undercut by the satire.

The exhibit closes with images that indicate that the descent is approaching the bottom of hell. Wishing that they had been born into a musical rather than into a play requiring them to emote, the exhibit members dance frantically until their faces suddenly freeze in zombie-like smiles while *"around them images of coon performers flash . . ."* (32). The degrading images are those of stereotypical black performers during Hollywood's golden era.

The bottom of Dante's hell is Satan encased in ice of his own making. In his fury to escape, he so beats his wings that the rushing air converts the water flowing into the pit into ice. "'Lo Dis, and the place where thou must arm thee with fortitude,'" Virgil commands the pilgrim on frozen Cocytus (*Inf.* 34.20–21). Dante must see himself in Satan, or Dis; he must see the potential for sin in himself. Once he does, because the admission of sin is the prerequisite for its purgation, he can climb over Satan, actually grip the creature's matted hair, at which time he leaves hell below him to begin the ascent to Beatrice and the Earthly Garden.

The bottom of Wolfe's hell is the exhibit "Symbiosis." Amusing though it is, it is curiously unfunny and I think intentionally so. While a character in corporate suit known only as Black Man throws objects from his past into a trash can, he is approached by a character in late-1960s street style known only as The Kid, who, visibly upset, demands an explanation for the trashing. The Man's answer is that his "survival depends on" dissociating himself from his heritage. "I have no history. I have no past" (34), he justifies his action. As he perceives his situation, to assimilate into mainstream American culture with its promise of corporate rewards, he must renounce everything that stigmatizes him as possessing a culture distinct from it, including the Kid. When the latter protests violently, the former overpowers him and stuffs him into the can. About to leave, the Man discovers a Temptations album on the ground. As he lifts the lid to toss in the album, the Kid "*emerges from the can with a death grip on* The Man's *arm*" (37).

The exhibit is farthest from the throbbing life of the opening exhibit and, as we shall see, from the life of the closing exhibit. Whereas Miss Pat warns her passengers to claim their baggage or have it trashed by the airline, the Man trashes it himself because he wants to dissociate himself from that part of himself that he cannot accept. Yet he can no more get rid of his past than he can his guilt. The Kid is the Man's guilt, stalking him so long as he is unrepentant and thereby denied by him because he is unrepentant. When Miss Pat tells the passengers, "You can't stop history! You can't stop time!" she is right about life but not about death. Time stops in hell, which is the eternal enactment of the condemned's torment. The Man and the Kid are locked in death's grip.

The two are mirror images, each of whom to be saved must see himself in the other. The Kid is the Man's past; the Man, the Kid's future. Locked in symbiosis, they need each other, for together they make an African-American heritage; alone, each is incomplete. If they could accept each other, the healing of the divided self could commence.

The ascent of Mount Purgatory, the second book of the *Commedia*, is the healing process. It reverses the descent into hell in that as the penitent purges his sin, the weight of it drops from his soul, allowing him to rise to the next higher level. The ascent reverses the descent in another aspect as well. Hell is man's isolation not only from God but from other men. Since expiation unites man with himself and with other men, the ascent is increasingly a communal experience: an acceptance of one's responsibility to life's fellowship.

In the first of the three remaining exhibits, Lala, a performer, at first denies having a mother in the audience and being a mother herself as inconsistent with her stage image. But gradually she comes to drop her phony name, accent, and stage "'*disguise*'" and accept herself as she is. Her divided self integrates as does her family when at the exhibit's end, she and her child, who "*mirror*" (45) each other, hug at centerstage.

Normal Jean of "Permutations" is not a divided self; neither is she disconnected. On the contrary, she sits on an egg, incubating it. Her mother is distressed, but she is very proud to be giving birth and wonders what accomplishments her offspring will achieve. The exhibit reverses the exhibit in which Aunt Ethel bakes Negro dolls that no one knows what to do with.

"Cookin' with Aunt Ethel" begins the descent through hell's sterility. "Permutations" ends the ascent through purgatory's new life. Dante's *Purgatorio* ends with the pilgrim "ready to mount to the stars" (33.145). "Permutations" ends with Normal Jean wondering about how far her children will go in life. As she says the word, she becomes enraptured by it: "Fly" (49).

From the Earthly Garden atop Mount Purgatory, Dante and Beatrice ascend into the heavenly spheres and then the Empyrean to encounter, in Wolfe's metaphor, the souls of those who in life claimed their baggage. The reward for accepting their Christian heritage is that following the purgatorial ascent, they are reunited with God in eternal life. In the concluding canto of the *Paradiso*, Dante is transfigured by the beatific vision. Returning to himself, he resolves to recreate the experience.

Parodying an episode in *For Colored Girls*, Wolfe's Son throws two black dolls out the window. When the Man tries to throw away the race's history, the Kid grips him. The first two exhibits following "Symbiosis" are the theatre work's counterpart to the *Purgatorio* in that the two speakers accept responsibility for their history in the persons of their offspring—their kids. The third, and final, one is immediately different in that the speaker announces that she will recount a visionary experience. In a *"hurricane of energy,"* Topsy Washington, the speaker of "The Party," has returned from a "function" that she connects to God, who did not rest on the seventh day of Creation but "partied." The one she went to began somewhere "between 125th Street and infinity" (50).

She is the second of the work's two guides, similar to Miss Pat in that each is witness to a supernatural experience, but the similarity stops there. The first one Miss Pat comments on as it unfolds for the audience in slide projections. Though Topsy can only describe the second one verbally, its energy lives in her. The first one, a condensed history of the African-American's past, Miss Pat attributes to a time warp. The second one, a vision of the African-American's future, Topsy cannot account for rationally. "The whole place just took off and went flying through space—defying logic and limitations." Transfigured, she bears the "madness" in her "head" (51).

Topsy's experience, comparable to Dante's mystic-rose experience in which he sees the heavenly assembly, is a vision of the future because all the guests are alive, whether alive (Eartha Kitt) or dead on earth (Malcolm X). From the experience she understands a higher truth that gathers into it the contradictions of life's journey, contradictions she manifests in her person. Black life is pain and suffering, joy and fulfillment mixed together. Being black is not denial but affirmation of life as lived by all the blacks who have gone before and are celebrating in eternity.

An earthly version of the heavenly party now begins. While exhibits reprise their roles against a backdrop of flashing images of diversified African-American life, Topsy sings the revue's theme song: "THERE'S MADNESS IN ME / AND THAT MADNESS SETS ME FREE" (53). Suddenly the action stops as Miss Pat's voice comes over the amplifier reminding the passengers to check the overhead. The work ends as it began except that in the interim, the audience has been given the baggage's contents in sensible form.

Just before the earthly party erupts, Topsy sums up her feelings about carrying the vision in her person. "And everything I need to get over in this world, is inside here, connecting me to everybody and everything that's ever been" (51). Wolfe's challenge as theatre artist was to connect his vision with a design that would manifest it. Every satirist faces the challenge of finding an appropriate form, especially if he/she loves what he/she is satirizing, for without a scheme the subjects are nothing more than objects of ridicule. Wolfe's challenge was more acute, though, in that he had to discover a design that yields connection in disconnection because the reason for the satire is that the subjects in the first half reject their sustaining myths and traditions.

I think that is why he chose the Dantean design, or configuration. Like Dante's poem, the play is both descent and ascent. It is not, however, a re-vision of the *Commedia* in Adrienne Rich's definition of "entering an old text from a new critical direction."[18] The contemporary scheme of damnation and salvation is comparable to that of the medieval work only in the sense that the playwright took the design as the principle for arranging the satire. Dante's classification of sins allows him to rank his sinners according to the increasing gravity of their disconnecting themselves from their heritage until at the bottom of hell, the Man denies his race for an assimilated self. He will be white in a white man's culture and black "only on weekends and holidays" (36).

Yet since the way down is the way up, once the spectator perceives the design, he can expect a correspondence of sorts on the other side of hell. Wolfe does not disappoint. The lady with hairpieces is bald. When Lala whips off her stage disguise to be herself, she has a full head of natural hair, for she, unlike her counterpart, is alive. The second half of *The Colored Museum* is alive. On the Celebrity Slaveship, Miss Pat informs the spectators-as-slaves that survival depends on abandoning "your God" (4) for the new-world god. When Topsy returns from the heavenly party, she tells the audience that she is filled with "my God" (51). Abandoning one's old-world god for a new-world god parallels the conflict in Wilson's Loomis and further supports the argument that Wolfe uses the *Commedia* only as a structural principle.

As if to prove the point, divine love is the prime mover of Dante's universe to be imitated by humans in their lives. In the architectonics of the tripartite poem, the concluding line of each division ends with "stelle." The concluding line of the *Paradiso* adds "amor": "l'amor che move il sole e l'altre stelle," translated "the love that moves the sun and the other stars" (33.145). Love is what Dante brings back from his visionary experience. It fills his poem.

Wolfe does not need Dante's concluding line. Although love fills his work too, the playwright can present it onstage in the finale by reprising images of African-American life around Topsy, who actualizes the love she brings back from her visionary experience in the madness and contradictions of her person. In the architectonics of his play, he saves the concluding line for Miss Pat's reminder about checking the baggage before disembarking in the new world. The African-American still has a choice that he can make about his heritage. He does not have to forgo history to create himself as the characters feel they must in the next chapter.

In satirizing a black who trashes his culture to be white, *The Colored Museum* is a fitting companion piece to *Native Speech*. It also is a fitting work with which to close this chapter. It reverses the descent into hell; the next chapter does not.

4

Exemplary Selves in Hell

In the second act of Gurney's *The Perfect Party*, a character appears whose name was not included in the act-1 guest list. He is the host's incorrigible brother Tod, whose name in German means death.

Tony, an ex-university professor, wants to give the perfect party. Yet even though the conception is a metaphor for the new-world American Dream, Tony, who is a member of the New England ruling class, gives an old-world party. It is a communal experience but limited to people he believes capable of a perfect performance. When Lois, the new-world newspaper stringer who wants to parlay a review of the party into a full-time position as reporter, declines to review the event because it lacks the element of danger, he informs her that his twin brother, Tod, a wrecker of parties, will attend.

Once the host discovers that the old world bores the new-world journalist, he has to fabricate interest. Since he knows only the right sort to invite, he fabricates the wrong sort: the antithesis of the guest whose breeding merits invitation, the individual whose name spells death for old-world values. He intuitively creates the self with whom she can identify.

In act 2 Tony appears disguised as Tod, the farcical version of the exemplary self, just as Nelson's Hopper is the farcical version of the same playwright's Charlie. Not satisfied with being the subject reporting himself as object, or reality, he fabricates himself as the reality, or object, to be reported. The object is not a created self but a fabricated image. Singularity is Tod's distinguishing characteristic in that he has a pronounced limp, which gives him a "certain Byronic appeal" but which disqualifies him as a "tennis partner" in doubles matches (220), irritating conversation, and an abnormally large penis. Changing her mind, Lois agrees to review the party, which climaxes with the two of them in bed.

Hwang's American Dream is the promise of the old-world community ful-filled in the new world, which welcomes all applicants, rather than just the privileged, into full participation in society. The Dream shrinks, however, in life and in literature such as F. Scott Fitzgerald's *The Great Gatsby*, into one of material success, which is the spirit's death, and individual fulfillment. "He," Tony says to Lois about his brother, "is in constant competition with me, and everyone else. He has hacked his way through life's dark wood leaving a long, bloody spoor of victims behind him" (221).

Despite the comic masquerade, Tony's impersonation of an invincible in-dividual cannot be executed. He and Lois must inevitably be disappointed given their false expectations. Each enters the bedroom vowing to outperform the other; each exits having fallen short of the mark. They mix metaphors by applying standards of competition to an activity that is neither competitive nor individual. On a scale of seventeen, reviewer Lois awards the event a seven.

Where they are not false is within themselves. They are basically likable characters with traditional values that they do not abandon and that adhere to their fabricated selves. They are not hollow. The death that Tony generates from within himself is farcical.

Though the party is not perfect, the play is as an introduction to this chap-ter. With the breakup of an order in which station was fixed by class and gen-der, Lois sees an opportunity to create a self as a reporter. Tony, who identifies with the old order, has no experience wedding the old and the new as imaged by the deed in the cup in the playwright's *The Middle Ages*, until she challenges him. He fails, just as the party does, because he fabricates a false self who, di-vorced from history, sets expectations that he, conditioned by history, cannot meet. On the spur of the moment, the host becomes an impostor, the first in this chapter who does not forge fresh metaphors that transform reality but who appropriates a false identity.

A character in Richard Greenberg's *Eastern Standard* fabricates on short notice not to wreck a party but to become part of it. Four yuppies who meet over lunch at a midtown Manhattan restaurant reassemble at the one's Long Island home. To this summer retreat come two non-yuppies. The first is the restaurant waitress, invited by the host when she breaks down telling him of her problems trying to live and work in the city. The second is an obnoxious bag lady, May, who hurls obscenities and drinks at the restaurant customers, also invited by the host when the waitress breaks down telling of her older friend's problems trying to survive on the city's streets. Yet though invited for the weekend, two weeks later both women are still there. Seeing an opportunity for a place to live, May has become a sweet lady trying to wheedle an invitation for them to stay on during the winter, until they learn that they cannot, at which time she drops the impersonation.

When one of the yuppies insensitively asks her what she wants from life, the homeless woman who must return to her impoverished street culture—the bag from which she lives—answers immediately, Money. Incredulous that the younger woman would not know the answer, she turns the question back on her. But the investment counselor, who can remain at the house for as long as she likes, has to think before answering, Happiness. The two exit with the ex-impostor's glacial laughter spreading over the stage. She leaves before the others are up in the morning, taking with her their watches and wallets, camera and earrings.

A character in Dennis McIntyre's *National Anthems,* not invited to the party in a Detroit suburb although he lives on the same street, fabricates a history as a fire-fighting hero in order to win recognition. When he, Ben, is exposed, he leaves so humiliated that he is unable to respond to the hostess's attempt to soften the blow to his ego.

Lacking resources and a supporting network of family and friends to create new selves but not lacking the courage to fabricate images of selves, May the bag lady and Ben are exposed as impostors and sent back to their old, impoverished selves. Other characters unwilling or unable to create selves yet not satisfied with fantasizing themselves into celebrity images circumambient in films and television retaliate with violence against those who humiliate them or suffer the defeat until they can retaliate by appropriating an image.

For the critic who approaches plays through genre classification, David Rabe's *Hurlyburly* is a bonanza. It can be variously interpreted: as naturalistic—for example, Rabe's declaration in the afterword that he wanted to construct a play with a "Darwinian assemblage of detail";[1] as surrealistic—his belief that in some way "'accidents' and 'destiny'" are the "same thing" (208); as theatre of the absurd—various characters' attempts to subject irrational experience to rational analysis; and as existential drama—the acceptance of irrationality as the reality on which the individual takes responsibility for his life.

Although I think that a critic can make a good case for each and that more than one genre applies, I want to enter the play through the statements of two characters. One of them, Eddie, shares a house in the Hollywood Hills with another character. In act 2 he offers his explanation for the unprecedented anxiety of modern life. Whereas the "Ancients might have had some consolation" from their faith that above them was a "divine onlooker," moderns have no such consolation (144). Moreover, the consequences of the old god's death are the birth of new divinities, science and materialism, and the disintegration of the old-world chain of being, so that humans are aware that they have been dropped from their hierarchical ranking below the angels and their place taken by things. Toward play's end the second character, a runaway from the Midwest who periodically takes refuge in the house, disagrees. From her point of view, life remains mysterious because there is no hierarchy. Existence is a flow equally indifferent to everything in it. If she were a student majoring in American literature, she could cite Stephen Crane's five-line poem "A man said to the universe" as illustration. She does not cite the poem, but she elaborates its idea when she says that how one feels about his relationship with everything else in the flow makes no difference to the flow.

She also does not say, but the play does, that how one feels makes a tremendous difference to him and the person to whom he expresses himself. Long and repetitious, the play dramatizes each character's attempt to win self-esteem in an existence whose purpose, if there is one, can no longer be discerned or affirmed as all of them bump "around in this vague, you know, hurlyburly, this spin-off of what was once prime-time life" (137). With its slamming doors and characters in perpetual motion, the play could be a farce, but although it opens with the principal character with his pants down and his and everyone else's self-esteem disintegrates, the action does not reverse to restore order.

Eddie and Mickey, two television casting directors, share a house in the Hills of Hollywood, the Babylon of the modern age. Early in the play, and repeated later, Eddie reminds a friend and aspiring actor, Phil, of the city's "game" (41). To produce a story, the guts of which are invariably cut out as being unsalable, a studio has to fill out the surface because the more authentic looking the surface, the less likely the viewer will catch on that the center is a hole, that he is viewing the same empty story for the umpteenth time with only the details changed. The role of casting director is to hire authentic-looking actors to give the surface its texture. But actors are no different from the other realistic details like cars and trees. They are no more than a "prop" (140) in the "background" (139).

The "game" is the play's metaphor. Following the death of the old order, which assigned persons their roles in society, everyone has a hole in the guts of his/her existence that he/she must fill with a self or must so fill out one's surface with authentic-looking and authentic-sounding details as to create the illusion of having a self. But whether one creates a self or fabricates an image of a self, one needs the participation of at least one other person in the game, with the result that this dependence on another for validation of one's own life is the source of the play's comedy and pain.

But for the perpetual motion, *Hurlyburly* resembles O'Neill's *The Iceman Cometh* in that a group of characters are driven to one another for the support they need to sustain their illusions, only to have their hope betrayed. In Rabe's play, Eddie, a divorced man and father of a daughter who lives with her mother, professes to love Darlene. This professed love feeds his illusion that he is creating the self of a loving, responsible husband and father. To support the illusion, for he is in fact emotionally unstable and drug dependent, he has to believe that Darlene is worthy of his love, when in fact she is a slut who goes to bed with whoever buys her dinner, just as she, to support her illusion that she is creating the self of a loving, responsible woman, has to believe that he is worthy of her love because he is a sensitive, understanding man. When he reacts with hostility to her revelation that years earlier she had an abortion but was never sure which of the guys she was dating was the father, each feels betrayed. They turn on each other, he accusing her of inhabiting a moral miasma and she retaliating by accusing him of lashing out at her to get even for the beatings his parents administered to him when he was a child.

But for the perpetual motion, Rabe's play resembles Sartre's *No Exit* in that each character in a group appeals to another to bolster his self-esteem, only to have the other character rip the mask off, revealing the reality beneath the propped-up surface. "Facade" (51), Darlene's word for the exterior makeup and clothes she puts on to greet the world, is most apt. Each torments the other by making him confront the truth beneath the facade: He is an impostor. And that knowledge drops him deeper into the hell of the emptiness within himself because he plunges into self-destructive acts such as taking drugs whose self-altering properties intensify his illusion that he is improving, only to have the facade exposed again when he appeals to another for confirmation that he is creating a new self.

The general hurlyburly sent spinning by the post-medieval breakup of the old order is agitated by the post–World War II upheaval in values caused by such sociological phenomena as the rise of yuppies and the advent of feminism: the sociological realities of *The Heidi Chronicles*. In the afterword, Rabe cites the advent of feminism as one of the factors that gave rise to the impulse from which he began writing the play. He was daily made aware of the new roles that the Women's Liberation Movement propelled men and women into with each other.

Disoriented by the new freedom with its loss of traditional roles and cultural-sexual identity, Susan in *The Heidi Chronicles* is swept away in the hurly-burly. Heidi, however, finds role models by recovering her lost heritage in the illuminating images of women painted through the ages by women. The illuminating images that the men and women of *Hurlyburly* recover from the darkness are the ubiquitous images of our culture, for the technology that creates television has supplanted the old-world faith. In its impact in changing a worldview, it is the contemporary equivalent to Newtonian physics in the seventeenth century, alluded to by the playwright in the afterword.

All of the characters in Rabe's play are in one way or another related to the image-making industry. They give their energies to working for it or trying to get jobs in it. They turn on the tube when they come into the room; they listen to it or with sound off watch it, even while moving about the room; they talk to it. The illuminated box is the electronic age's deity, the center of people's living rooms and lives because having been created by people in their image, it mirrors them. Every program contains the obligatory smiling face that speaks at, while looking through, the viewer. Every program is an authentic surface concealing an empty core, just as every viewer is authentic in speech or mannerisms but hollow inside: an image that conceals emptiness—the facade of a self.

At one point Eddie yells at the prostitute to whom he introduced Phil, "I'm not a goddamn TV image in front of you, here" (147). But he is. Each character is to the others. Being no more than an image in another's eyes is an extension of the game-playing metaphor. Eddie himself uses the same word for the role of people to one another and the role of actors in a television story: "background" (137, 139). Each character is so self-absorbed that he comes to another not as an existential self but as confirmation for himself. They are exemplary selves craving interactive relationships not so that the self can develop through interaction but to confirm its existence. If someone listens, even pretends to listen, a rational self must be transmitting from behind the face to listen to. Invariably, however, the other character rips off the image, exposing the fabrication and sending both of them spinning back into the hurlyburly.

In the afterword Rabe offers a Jungian interpretation of his play, revolving around Eddie's acceptance of the aspiring actor Phil. Whatever Phil is in Jungian terms, he is the least sophisticated and the most violent of the four male characters, the one whose sense of self is most tenuous. When he bursts into the opening scene to tell his friend of a fight he had with his wife the previous night, he relates how just before he hit her, he had the sensation of seeing her disembodied face in front of him making him feel "like shit" (14). In act 2 Eddie introduces him to a prostitute, who leaves with him in her car. She returns to the house a battered woman because he threw her out of the car while he was driving it. She cannot think of anything that she did to anger him, she tells Eddie; all that she did was smile at him. Yet when Phil returns, he claims that in her smile he saw the look of a woman seeing through the "personality" with which he is trying "to make do," thereby rendering him "invisible" (139).

The characters' rage at having their fragile selves nullified reflects their fear that life is nothing more than an image concealing the death whose gravitational pull ultimately sucks in everything. Television producers are snakes who devour actors "alive" (44). Women "undermine" (183) a man's self-respect. Before Phil's argument with his wife became a fight, their conversation became an argument when she made such fun of his ideas that they disappeared, leaving only a "hole" (13). Mickey dismisses any higher intention in Phil's death: "He was in the wrong place; this big hole opens up, what's he gonna do?" (177). Everyone so betrays everyone else's expectations that the American Dream has become one of longing for the inevitable "oblivion" (114).

Ricocheting off one another in the random bumping of their atoms, the characters clutch at the development of a self as their stability. Forms of the words "desperate," "associate," "connect," and "relationship" are repeated throughout the play. If they can associate or connect, they can forge relationships; if they can forge relationships, they can arrest the downward pull to darkness. Hence they analyze their thoughts and feelings through absurdly comical loops in the desperate hope that they are real and substantial enough to sustain a coherent self. Hence they plead with one another to listen to them as they analyze, and if they are not interested, to maintain the illusion that they are.

In *Hurlyburly*, language is a tool for demonstrating the existence of a self. Articulating one's thoughts and feelings—asserting a coherent self—mandates two conditions. One must have a listener, whether genuinely interested or only pretending, because a listener validates at least the illusion of communication. It is not necessary that the two talk to each other; they can take turns talking. That is playing the game in which each is background for the other. Eddie agrees with Phil that his wife should not have interrupted him while he was talking. In "civilization," people "take turns" (13) talking. And if one has no other with whom to play the game, one must take what is available: the television set with its talking heads.

One also must keep talking even when one has nothing to say. "'*Blah-blah-blah*' and '*rapateta*'" are sounds uttered throughout the play, which according to the stage directions "*should be said unhesitatingly with the authority and conviction with which one would have in fact said the missing word*" (5). The implication is that once the transmitter is shut down, the self begins to disintegrate. If the speaker is shut off for too long a period, the self is annihilated. In this sense Rabe's play is like Beckett's great existential drama in that the two tramps must continue ad-libbing, because once they stop, *Waiting for Godot* is over.

Eddie, unlike Mickey, continues to hope that there is something other than the nothingness that he sees mirrored in the television screen and in others' faces and feels in the depths of his being. He becomes convinced that Phil's death note yields a meaning, and perhaps he is right. But although Rabe agrees, the antinomies are reconciled on another plane of existence. Life in the play's imaginative world is a hurlyburly. The community fails to develop not because the characters lack a common language in which to communicate their thoughts and feelings but because each speaks not to another but from his self-absorption. Her fragile self nullified by him, Darlene exposes Eddie's self as forced and disjointed. "I don't have time," she spurns his request to follow his argument. "I mean, your thoughts are a goddamn caravan trekking the desert, and then they finally arrive and they are these senseless beasts of burden" (54).

David Mamet's *Glengarry Glen Ross* also mandates a listener, but silent listening is not enough to satisfy the speaker. Act 1 consists of three scenes in a restaurant, each a dialogue in which one of the participants is a seasoned real-estate salesman trying to get the other participant to do something. Alternately belligerent, indignant, and pleading, down-on-his-luck Levene wants office manager Williamson to give him premium leads so that he can get his name on the board recording sales performance and preserve his job. He cannot, the manager wants Levene to understand, because the rules set by the owners are that during the contest to determine the top man, a salesman does not qualify for premium leads unless the number of his sales puts him on the contest board. He is corrupt enough to sell them to Levene, but the salesman is too broke to buy, and the manager demands the money in advance of, not after, the closing that a premium lead is expected to effectuate.

"If you'd *listen* to me,"[2] Levene urges Williamson on the assumption that by giving his full attention, he will be moved to act. The veteran proceeds to cite his sales record over the years. "Are you listening to me? . . ." (19), the manager interrupts, citing the rules and forcing the salesman to shift his argument. And each time he shifts, Williamson rebuts him until finally, in desperation, Levene drops the argument about his service to the company and asks as a personal favor, but to no avail. No argument or entreaty can persuade Williamson to act. Only bribery can. The manager will consent on condition that the salesman puts cash on the table. When he cannot, the lunch is over.

"You listening?" (29), veteran Moss asks his younger colleague Aaronow in the second scene. After commiserating with him on what he has to do without premium leads to get on the board so as not to lose his job, he goes on to tell the junior man of someone they know who has beaten the system by buying leads and going into business for himself. They could get back at the owners for making the contest rules by stealing the premium leads, selling them to the person who buys them, and going to work for him. Aaronow must do the stealing, though. If he refuses and Moss, who has made the deal to sell the leads, has to break into the office and is caught, he will name the junior colleague as an accomplice. "And why is that?" Aaronow asks. "Because you listened," the older man answers (46).

For Moss the "hard part" of going into business for oneself is the "act." He means the decision a person makes to go on his own because most people still live in a "*medieval*" world in which they are "in *thrall*" to somebody else's rules (32–35). In the play's context, however, "act" takes on more meaning than a decision. The "hard part" for a salesman is getting a customer's will to move so that he will commit himself to a course of action such as signing a contract. Arguments and entreaties do not work for Levene, and a threat does not work for Moss.

The third scene is the persuasion that works. A virtuosic performance of the playwright's ear for patois, it is essentially a monologue spoken by the top man on the board, Roma, to a stranger in the next booth, a man named Lingk, whose attention he gains by thinking aloud so as to presume that they share the view of inhabitants of the world unhinged from its traditional stabilizing center. "You think that you're a *thief*? So *what*?" To allow such a thought to inhibit action is to be "befuddled by a middle-class morality," the top salesman observes, duplicating Moss's reminder to Aaronow that they are by honoring the owners' rules. "You fuck little girls, so *be* it. There's an absolute morality? May *be*."

The musing speaker then asks the stranger, who is being set up to be a customer, specific questions to establish a bonding. While Lingk pauses to think, Roma gives his recollections of memorable sexual experiences. They are sensations and impressions because life in the hurlyburly is disjointed. "And that's our life," he leaves the attention grabbing introduction to move into the issue guaranteed to hold the listener's attention, that of providing for his family in the event of illness or accident (47–48).

Once a man, the salesman continues, accepts the dissolution of the old order and all experience predicated on an absolute value system, he is free to take responsibility for his life and the lives of those for whom he accepts responsibility. No longer inhibited, he can act, for the sales pitch, which builds through two more pages of script, incorporates the word "act" three times and "acting" one time. Life is not absolute but what one makes of it by "*acting each day*" (49), which builds the strength of character to act when encountering life's contingencies, absurdities, and opportunities—such as purchasing a property, a guide to which Roma spreads on the table.

If Eddie in *Hurlyburly* spoke the monologue, it would fit Darlene's description of a caravan of senseless beasts of burden, but it would be an honest attempt to forge his thoughts and feelings on his responsibility to his ex-wife and daughter into a coherent self. Though they are more insensitive than caring and they have their psychological quirks, Eddie and the other denizens of the Hollywood house are not vicious, and they have their moments when they feel guilty for being disconnected from traditional values. In contrast, Roma's monologue seems noble in that existential man can integrate himself by taking control of his life. Yet the thoughts and feelings are dishonest. They are not the salesman's groping attempt to articulate himself or understand life, but a facade. The surface disjointedness conceals a pitch calculated to seduce. And that is the difference between the moral universes of the imaginative worlds of *Hurlyburly* and *Glengarry Glen Ross*. The one pleads for engagement; the other manipulates to entrap.

Mamet's verbal images are so blistering that the theatregoer can overlook his stage images. I remember a production about which a woman reviewer, incensed by the demeaning language in which the all-male cast refer to women, asked, "What set?" But of course there is a set, and it is as important as the language.

Act 1's set is a restaurant in which three dialogues take place, only one of which culminates in eating or imbibing. Toward the end of his monologue, just before he spreads the map on the table, Roma calls for another round of drinks for himself and Lingk. In act 2's set in the real-estate office the next day, the audience learns that the preceding evening Roma went home from the restaurant with Lingk to meet his wife and to close the deal. The three celebrated with a meal cooked by Mrs. Lingk. During the act Levene comes into the office exuberant because he believes that he has sold eight units to a couple. As he describes the closing that morning at the couple's home, it began with him in the kitchen eating crumb cake and ended when the three celebrated the signing of the contract with a toast of shot glasses.

One passage in the act I must quote. In the office, Moss and Roma argue, the former accusing the latter of being arrogant because he is top man on the board whose closing of the Lingk sale makes him the contest winner. The latter turns the argument back on the way the former acts after he has closed a deal. "Fuck *you*, Dave," Roma snaps at Moss, "you know you got a big *mouth*, and *you* make a close the whole *place* stinks with your *farts* for a week. 'How much you just ingested' . . ." (70–71).

The last word should ring a bell, for ingesting is the process by which the ego creates a self. Characters in this chapter, however, do not create selves because something has happened to the ingesting. To become "#1," Nelson's Charlie creates images to consume, but ever since, characters driven by the same obsession yet unwilling or unable to merge images from the unconscious with those from the sensory world have resorted to fabricating images of selves in a vain attempt to satisfy the insatiable hunger that the obsession activates.

We traced this hunger through various fabrications until we reached that of an image of a successful competitor concealing a deficient self—an emptiness within. Mamet's imaginative world drops us through the fabrication, the facade, into this hollowness, this maw. In a society disconnected from traditional values, a society in which only the fittest predators flourish, the salesman gets to be #1 on the board by ingesting other selves, of clients and of competing salesmen.

"Life=power=food, the earliest formula for obtaining power over anything, appears in the oldest of the Pyramid Texts," writes Erich Neumann. A few paragraphs later, he puts the thought into a concrete image: "'Being swallowed and eaten' is an archetype that occurs not only in all the medieval paintings of hell and the devil; we ourselves express . . .'"[3]

The restaurant in *Glengarry Glen Ross* is life, where one eats or is eaten. The real-estate office is hell, where the predator processes his transactions with his prey and where, from the files in the kingdom of the dead, he collects leads to new prey, though many of them are dead. Roma tells Aaronow, who has lost his self-confidence because he cannot close a sale, that he cannot be expected to, not with the old leads the office manager gives him. "That shit's dead" (56). Following a lead to a Polack or an Indian is a waste of time too; they are "deadbeats" (28, 62) who talk to salesmen but never sign a contract. To Moss, Indian "broads all look like they just got fucked with a dead *cat*" (30), and to Roma, a lead to an Indian is a lead "from the *morgue*" (62).

The triumph is closing with a live person because by getting him to sign a contract, the salesman consumes his vitality. Although Levene does not know that the couple's contract on the eight units will kick out, in his description of the signing ceremony, he waxes as they wane:

> They signed, Ricky. It was *great*. It was fucking great. It was like they wilted all at once. No *gesture* . . . nothing. Like together. They, I swear to God, they both kind of *imperceptibly slumped*. And he reaches and takes the pen and signs. . . . I shake his hands. I grasp *her* hands. I nod at her like this. . . . I'm beaming at them. (74)

Having gotten the customer's commitment to purchase the property, the re-animated salesman deposits the contract in the office. Sometimes the signer follows, hoping to reclaim his signature. Lingk, who comes looking for Roma, is a shell of a man, having lost his self-respect, who pleads for the contract back because his wife sent him to cancel the deal and who in his humiliation has to admit that he lacks the "power to negotiate" (92). Only a mistake by Williamson allows him to phone the State's attorney to nullify the contract, and even then as he leaves, he apologizes to Roma.

Were it not for the office manager's mistake, Lingk would have to abandon hope in the office. He has come to the wily devil's pit, where all is subterfuge. On this level of suggestion, the office is a Dantean hell. The salesmen do not change shape as Dante's thieves are condemned to do as they eternally enact the sin that dropped them into the seventh bolgia, or ditch, but they change roles and in the police interrogation for the break-in, they are subjected to verbal and physical abuse. To trick Lingk into believing that there is enough time to nullify the contract after he returns, Roma has Levene play an important client whom he must get to the airport for his flight. When Williamson discovers that Levene is the thief, he turns him over to the interrogating detective, who manhandles him. After the apprehended salesman is taken into the inner office, Roma announces that he is appropriating his property. "My stuff is mine, his stuff is ours. I'm taking half of his commissions—" (107).

An office broken into with a board covering the broken window and the cavity within, the leads and contracts having been stolen, the act-2 set is a stage image for the hollow self: an image covering nothing. In this hell, predators do to one another what they do to clients in life. They prey on them in an attempt to satisfy the hunger within themselves.

When a salesman closes on a customer, he gets his name on a contract, the possession of which puts his, the salesman's, name on the board. The more signed contracts that he can deposit in the office, the more times that he can see his name go up on the board until he is #1: the one who has consumed more customers than anyone else.

Yet since the salesmen are in competition with one another, the more customers that one predator ingests, the more he becomes prey to the other predators. By stealing his leads and signed contracts, thereby nullifying them, they cause his name to be dropped down on the board until it is removed. Like the customer's self, his self is negated, devoured by them. Hell, then, mirrors rapacious life in that it is the perpetual theft of one another's property: his self.

But theft is to no avail. It does not nourish because salesmen steal one another's emptiness. The play's irony is that the surface disjointedness is a mask, an image, to disguise the entrapping sales pitch, but that sales pitch itself masks a real disjointedness. The cavity Mamet's characters conceal beneath the image of the successful and sympathetic seller of the American Dream of wholeness for one's family is the negation of moral obligation, a spiritual death that cannot sustain life. Thus the characters are insubstantial images or selves without souls.

Roma, who told Lingk at their first meeting that he does not believe in hell in the afterlife or on earth, leaves for the restaurant to replenish himself on the living. Aaronow, who believes in hell, cannot leave. Since he cannot close on a client, he remains in the office, wailing, "Oh, God, I hate this job" (108).

As Head of Production for a Hollywood film studio, Bobby Gould in *Speed-the-Plow* likes his job. It is a position of power. Of all the scripts that come through his office, he recommends to the top studio executive those that he thinks will be successful films. To be successful, a film must make money; to make money, it must present images that the public will pay to see. There is no doubt in his mind about his knowing what images people want, and not only what they want, but "what they require."[4]

People require this year the images that they paid to see last year. All films in *Speed-the-Plow*, like all television productions in *Hurlyburly*, are the same old story. Their surface details change to give them the look of authenticity, but they are empty at the core, endlessly repeated variations on the half-dozen or so categories of successful films such as the buddy film or the prison film. Producers like Gould and his assistant, Charlie Fox, who brings his boss a commitment from a box-office star to make such a film for their studio, know that they are hollow. Yet their role is not to change the Hollywood system but to make money for the studio by satisfying public demand and in the process to satisfy their hunger by making money for themselves.

In this blackest of comedies, studio producers project onto the public their own cynical motivation, a cynicism that is reflected in their films. Like the image fabricators of *Hurlyburly* and *Glengarry Glen Ross*, who project onto the television screen or into the sales pitch images that disguise their negation of moral obligation, the image producers project onto the movie screen images that disguise their negation of principles, a negation that Gould admits "is hell" (44). But the Hollywood of *Speed-the-Plow* is hell on a scale larger than that of any theatre work examined so far, with the possible exception of its satiric treatment in Nelson's *Jungle Coup*. In each work, images that reflect not an objective reality but the transmitter's subjective reality are projected as fulfilling national and international audiences' requirements.

Bobby Gould appears in more than one Mamet play, one of which is "Bobby Gould in Hell," but the character surely is in hell in this play too, trapped in his image of himself as a producer of superficially active, spiritually dead films. Since he has convinced himself that a spiritually dead public has forced him to fabricate the self-image and since he will not test his argument that public taste necessitates maintaining the self-image, he projects into his films the image of a superficially active, spiritually dead self, a self without a soul.

Yet he is offered freedom from the entrapping image by a more powerful, spiritually active image. Were the play written by T. S. Eliot, were the secretary

named Beatrice or Grace rather than Karen, the audience would be more receptive to her as the play's stage image of the new life. Mamet skillfully introduces her even before her appearance. She is the party on the other end of the
telephone line, the temporary secretarial replacement to whom Gould has to
explain in a series of interoffice calls how to phone the top studio executive
and where to get the coffee that he and Fox want.

Visually different in that she is a woman in a male sanctum, Karen is verbally different too. Her words are free of cynicism and greed, of scatological
jokes about getting ahead in life and getting even with the competition when
once ahead. She does not have greater conviction about her view of existence
than does Fox about his, but her response to the book Gould asks her to read,
which is different from Fox's predictably contemptuous dismissal, reveals an
idealism that the Head of Production has long since discarded. Everything
about her is different for Gould, but most of all is that she seems genuine in
herself, as opposed to fabricating an image, and genuinely interested in him,
as opposed to manipulating him as the people around him always are trying
to do. Thus the longer they talk about her motive for being with him, the more
he becomes unsure of himself and his motive for asking her to come to his
home. "I don't understand" (59), he blurts out three quick times.

The new life that she offers Gould is the life of the spirit to which she awakens him when she comes, at his invitation, to his home in act 2 to present her
critique of a book, submitted to the studio as a possible script for a film, which
he asks her to read. Despite his objection that the book would not make a com-
mercially successful film, she argues for it as a change from the spiritually degrading films that Hollywood makes and one that the public would pay to see
because it speaks to a hunger in people ignored by the entertainment industry because the media deny its existence. The change must come from within,
however. Films cannot change from without, and they will change only when
image makers realize that they have the same gnawing hunger that the public
has, that it exists in them as well as in the public.

Spiritual nourishment satisfies the hunger, she appeals to her host. Knowing the feeling of emptiness, she recognizes it in him, but he has fabricated
his superficial self-image to hide behind because he is afraid to test his feeling.
If he can admit that he has been wrong about what people need, then he can
understand his motivation behind asking her to come to his house. She knows
that he wants to take her to bed, yet it is love, she tells him as she attempts to
make him penetrate his mask, that unlocks the prison of self-isolation. Let love

enter his life and he will create a new self and from that a new image. He can project the new inner reality into a new image for himself and into new film images for the public.

Karen is the new, temporary reality in Gould's office that breaks the fetters of his infernal dialogue with Fox and that seeks a more permanent relationship with him. Just as Fox sees the box-office star's commitment to make a film for the studio the intervention in his life that frees him from his "historical self" (28) as assistant producer to become co-producer, and just as she sees Gould's request of her to read the book as her opportunity to change her life, so she intervenes in his life, offering him the opportunity to change. He does not have to retreat into prayer and fasting or be crucified on an island. All that he has to do is respond to her in his home, to which he invited her and to which she, understanding herself and him, has come. He does not have to be afraid with her, for she has been a bad person herself. But she believes that experience can transform: that lust can become love—that together they can create new self-images and new film images.

She can awaken him and she can stir him, but only he can act. She so persuades him that his will moves.

Act 2 is Dostoyevskian, yet act 3 yields no salvation. The pattern of Karen's appearances suggests that she and Fox contest for Gould's soul. Her entrance in act 1 displaces the assistant, who leaves. She remains with the Head of Production till act 1's end and then shares the stage with him in act 2, where she is at her strongest. Her force begins to weaken in act 3 when Fox, who is alone with the producer, learns that Gould intends to recommend the book that she read and not the script for which he has the star's commitment, thereby terminating his opportunity for co-producer status. He attacks the producer physically and Karen verbally when she appears. She is at a disadvantage, though, in that she cannot attack him. Any attack would be futile, for she cannot hope to dispel his cynicism with her idealism. He does not respond to it. For him she is an impostor: the competition posing as do-gooder.

Since she is only as strong as the strength she has given Gould, when he capitulates, she has lost. He does when his assistant makes him see that, though seemingly frank, she is disingenuous. Her motivation no different from anyone else's in Hollywood—his own included, he cynically observes—she is manipulating him to achieve her end, which is making a film with him. With the producer's wail, "Oh, God, now I'm lost" (78), Fox vanquishes the secretary.

Karen's behavior needs no defense. She never pretended to be a saint and admits to being a sinner. Her motivation, like all human motivation, is ambiguous because less than perfect. Yet her interactive self awakens other selves to change through the interaction as Fox's exemplary self does not, and her idealism revitalizes the spirit to create new images as Fox's cynicism does not. Her only request is that she be allowed to participate in the change, in the creative process. That she is going with the producer into the meeting says more about his change than her alleged machinations.

Anticipating heaven, however, Gould plummets back into his old, spirit-negating self. "And what *if* this fucken' 'grace' exists? It's not for you," Fox consoles his partner. "You know that, Bob. You know that. You have a different thing" (81). With the new life expelled, the two men, who mirror each other, together will produce the thing: superficially active images that conceal spiritually dead cores. Toby Silverman Zinman has written an article that studies the rhetorical device crucial to the playwright's style. After explaining how the device, Jewish aporia, demonstrates loss, she concludes that Mamet's rhythm of speech gives "Nothing shape and sound."[5] I see the nothingness as the emptiness within the characters and their hell, for in this play's final irony, the two men do not escape their historical selves but switch them, and that is hell.

We do not know what would have happened to the relationship of Gould and Karen had they gone into the top executive's office. We know what happens to the relationship of Gould and Fox. By making the producer see that Karen's motivation is the human one of power, the assistant gains power over his superior, not only becoming co-producer but having his name precede that of his partner. In the hell of *Speed-the-Plow* as in the hell of *Glengarry Glen Ross*, one must devour or be devoured.

The occasional theatregoer who saw the above two plays might conclude that for Mamet, woman, in the person of Karen, for example, is not driven by the same hunger. He obviously has not seen *Oleanna* and probably not passed the Orpheum Theatre when it was staged in New York. A poster out front announced it as "A Power Play."

Act 1 opens in the office of a university professor, John, who is distracted, as he will be throughout the act, by telephone calls that interrupt an unscheduled office meeting he is having with Carol, a student who sits and waits until he can return to her concern. Failing his course, she wants to discuss her grade. Since he understands the course material, having written a textbook on it, he cannot understand why she cannot understand intellectually unless her problem is psychological. To bolster her self-confidence, he adopts the strategy of talking personally. He thinks that he puts aside his professorial mode to be on her level, a strategy that, when added to what he considers his natural charm, will help her overcome feeling stupid.

Since they inhabit different universes, Carol cannot accept as professional his personal manner. As she listens, she hears an ulterior motive when he volunteers to change her grade to A and when he tells an off-color anecdote to illustrate a point, and she feels one when he puts his arm around her shoulder. The situation is aggravated by her feeling of disfranchisement from the entire educational process, which he, a member of, mocks in his adversarial mode because he cannot stop being professorial and, from her point of view, patronizing. Hearing in his adversarial mode a mockery of her educational aspirations, he becomes for her not merely another instance of privilege humiliating while exploiting the disfranchised but the proverbial straw that breaks the camel's back. Between acts 1 and 2, she files a report against him with the university committee that recommends to the governing board whether a professor should be granted tenure or should be dismissed.

When, in his office to which she has come at his request for a meeting in act 2, he tries to neutralize her charges by implying that she misunderstood his motive in act 1, she replies that the events that took place are not what he "*said* they meant."[6] He must understand that a new day has dawned. She is no longer to be exploited. "I don't *care* what you feel," she says to him. "Do you see? DO YOU SEE? You can't *do* that anymore. You. Do. Not. Have. The. Power" (50). When he pleads for civilized discourse, she responds that she will not allow his wish, to discuss their differences privately, to prevent her from availing herself of due process. The act ends with his attempt to stop her from leaving the office before they can address the differences.

Act 3 completes the play's series of reversals. She becomes the teacher, instructing him in the uses and abuses of power. Losing his job, he has lost power. By reporting him to the tenure committee, which ruled in her favor, she has gained it. When he protests that his putting his arm on her shoulder was devoid of sexual content, she reminds him of their new relationship: "Don't you begin to understand? IT'S NOT FOR YOU TO SAY" (70). Possessing power, she uses it. She presents him with an agenda for change in a list of books that if he will substitute for books he presently requires for his course, she and her group will consider speaking to the tenure committee on his behalf. He refuses, ordering her to leave his office.

Act 3 also completes the play's unmasking of both of them. Before Carol leaves, John learns that she has accused him of trying to rape her when he re-strained her from leaving the last time she was in his office. And before she leaves, she instructs him in the correct way to address his wife on the telephone. Enraged, he knocks her to the floor and is about to hit her when he stops and says, "I wouldn't touch you with a ten-foot pole. You little *cunt . . .*" (79). The play ends with her repeating, "Yes. That's right" (80). I understand her to mean, 'Yes, that's right. At last we are facing the truth of our relationship.'

Carol does not have to be duplicitous when she arrives at John's office. She can have come to discuss her grade. But the longer she listens to him, the more he confirms her classroom impression and the more the discussion draws her out until she reveals herself. For her the value of education is not academic but political, and since it is the vehicle for gaining power in life—in job opportunities and earning potential, for example—her real motive for being in the classroom is power. She wants it, and once she has it, she knows how to use it.

The play's ambiguity has sparked much commentary in the newspapers, with most of it sympathetic to John because the consequences of the action are more severe for him. I do not think, however, that Carol has received enough credit for drawing him out. Midway through act 3, she confronts him with the following charge: "YOU BELIEVE IN NOTHING. YOU BELIEVE IN NOTHING AT ALL" (67). Though written before *Oleanna* was produced, the Zinman article referred to above applies to this play too in that rather than being attributable to distractions, John's mental meanderings and verbal im-precisions give shape and sound to an emptiness within him.

Carol does not accuse him of not understanding the subject he teaches but of not being honest about his real motive for being in the classroom. It is the same as hers: the desire for power, in his case of requiring texts and giving grades. The intellectual skeptic and classroom adversary are fabricated images to mask an insatiable hunger to devour students. Since he uses the power of grades to deny her the opportunity for the power of a job, she has no recourse but to deny him his power. She corrects his admission that he hates her. "Lis-ten to me, Professor. *(Pause)* It is the power that you hate" (69).

Oleanna exposes human activity as an exercise in power with those who have it using it and those who lack it wanting it. Interaction in which the par-ticipating selves mutually grow is an illusion because a relationship in which one is the master and one the slave denies equal participation and growth. The master increases but at the other's expense.

Given life's reversals of fortune, however, master and slave can switch places. Twice John appeals to an old, civilized order as the basis for discourse. The first time, which occurs early in the play, he does not finish the thought. "We are two people, all right? Both of whom have subscribed to . . . certain arbitrary . . ." (10). Carol does not respond to the thought at the time, but she does throughout acts 2 and 3 after she has gained and he has lost power. She makes it clear that the arbitrary standards to which he subscribes are not those to which she subscribes. His are patriarchal. When she substitutes her list of books, she says, "If you can choose them, others can. What are you, 'God'?" (74).

Oleanna is hell because it completes Finley's attack on "one male god," not through interaction but through inversion. In place of the male's repressive culture, Carol and her group will substitute an equally repressive culture, that of one female goddess. We know Mamet's attitude toward inversion in *Speed-the-Plow*. The co-producer replaces Gould over Fox with Fox over Gould on screen credits. But the partnership creates no new images; it reproduces the past.

Oleanna is hell because it completes Charlie's consuming appetite in *Conjuring an Event* to include human beings. Since interaction is, in Carol's words, not only "'unlikely'" but "*impossible*" (69), one must fabricate an image—naive student or paternal mentor—to conceal the ravenous exemplary self that life forces the person to be. Unmasked, Carol and John feed on each other.

To exit the hell of this play, we will go through another play that dramatizes circumstances that would make cannibalism not morally acceptable but understandable. Yet the characters do not feed on one another and thereby affirm humanity's values.

We are beginning the book's reverse movement into the second half. And since climbing out of a pit is more difficult than falling into it, we will proceed more deliberately.

The immediate objective is to determine what humanity can recover from the disintegration of values that is the hell of chapter 4 and how it recovers. That is, what agency or faculty makes the recovery possible? Once we determine in chapter 5 what can be recovered and how it is recovered, we will focus on the selves in chapters 6 and 7. Chapter 8 will bring us to the contemporary American theatre at century's end.

5

Interactive Selves

The playbill for Ted Tally's *Terra Nova* implies that it is so grounded in history it is a docudrama of the ill-fated 1910–13 British Antarctic Expedition. The playbill typically cites the play's debt to the journals Captain Robert Falcon Scott kept on the expedition and may even include a map contrasting the routes taken by the Englishman and the Norwegian Amundsen in their race to the South Pole in 1911–12.

No playbill, however, can indicate the playwright's artistry, for although *Terra Nova* incorporates passages from Scott's Antarctic journals and actual slides from the expedition and the title is the name of the ship on which the British Antarctic Expedition sailed from England in June 1910, it is demonstrably more than a docudrama. The rudimentary critical exercise of comparing the play with the relevant sections of the historical journals yields radically altered details in the play as well as patterns of details not found in the journals. These alterations and additions—Tally's artistry—transform the reenactment of a physical expedition into the enactment of a spiritual journey that connects history and imagination.

The play opens and closes with the character Scott in front of the tent that will become his grave writing in his journals. Because the "Message to the Public" is an authentic journal entry, the seven words he articulates while composing in the prologue—"The causes of the disaster are these"[1]—create the impression that acts 1 and 2 will dramatize these causes.

The impression is misleading. The historical document, the "Message to the Public" printed as the last entry in Scott's Antarctic journals, begins: "The causes of the disaster are not due to faulty organisation . . ." followed by the causes enumerated. The first is the loss of the pony transport in March 1911.[2]

Terra Nova makes no mention of the expedition's reliance on ponies to pull the heavy sledges; the loss of the transport; or the shooting of the remaining ponies some nine months later, the meat to be fed to the dogs, who went as far as the Lower Glacier Depot before returning to the base camp with one of the support parties, and stored in depots as provisions for the Polar party's return marches. From the opening scene, therefore, the play moves away from a strict reenactment of historical events, although these events remain the matrix from which the action develops.

One cause of many given in the historical document is the "astonishing failure" of Petty Officer Edgar Evans, but for whom the "advance party would have returned to the glacier in fine form and with surplus of food" (476).

In the journal for January 7, 1912, Scott notes that Evans had a "nasty cut on his hand" from sledge-making. The next day he wrote, "Evans' hand was dressed this morning, and the rest ought to be good for it" (416). Despite being deflated by the realization that Amundsen had beaten them to the Pole, the members of the Polar party were in good health as they began the return marches on January 18, until January 23 when they discovered that Evans's nose was frostbitten and his fingers blistering. From then on his condition deteriorated rapidly. In early February he was "dull and incapable" (437) after falling; days later he was "going steadily downhill" (439); by February 13 he was powerless "to assist with camping work" (444). He died on February 17. According to Scott's journals, Edward Wilson, the Polar party's medical doctor, opined that he died from brain injury suffered in one of his falls.[3] His death demoralized the others because he was the fittest of the group, but it eliminated the necessity for making a decision about how to proceed with him. As Scott explained, "The safety of the remainder seemed to demand his abandonment, but Providence mercifully removed him at this critical moment. He died a natural death, and we did not leave him till two hours after his death" (462).

The petty officer's "astonishing failure" is the basis for the play's act 1, but Tally has so radically altered the details of this failure that the dramatically conceived Edgar Evans bears little resemblance to the journals' Edgar Evans. The exterior action of *Terra Nova* covers the period January 15, 1912, to March 29, 1912, and, again in terms of the exterior action, contains only the Polar party. That is, act 1 opens the day before the discovery of the remains of Amundsen's camp by Scott and the four men chosen from the Summit party for the final assault on the Pole: Lieutenant Henry Bowers (added at the last minute to what should have been a four-man team), Captain Lawrence Oates, Evans, and Wilson. Act 2 closes with Scott, Wilson, and Bowers pinned down by a blizzard eleven miles from the One Ton Depot. Evans had died on February 17, one month earlier than Oates's heroic act of self-sacrifice.

Moments into the play, even before the character Scott announces that the date is January 15, Oates calls him aside to tell him that Evans is "not pulling his weight, sir" (5). After Wilson dresses the wound, he describes the hand as "badly frostbitten." To Oates's question, "Gangrene?" the doctor answers, "Not yet," but the "fingers are swollen like sausages" (16). While the commander goes into the tent to examine the petty officer's wound, the others, outside, discuss the implications. Oates introduces the theme of moral choice: "Evans knows his duty, same as the rest. If he was any sort of man, he'd do what has to be done" (18). The injury means that since he cannot pull the man-hauling sledge, the others must pull for him and on short rations.

Inside the tent Scott accuses Evans of putting his self-interest above that of the team by concealing the wound so that he would not be replaced on the Polar party and sent back with a support party. When the petty officer attempts to explain, Scott interrupts him. "Damn it, Evans, stop pretending! Your hand is dead, do you understand that? Dead! It's going to swell up and turn black and rot off your arm!" (19). He then strikes the subordinate in the face.

Tally's conception of Evans transforms an "astonishing failure" of stamina in the journals into an astonishing failure of character in the play. By not apprising his companions of his injury, the petty officer has put his self-interest above a concern for the team's welfare. Tally also has added characterizations based on persons only referred to in the Antarctic journals. Yet they are not members of the Polar party. Because Amundsen and Scott's wife, Kathleen, appear only to the commander, either one's appearance onstage signals a shift to the play's interior action. When Scott leaves the tent, for example, he is visited by Amundsen. Together they review the situation: Since Evans cannot survive, he must be abandoned. Scott at first agrees; coming to his senses, he objects.

The party proceeds toward the Pole, periodically stopping for Evans to catch up. Once they realize that Amundsen has beaten them, Oates turns on Evans. His injury so slowed them down that it cost them the honor of being first. "How do you like this nice piece of work you—(*moving to Evans*)—weakling, you bloody pathetic liar—and coward!" (27). Ignoring Scott's command to leave Evans alone, he squeezes the injured man's hand until he screams in pain. Bowers leaps on Oates and pulls him away from the collapsing petty officer.

Act 1 ends with the five men posing for the famous photograph of the British Antarctic team at the South Pole. Evans does not die until midway through act 2.

Another cause of many given in the historical document is the "sickening of a second companion, Captain Oates" (477). Disabled by frostbite and knowing that he was holding back the others, on the morning of March 16, 1912, he walked out of the tent and into the blizzard. The previous Sunday, March 11, his condition forced the others to evaluate their own chances for survival. Scott "practically ordered" Wilson to hand over the opium tabloids, which were distributed among the men, but by March 22 the three still alive had resolved to die "natural" deaths (460–63).

Act 2 is an almost faithful reenactment of these events, except that by expanding the scenes, act 2 expands the theme of moral choice introduced by Oates in act 1 to include being true to oneself; accepting one's fate, tragic or otherwise; and being responsible to others, even if that means self-sacrifice. On the verge of injecting the gangrenous Oates with a lethal dose of morphine, Scott desists because he regains consciousness, drinks some tea, and stumbles out of the tent. Amundsen then appears to convince Scott that opium is not for him; it is "for men who have no choice" (53). Though the scene does not change, from Scott's comments it is clear that the three still alive have pushed on until pinned down by the blizzard, at which time the commander is, as he was in the prologue, composing the "Message to the Public."

Had Tally merely eliminated some of the causes to focus on others, the play still could be a docudrama. After all, conflict between men is more interesting than conflict between men and ponies. But as pointed out, Tally created the conflict; it is not in the journals. Of course, one could argue that he had to because without conflict, he had no drama. Yes, but he not only altered the details to create the conflict, he altered the chronology of events.

Leonard Huxley, the editor of Scott's Last Expedition, graphically illustrates the chronology in a footnote that moves from narrative analysis to table of distances contrasting the lengths of the outward and return marches. (Bear in mind that the return marches were expected to be faster and fewer. When all of the parties, advance and support, with ponies and dogs left the base camp, they were heavily laden with provisions to be dropped off at each depot for the return marches. By the time the Polar party was formed, Scott and his companions had lightened considerably the load on their man-hauling sledge.) "The return journey on the Summit," Huxley summarizes, "had been made at good speed, taking twenty-one days as against twenty-seven going out, the last part of it, from Three Degree to Upper Glacier Depot, taking nearly eight marches as against ten, showing the first slight slackening as P.O. Evans and Oates began to feel the cold. . . ."[4]

The slackening did not begin until two weeks after the party left the Pole. Yet Tally has the slackening begin on the outward journey, before the party reaches the Pole. Clearly the playwright has structured *Terra Nova* into three units: approach to the Pole with conflict caused by Evans's failure of character; climax at the Pole followed by a banquet at which there is no food; and resolution of the journey. To understand why Tally structured his play this way, we must examine both the play's interior action and the banquet scene.

The interior action takes the form of recurring daydreams in which Scott is visited by either Amundsen or Kathleen. Conceived in Dantean terms, they are Scott's guides through his inner life, but because *Terra Nova*, unlike the *Commedia*, is a staged play, their appearance is determined by drama's conventions. They appear as characters, but visible only to Scott, who spur him on his journey. The Norwegian explorer is the voice of reason—as when he defends the use of dogs because they can pull sledges and they can be converted to protein—and of conscience—as when he convinces the Englishman not to take opium. Kathleen is the wife Scott left in the garden, the woman to whom he wants to return. As he says to her, "I've been happier here, I think, in this garden—than anywhere else in my life" (9). Each taunts him about his motivation. The former tells him that he knows the rules but "not one dark corner" (23) of his heart; the latter senses that inside him is a "fearful yearning" and a "kind of terror" (39). Since none of these passages is in the journals, the effect of Tally's additions is to internalize the action, to underscore the spiritual journey into the unknown, which is initially the landscape of Antarctica but ultimately the landscape of humankind. Stated as simply as possible, the journey in *Terra Nova* is a test of humankind's "unaided" (6) ability—unaided by dogs, for example—to penetrate the unknown, to turn around, and to return home.

The experience would seem to be a failure. Scott and his men have been beaten by the Norwegian team, and they must return eight hundred miles to the base camp unaided by dogs or any external support. The play's climactic passage is spoken by Wilson at the Pole: "North—north in every direction. Think of that. *(Pause)* Strange that it's no different, really, from any other . . . I mean somehow I'd hoped—perhaps it might. . . . *(Pause)* Childish, I suppose" (27). The unknown is not charged with significance; it is devoid of it. The journey is analogous to the experience in the snow in Wallace Stevens's "The Snow Man," where the listener, "nothing himself, beholds / Nothing that is not there and the nothing that is."[5] I am not suggesting that Tally is echoing Stevens, but he has Bowers say, "I can't get used to that, the sound of nothing. If we were here a hundred years I'd never get used to it" (42). When Tally writes in his own voice, explaining in the prologue the use of actual expedition slides for the play's setting, he describes the final one brightening until "it shows no contrasts at all, but is just a blank square of light."

Act 1 ends with the Polar party at the South Pole. Act 2 opens with the five men, in formal evening dress, celebrating what is presumably the mission's successful completion. Evans proposes a toast, Scott makes a speech, and all eagerly await the serving of the meal until Amundsen announces, "There is no food" (35).

The banquet scene is unquestionably theatrical. When Amundsen, who up to this point has appeared as a "dicey-lookin'" (33) French waiter, lifts the edge of the tablecloth, the table is revealed to be the sledge, which, given its rectangular shape, is a hearse. But the scene is not a trick to catch an audience off-guard after intermission. Scott's ill-fated adventure is common knowledge; what is not, what Tally cannot expect theatregoers to be familiar with, is the record of the adventure kept by Scott. The scene therefore is not played to disabuse the audience of the belief that Scott and his companions survived the expedition. It does, however, force the audience to recognize that the historical experience is being recast, for this is the play's one interior scene in which Amundsen appears to the five men. It takes only a moment's reflection to realize that since the Polar party cannot be having a collective dream, the journey has been radically transformed.

With the banquet's dissolution, the Polar party must return to their Antarctic gear. There is no nutritional sustenance to get the men home. Neither is there spiritual sustenance on this pitiless wasteland. *Terra Nova* removes the television screen in *Hurlyburly*, the camaraderie in the sales pitch and the board in the window in *Glengarry Glen Ross*, and the movie screen in *Speed-the-Plow* to expose the hole within. Since the explorers do not have a restaurant to which they can adjourn while waiting for the next lead, the expedition into the blank square of light forces them to confront the nothingness in the universe and in themselves.

Then why not abandon Evans the instant he slackens? Why not inject Oates with a lethal dose of morphine the instant his feet are frostbitten? If Amundsen's party can kill dogs for protein, why not cannibalize the vulnerable, as John and Carol do to each other in *Oleanna*? In a universe devoid of transcendence, what difference does it make?

Humanity makes the difference; humanity dictates moral choice. When Scott comes to his senses after agreeing with Amundsen that Evans should be abandoned, he takes his stand at the threshold separating responsibility from expediency because he knows that should he cross the threshold—scale the wall—he no longer will be human.

> There's a wall. I can see myself approaching from a great distance—and at last I come to it. On this side I'm something like myself. On the other side I'm lost. I have no name. *(Pause)* Can't you understand? Where is the point at which the entire thing becomes worthless? After one man dies? After two? (22)

Rather than being a docudrama about one of the last chapters from the heroic age of exploration, *Terra Nova* is an existential drama. Bereft of support because the provisions stored at the depots turn out to be inadequate, the Polar party must trek across eight hundred miles of alien landscape under conditions hostile to life—only to die. Death is the journey's goal whether at the blank South Pole or in a raging blizzard eleven miles south of One Ton Depot. Yet in an image worthy of Camus's *Myth of Sisyphus*, the men continue to drag their sledge long after it has served any purpose, just as, in an image worthy of Beckett's *Waiting for Godot*, they continue to "huddle together for warmth," even though each is "still alone" (53).

Tally's Antarctic play opens the book's second half because it reverses the descent into hell that closes the first half. The audience sees images of something in the nothingness. And they are not images of life devouring life, which is death, but of life sustaining life as long as possible. Tally's artistry, his alterations of and additions to the journals, transforms history imaginatively. *Terra Nova* makes connections.

"Where will you find the rules?" Amundsen asks following the abortive banquet as the explorers prepare to meet their fate on a frozen landscape, to which

Scott replies, "In myself" (35). The images of the appearing and disappearing Kathleen and Amundsen and the banquet scene manifest the commander's interior life. He is aware of his hopes and fears, even absorbed in them, but despite drifting into reveries in which he is visited by his wife and Norwegian competitor, with whom he expresses them, he is not isolated because of them. True to himself and responsible to others, Scott, in the play's most poignant passage, writes to his wife:

> My darling Kath—I want you to know I shall not have suffered any pain. We simply stop being. Therefore you mustn't imagine any great tragedy. You know I cherish no sentimental rubbish about remarriage. When the right man comes along to help you in life you ought to be happy again. I wasn't a very good husband, but I hope I shall be a good memory. (55)

The visual and verbal images are not a mask or facade concealing nothingness but guides to the life within the nothingness, for meaning does not have to reside in the hurlyburly but can be in people themselves, the explorers of the blank square of light. In a universe in which people must charge the unknown with significance, they discover spiritual sustenance within themselves as they quest. The South Pole is blank, and the play's setting, as Tally indicates in the production notes, should suggest "abstraction." For the voyager who has confronted the unknown, however, life is neither blank or abstract.

Reconnected with themselves, people can interact with others to form a community and under the most trying of adversities. The conflict of self-interest dramatized in the playwright's alterations to the journals' Edgar Evans takes the men into nothingness; the sacrifice of self-interest in concern for one another on the return marches brings them out. Paradoxically the sacrifice contributes to the creation of a self by developing one of its components, character: the moral fibre or constitution accruing to the nature of people as they go through life that enables them to meet adversity.

Evans, whose character failed in act 1, shows the way to a new self in act 2. Suffering from concussion and gangrene, he nevertheless keeps moving by putting "one foot in front of the other" (37). And when he can no longer continue moving forward, he sings, "'Eternal father strong to save, / Whose arm doth bind the restless wave. . . .'" Scott cries out, "Christ Jesus," and Oates chants the *Kyrie Eleison*: "Lord have mercy on us, Christ have mercy on us, saints have mercy on us all . . ." (44–46). His death frees the others to keep going, one foot in front of the other. Oates throws himself into the blizzard, and the others push on until death claims them, naturally and with dignity.

Elemental theatre, *Terra Nova* is a new land of self-discovery. On "close to a bare stage," five actors wearing Antarctic gear haul a sledge. After Evans dies, there are four; after Oates's death, three. But the journey is not meaningless. By creating images that are guides to an interior life for real persons whose fortitude is documented, Tally's artistry reconnects history and the imagination disconnected by the fantasizing in the previous chapter. The surface embodies the inner life, which motivates the outer action.

In the existential play's stage images of something in the frozen nothingness, the playwright reconnects the image and the self disconnected in the previous chapter. Act 1 limits the explorers to a time and place established by such historical materials as journal entries and photographic slides. With the banquet's dissolution, act 2 cuts them loose from civilization's restraints; bound only by inevitable death, they are free to create themselves in the blankness. As they trek and huddle, dream and record, they not only create themselves interiorly in exterior action, they create themselves exteriorly in images that fit their historical images. And these images transcend their deaths. By cradling the dead Evans in their arms, his companions sculpt an Antarctic Pieta. And at play's end, while Scott writes the last of his journal entries, Amundsen sketches a portrait of the British team as Vikings whose frozen bodies a dislodged iceberg will one day carry home "into the sun again" (57).

The published edition of *Terra Nova* contains an excerpt from *The Edwardians* in which J. B. Priestley notes that had Scott beaten Amundsen to the Pole and then returned to England, he soon would have been forgotten. What fires the imagination, he goes on, is the "idea of Scott and his companions doomed in that remote howling wilderness of snow and ice." Since Tally altered details in the journals for his play, I would like to alter a detail in the excerpt for this chapter. What fires the imagination in *Terra Nova* is not that humankind is doomed but that on a landscape inimical to humanity, humankind's humanity triumphs.

Humanity also is the source of inspiration in Tina Howe's *Painting Churches*, not because there is nothing at the center of the play's universe but because what is, is dying. In their Beacon Hill townhouse in Boston, Gardner Church and his wife Fanny are packing, preparatory to their move to their Cape Cod cottage, the traditions that have sustained them. Each comes from a distinguished New England family, but he is the more eminent of the two because he has been a creator of his tradition. A Pulitzer Prize winning poet, he was at the center of creativity in his day, acknowledged as the poet to whom all subsequent poets were indebted, the one who "'led the way.'"[6]

Gardner is presented as godlike. When he and Fanny mug for their visiting daughter, a painter, he plays the dead Christ to his wife's Mary in Michelangelo's *Pietà*. For Michelangelo's *The Creation*, Fanny insists that she be Adam to his God. Mags, the daughter, remembers a time as a girl when she and her father went swimming in the phosphorus-laced water off the Cape and he was brilliant and iridescent.

He is a dying god, though: in his seventies, going deaf and senile, and unable to create anymore. He works in his study reproducing the past by typing his favorite poems on manuscript pages for a projected volume of criticism that will never come to light because he cannot analyze the poems. All that he can do is type them, recite them, or teach them to his parakeet. He can no longer contribute to the tradition.

Fanny's tradition is social rather than literary in that she has known all the right people in all the right settings. But her tradition is dying too because at her age, in her sixties, death is shrinking the circle of friends with whom she and Gardner socialize. With little to occupy her while he types and with a deadline for moving, she has assumed the responsibility for deciding what of their traditions—her Paul Revere teaspoons, for instance, and her husband's favorite volumes of poems—they can take to a cottage one-eighth the size of their townhouse, on which incidentally they can no longer pay the taxes.

With the poet's creative well gone "dry" (367), so that he can no longer create new poems but can only mechanically reproduce past glories, Fanny becomes the caretaker of Gardner's legacy, just as she will care for her senile husband in their waning years in their retirement cottage. Her rationality fills the vacuum left by his collapse, but it is as mad as his spirit is impotent. An advocate of "system" (400), she stacks books according to the binding's color and not according to the contents. When that system does not work, she devises one in which he can participate. She divides piles of manuscript pages between them, and they dive-bomb sheets and packets into open cartons.

Were it not for Mags, the heritage that survived the dispersal would wither away into nothingness stored in boxes in an attic or garage. She is a New York-based painter who has come to Boston to assist in the packing on condition that her parents allow her to paint them. On one level the play records the passage of the center of artistic life from Boston to New York. The daughter will take the creative future with her, prefigured in her narrative of the phosphorus swim when she was a girl. While Fanny washed dishes in the house, Mags, "laughing and iridescent" with Gardner (405), held onto her father in the water for as long as she could before he slipped from her grasp.

She must, however, find her own medium in which to create. She did when she was a girl, as she relates in the story of her melting crayons on a hot radiator to create a magic cake of shimmering colors. "I FOUND MY OWN MATERIALS! . . ." (388), she repeats at story's end, and it is with these materials, rather than her parents', that she revives the heritage.

Were Mags to think of expressing herself in poetry, she might be so awed by her father's stature that she would be unable to create. She also lacks her mother's social skills. Although she feels dwarfed by her parents, finding a medium congenial to her temperament frees her to see them as two persons she loves and respects, and frees her to image them as she sees them. Just before they look at her portrait of them, Fanny tries to get Mags to see them, not in her imagination, but as they are: decrepit has-beens. Mags then turns the perception around and gets her parents to see themselves, not in their self-image, but as she images them: as temples of the heritage.

Mags's painting stimulates their imagination and they not only see her images of them as suggesting the gaiety of an Impressionist painting of a couple dancing, they become the images. As they become animated, they once again become vital Bostonians. For as long as they dance, they are their images. They create new selves, as does she by winning their respect for her ability.

Terra Nova is a new land of self-discovery because spun loose from sustaining traditions, humans are free to create themselves. *Painting Churches* also is a new land of self-discovery because by creating, Mags creates a new self and renews the tradition. Gardner and Fanny have given their daughter a talent that enables her not only to create them in her image of them but to induce them to reconnect themselves with their images despite the parents' tendency to be exemplary selves. Dialogue in a Howe play bears the playwright's signature just as does dialogue in a Rabe or Mamet play. Hers is not interactive. Characters do not speak in response to one another; only at rare moments do their lines intersect.

The play's closing scene is one such rare moment, as luminous as Mags's story of crayons melting on a radiator, which brings to life a magic cake. Sustained by her image of her parents, Mags, in the act of creating that image on canvas, brings them together. The portrait and the stage come to life as the parents, interacting, verbally describe the scene that their dancing bodies are visually creating in the image of their daughter's portrait of them.

New lands of self-discovery, the two plays are connected by images of image-making, or the imagination. In the remainder of the chapter, we will look at a cluster of plays that dramatize the imagination in action. Dramatizing the creative process, they release images from the storehouse of man's heritage in his unconscious so that by seizing them, consciousness reconnects him to himself and his ability to create a new self.

The first is a play that develops the old-world ideal that Gurney in the closing of *The Middle Ages* suggests has to be wedded to the modern-world ideal for the American Dream to be realized. Only toward the end of his play, however, does this playwright introduce the cup as a symbol. For most of the play, he relies on a tradition in which the medieval ideal takes another symbol.

Len Jenkin's *Gogol* is a drama that integrates antinomies in a healing experience. That the antinomies are embodied in two historical figures who never met in real life connects history and imagination. That the integration is accomplished by their undergoing an initiation enacted in literature and opera places the drama in a sustaining tradition in which a young knight quests for the symbol of the supernatural healing power: the Holy Grail. The tradition's best known ceremony is that of Parzival, Anfortas, and the Grail maiden in Wolfram von Eschenbach's thirteenth-century narrative poem, *Parzival*.

Before we can look at Jenkin's recreation of the ceremony in *Gogol*, we have to identify the play's two antinomies to be healed in the ceremony. They are embodied in the play's two principal characters.

Though he does not identify himself as Nikolai Gogol, the assumption is that the first speaker is the Russian novelist, short story writer, and dramatist. As he explains to the audience in the prologue, entitled "Gogol Alone," he will be "hosting a little party for a friend."[7] Since he has a troupe perform his theatricals at the party, which is act 2 of the play proper, he is a dramatist. He also shares with the author of "Diary of a Madman," "The Nose," and "The Overcoat" the creation of realistic images turned loose in a fantastic universe. "Welcome," he begins the prologue, "I am Gogol. I am not lights and shadows.

. . . I am Gogol, cloud and mud. I am extinct. I run the roller-coaster at night. I am a go-go dancer and a fool." These images have a mad quality to them characteristic of those in his counterpart's St. Petersburg stories. And like the Russian artist, Jenkin's Gogol is slightly mad. He interrupts his imitation of a choo-choo train to tell the audience about the party for his friend, yet as soon as he does, he corrects himself. The friend is not a friend. He is an "acquaintance, a pen-pal, a colleague." But he is none of these either. "To be honest," he confesses, "I've never met the man" (5).

Madness and spiritual illness unite the real Gogol and the character in the play *Gogol*. The difficulties he encountered writing his masterpiece, *Dead Souls*, Nikolai Gogol recorded in *Author's Confession*, difficulties which he sought to resolve by regenerating himself spiritually. The very conception of the narrative of which the published novel is only the first part was interrelated with his spiritual condition. As he confided in a friend, the epic would "'finally solve the riddle of my existence.'"[8] He never completed the work, burning the second part days before dying in 1852. The quest had taken him to "insanity and suicide."[9]

At the end of act 1 of Jenkin's play, Gogol has his accountant burn the books, but this is a minor detail compared with the major one. Gogol suffers from an unnamed illness, which he connects with a wound he received from a spear that fell from the props being shelved backstage and pierced his side. Holding his reddening side, he laughs madly as he exits the stage on the back of a giant turtle.

In the play, Gogol is the artist: collector of images in the house he inhabits with mistress and animals outside of town, the "one with the iron gates made with strange pictures" (34). He rules a kingdom of the irrational: a house with gates that make it a castle, a realm of death from which he releases images of life in the form of theatricals. The antinomy he embodies is the unconscious.

The friend who is not a friend that Gogol invites to the party, the character for whom the artist stages the theatricals, is Doctor Franz Anton Mesmer. Since he gives his full name and profession in the second scene following the prologue, entitled "Mesmer Alone," there is no question about his identity or the antinomy he represents. He is the voice of consciousness who announces, "I am a doctor. I heal the sick. I would wager my life on it" (9). A passage from an authoritative encyclopedia defines the position of the originator of the doctrine of animal magnetism, later called mesmerism, by contrasting it with that of his followers:

In fact, in the hands of the mesmerists animal magnetism became a multifaceted biophysical entity which could account for just about anything. For Mesmer, animal magnetism was and remained a biophysical agency belonging to the Newtonian scheme of things, of interest primarily as a way to understand illnesses and a way to cure them rationally.[10]

The play proper opens with Mesmer under attack for being a quack, a charge the character admits is partially true because he does not understand the source of his healing power. He knows that he has it, and the first scene of the play proper, the scene between Gogol's monologue in "Gogol Alone" and his monologue in "Mesmer Alone," shows him with a revitalized patient emerging from the healing bath. "Maybe I did something for God without knowing it," he quips, "and he's paying back in pieces" (10). A fool, though not totally guileless, is a better designation than quack because in his lack of judgment he has on occasion been sexually intimate with patients. The consequence is that since he is discredited in the medical community and since he has so angered influential husbands that he can anticipate the police harassing and even arresting him, he is forced on a quest for a place to continue his medical work.

Like Gogol, Mesmer is spiritually ill but of a disease that "refuses to develop symptoms" (10). The explanation for both men being maimed—never stated in the play but implied throughout it—is that the two need each other to be whole. They impersonate formerly unified activities whose separation into antinomies has divided the human being into an unconscious mind mired in the darkness of the psyche's interior revealing itself in images and a conscious mind adrift in the atmosphere and expressing itself in speculation. Gogol's illness is manifested physically, forcing him to wait for the coming of the hero who will liberate him from his suffering. Mesmer's illness is manifested mentally in that he is blessed and cursed with a gift that drives him to drain "away a lifetime of poisons" (7) from patients.

Together they can become whole. Gogol releases in his castle the energy that Mesmer needs to focus as "magnetism, psychic forces, energy channels." Whatever it is named, the doctor goes on, "I suck it up and deliver free, except for a small service charge" (11).

To deepen the mystery of the quest for the power that heals, the play intersects it with other quests and questers. For example, act 1 introduces two characters steeped in mystery in history and fiction. The Resurrection Man is a character named for nineteenth-century grave robbers who not only disinterred bodies to sell for dissection but who sometimes murdered for that purpose. The Resurrection Man wanders in and out of scenes in *Gogol* attempting to sell to Mesmer the corpse of a young woman in a mud-spotted shroud. The irony in his name is emphasized whenever she begins to revive. He has not raised her from the grave to bring her back to life. He bops her on the head with a wooden mallet, knocking her unconscious.

Dickens's Inspector Bucket is the other character. From a passage in the "Hotel" section of Jenkin's *Limbo Tales*, which alludes to the detective's and Esther Summerson's night journey in chapter 59 of *Bleak House* and which the playwright connects in that play with allusions to Eliot's *The Waste Land*, Dickens's novel would seem to be a favorite of his. The "pestiferous and obscene" graveyard, the entrance to which is an "iron gate,"[11] connects the night journey's destination with Gogol's iron-gated castle, but only in detail. Like the presence of the Resurrection Man, that of Bucket establishes the presence of the poles of death and life in *Gogol*, but the characters are ineffectual in the play.

Dickens's relentless detective is out of his element because the mystery in Jenkin's play is of a different order from those in the novel: solving Tulkinghorn's murder or, with Esther on the night journey, tracking Lady Dedlock to the graveyard's iron gate. The Resurrection Man also is irrelevant. In act 1 he urges Mesmer to go into a commercial theater and watch the show, a comedy routine performed by Bucket's assistants, who are mechanical windups, culminating in a *"grotesque parody of religious ecstasy"* in which they mock the doctor as the "Prince of Peace" (21) for his alleged cures. Ironically, they are much closer to the mystery than they realize.

So, too, are we close to the mystery. At his house, Gogol gives final instructions to the members of his troupe—which among others includes his mistress, two bears, and the turtle—this night, their "last performance together" (28), for the guest whose knock at the door ends act 1 and begins the recreation of the medieval ceremony.

Wolfram von Eschenbach's medieval German poem, *Parzival*, narrates Parzival's quest for the Holy Grail, with chapter 5 relating the young knight's first adventure in the Grail castle. Coming upon the Fisher King and his attendants in a boat on a lake, Parzival asks directions to a place of shelter for the night. The older man, described as a "man of sorrows,"[12] directs him to his castle on the mountain. There, after being dressed in a cloak belonging to the queen of the castle, Repanse de Schoye, he joins the Fisher King, more "dead than alive" (123) on a sling-bed, and his company in a great hall, where he witnesses a marvelous ceremony. First a page runs in carrying a bleeding lance, the sight of which evokes weeping and wailing from the company. Then each wearing a garland of flowers as headdress come resplendent maidens carrying trestles, tabletop, candles, and silverware. When the articles are assembled in front of the wounded king, the queen, her face refulgent, enters carrying the Grail, which she sets before his lordship. A banquet follows, a communion service in which the Grail supplies food and drink in plenitude, for all that one has to do is stretch his hand in its presence and whatever he desires appears for him to fill the golden bowl distributed to each member of the company by chamberlains.

Parzival is filled with wonder but because of his breeding does not ask any question, not even when a page presents him with a magical sword or when, the ceremony over, he takes leave of the host and mournful company to retire for the night. Awakening in the morning, he finds the castle empty.

Parzival's confusion is compounded when a page at the drawbridge rebukes him for failing to ask the Grail, or Fisher, King "the Question" (131). He protests that he does not understand but to no avail; slamming the gate, the page disappears into the castle. Later in chapter 5 his cousin Sigune curses him for the same failure. She gives him the reason why he should have asked "the Question." Had he shown compassion for his host, Anfortas, by inquiring about his suffering, he would have released the stricken man from the state of "living death" (134).

Jenkin's play recreates the ceremony in contemporary terms. Though Gogol is suspended between life and death in his house, which is his body, he does not symbolize matter and Mesmer does not symbolize spirit. The madman and artist is as much spirit as is the doctor and scientist. Dying in his body, he must find a new body in which to incarnate his spirit, the energy he releases as images in a play-within-a-play he composes for the occasion. He, the host, is the wounded Anfortas who remains suspended until the guest whose knock ends act 1 assumes the role of the questing Parzival who will ask "the Question" that will cure both of them.

The first scene of act 2 functions as a prologue to Gogol's theatricals. Dressed as if they were guests, the two actors and two actresses in the troupe tell one another rumors about three areas of their host's life: his wealth, illness, and amorous adventures. Three times they stop the conversation to ask the invited guest, "What do you think, Doctor Mesmer?" (31–32), but in the first two instances, before he can answer they resume rumoring. The purpose is to whet his curiosity so that he will ask about his host, intensified by the third request. This time before he can answer, Gogol's mistress draws him away from the troupe.

The prologue over, Mesmer takes the only seat available to him "*in a row by itself*" in the audience section "*for the small red-curtained stage on stage*" (35). It is forward of the other seats, which are taken by Gogol, his mistress, and the other members of the troupe when not performing in the staged scenes. Once he does, the stage goes dark except for the light shining on him and the red curtain.

In the first scene a girl approaches the doctor and introduces the wooden pig she drags behind her as the Porker Pundit who can answer any question. She appeals to the onstage audience to ask one. When no one does, she turns to the spotlighted guest, "Please, sir, why don't you try? If no one asks a question my part here is done, and I return into the nighttime." Mesmer obliges, but it is the wrong question. Instead of inquiring about his host's health, he asks, "What will become of me?" (37).

After years of searching for the Grail castle, on a Good Friday Parzival surrenders himself to God's will, at which time his horse takes him, in chapter 9 of Wolfram's poem, to the hermit Trevrizent, who is the brother of Anfortas and Repanse de Schoye. The hermit tells him the story of the Grail, a talismanic precious stone with the power to confer life on whoever looks at it. Every Good Friday a dove descends from heaven to place a wafer on it, renewing its power to sustain life with food and drink.

Parzival exclaims that given his knightly prowess, he deserves to be among the company of its guardians. Trevrizent reminds him that pride is a sin and then relates the story of Anfortas's wound. It is a punishment for pride as manifested in his brother's pursuit of unchaste love. One day, seeking "adventure under Love's compulsion" (244), he was pierced in the scrotum by a poisoned lance while engaged in a joust. Sustained by the Grail, he cannot die, yet incapacitated by the wound, he cannot live because natural medicine cannot remedy his condition. In the state of living death, he must wait for his redeemer, a knight pure in heart who by asking "the Question" (246) will liberate him from his suffering, thereby succeeding him. God alone appoints the successor to the Grail kingship, declares the hermit. It is during this part of the tale that Parzival and his tutor discover their relationship. Trevrizent and Anfortas are brothers to Parzival's mother and therefore his uncles.

After the girl and the Porker Pundit depart, a man enters the onstage stage from behind the closed red curtain. Introduced by Gogol as Henry M. Stanley, explorer of darkest Africa, he approaches the guest. "Doctor Mesmer, I presume!" (38). Mesmer admits that is his name but questions the identity of the doctor for whom Stanley should be searching in an exchange that reveals his indifference to the drama. Though he has a reputation for possessing a modern stone, or magnet, with a mysteriously curative force, he does not hear the pun on the medieval stone with a mysteriously curative power:

MESMER: Aren't you searching for Doctor *Livingstone?*
STANLEY: Living who?
MESMER: Livingstone. (39)

Insisting that his quest is for him, Doctor Mesmer, the actor playing Stanley turns him around to face the onstage stage. This scene, entitled "Here in the Castle," depicts the nature of the stricken Gogol's illness, which is every human's condition. The red curtain parts to reveal a young woman chained to the castle wall. Bound and gagged in suggestive clothing so that her writhing is both erotic and painful, her spirit struggles to live while chained to a dying body. The liberator is not the Resurrection Man, who bursts upon the scene and begins to paw her. Neither is he Mesmer, who grabs the Resurrection Man's arm. The cure in *Gogol* is not having someone physically break the chain any more than the cure in *Parzival* is pulling Anfortas from his sling-bed. Since Mesmer does not comprehend, Gogol intervenes and orders silence.

The characters Gogol and Mesmer are brilliantly conceived embodiments of the antinomies whose drama of reconciliation is enacted in apposite metaphors from medieval literature. As the embodiment of the unconscious, the artist is maimed. Confined by his illness to the castle, he can communicate only in images of life in its passionate struggle with death. The embodiment of consciousness, the doctor also is maimed. Alienated from his roots in nature, he cannot interpret the madman's nondiscursive symbols; because he does not share Gogol's involvement in life, they do not speak to him. The play's early scenes dramatize his emotional distance from his patients, whether or not he is sexually intimate with them.

Because he is a doctor reputed to have extraordinary healing power, which is exactly what Gogol's illness requires since it does not respond to natural treatment, and because he is adrift without a laboratory in which to practice his profession, Gogol invites Mesmer to his underworld castle to cure him and thereby become king of the assimilated conscious and subconscious minds. To do that, however, the guest must show an interest in his host.

Mesmer is not callous. He intercedes on behalf of the chained woman, but his interest in healing is scientific and not personal. He does not ask his host what is wrong with him because he does not empathize with him. Both are maimed, but only the artist knows the nature of the illness. Only the artist knows that he is dying. The scientist does not, though the irony of their relationship is that together they can restore each other to wholeness. They need each other, but so long as the doctor does not speak to the patient—so long as the conscious mind does not respond to the subconscious mind's signals—the human being remains divided between death and life. At the one extreme, he is imprisoned in a festering body; at the other extreme, he is driven to wander on an alien landscape in quest of his physical and spiritual home.

Mesmer lacks imagination. He has not discovered the Grail, which in Jenkin's theatre is the imagination.

In *Parzival* when Repanse de Schoye enters the hall carrying the Grail, Wolfram's poetry reads as follows:

truoc si den wunsch von pardîs,
bêde wurzeln unde rîs.
daz was ein dinc, daz hiez der Grâl,
erden wunsches überwal.[13]

In Hatto's prose translation, from which I quote throughout this comparative study, the medieval poet extols the Grail as the "consummation of heart's desire, its root and its blossoming—a thing called 'The Gral', paradisal, transcending all earthly perfection!" (125). In the following verse translation, the Grail also is a transcendent "thing," a talismanic precious stone:

She bore the pride of Paradise,
Root and branch, beyond all price.
That was a thing men call the Grail,
Which makes all earthly glory pale.[14]

Jenkin's translation is different. As the castle prepares in act 1 for the party in act 2, Gogol assigns his mistress her role in the theatricals: "Roots, then branches, then almost anything you can imagine" (25). The mistress, only tangentially a Repanse de Schoye figure, will participate by stimulating the imagination. For the contemporary Grail is the imagination, and the party is meant to awaken its inexhaustibly renewing power by recreating the medieval Grail ceremony in the play-within-a-play.

Parzival's quest prepares him for his second adventure in the castle in the sixteenth and concluding chapter of Wolfram's poem. An anguished Anfortas asks the knight to keep him from the Grail so that he may die, but Parzival, humbled by the realization of his failure the first time he was at the castle and his years of searching separated from his beloved wife, Condwiramurs, now feels the king's suffering as he did not before. He asks the question, "'Dear Uncle, what ails you?'" Anfortas is immediately "whole and well again." And Parzival becomes "King and Sovereign" of the Grail castle (395), to be reunited with wife and family. His sacrifice modeled on the mystery of Christ's incarnation, the knight, entering the stricken man by identifying with him, cures his uncle and himself. In the celebration that follows, Parzival's infidel brother marries Repanse de Schoye, for love, like the Grail, is inexhaustibly renewing.

Mesmer, however, fails to act in the double sense of failing to move his will and failing to assume a role in the staged scenes. We are in hell again, traversing an endless circle. The doctor-scientist cannot participate because he lacks imagination. He lacks the ability to empathize with his host, and he lacks the image of himself in a new role. The images that Gogol releases would reconnect the two of them so that Mesmer could see himself in the patient and see in himself the artist who creates a new self by essaying new roles, but to do that he has to seize the images.

They come to the surface because *Gogol* descends into their storehouse in the unconscious, where the castle's host releases them in the theatricals for his guest's attention. But because Mesmer is disconnected from the creator-artist in himself, he fails to ingest them. The play-within-a-play is for him a sequence of disconnected scenes so that he neither revives a tradition nor creates a new self. He is not even a Parzival in that he is not curious about his host or the scenes. Yet he should be, for the interior play is the dramatic equivalent to *The Waste Land* in that the released images are the fragments that the quester must shore against his ruin by connecting them. When the doctor does, he will have found his heritage, his home, and himself.

Since Mesmer fails to ask Gogol "the Question," since he fails to exercise the freedom the *Terra Nova* explorers discover, the play asks the question,

What must theatre do to engage the spectator's imagination so that he will participate?

Putting aside the medieval romance, the host answers by calling for the theatricals to resume with another set of images consistent with the onstage staging: a curtained area, small enough to be portable, from which actors emerge in a procession of enacted scenes. A character from late medieval literature, Pontius Pilate, comes forward to stand trial for ordering the execution of mankind's Savior. The subtitle of *Gogol* gives the medieval tradition to which he belongs: *A Mystery Play*.

Recognizing mystery plays as composing a cycle from Fall to Doomsday,[15] we can understand why when Gogol begins staging scenes from the cycle, he begins with that point at which Christ is dead. Mesmer's failure to assume the role of Parzival, who sacrifices himself for his host's suffering, denies mankind redemption because Parzival is a figure of the Redeemer. Pilate's trial scene also gives the doctor one more opportunity to get involved in the action in a role he may find more congenial. If he will not play the Savior, perhaps he will play the executioner of the Roman procurator. But he will not, despite Gogol's mistress's attempt to goad him into acting by criticizing his refusal to participate as "spoiling the play" (46). Sentenced to death, Pilate has to force Mesmer, over his objection, to execute him.

"A Little Epilogue" returns to the prologue's contemporary setting but without the party atmosphere. The guest for whom the party was held remained a disengaged spectator. The castle with its Grail ceremony disappears into the landscape of a modern wasteland on which a cast member in work clothes mourns the death of his dog, hit by a car. As he sits on the onstage stage, praying to "Jesus Christ" to "have pity" on him "here alone" (47) in his self-isolation, he thinks he sees a woman on the horizon who will rescue him. His hope is short lived. Once he realizes that no one is coming for him, his head slumps. The theatricals concluded, the troupe forms a backdrop for the play's final scenes.

Confronting his guest, Gogol tells him why he was summoned. "Even yet, you don't see" (48). The doctor is to cure him, not of pain of which there is none, but of death. Forced to try over his objection that he cannot, Mesmer is unsuccessful. "So be it," pronounces the host. "I have no choice. It is now necessary that I cure *you*" (51). Again the doctor protests against becoming involved by insisting that he is "fine" (51), but the artist will not leave him alone.

"You have been a fool," he says to the reluctant Parzival. "This will cease. You are to become my cup" (55).

"My cup" returns to the Grail symbolism, but that which Gurney uses in the closing image of *The Middle Ages*, for the healing experience's second and decisive ceremony, this one extraordinary. Gogol initiates the medieval romance's miraculous transformation by becoming a figure of Christ, the blood from whose lance-pierced side, according to one legend, was collected in the Grail-as-cup by Joseph of Arimathea. Giving a dagger to his guest and ordering him to drive it through his skull, he makes him the vessel in which the two of them will live. "You will save us both" (57), he says as he sacrifices himself to the reluctant knight. To cure Mesmer's crippling detachment from life, Gogol has him spill his blood so that the artist can die in his body to be resurrected in the doctor's body. "One stroke, and clean. I don't wish to flop about like a fish" (57), he bids farewell to the maimed Fisher King incarnation. Together the two become a whole person, Mesmer-Gogol, king of the Grail castle.

The transformation can be explained in psychological terms. Gogol's pressure on Mesmer to respond to him is the pressure of the repressed unconscious to be accepted by consciousness. If accepted, as in an individual's normal growth, consciousness assimilates contents of the unconscious into a whole, integrated, self. If rejected, the individual's growth is maimed. In the play, Gogol is the reality of death that Doctor Mesmer in his desire to heal with animal magnetism has repressed in his unconscious until forced to confront it by executing Pilate and destroying Bucket's mechanical assistants, whose arrival at the house is a sure sign that the police are closing in. Once Mesmer accepts the reality of death, he is free to live to the fullness of himself. The reconstituted self is called, in the play's last line, "Mesmer-Gogol."

Certainly *Gogol* contains a psychological dimension. Jenkin, though, does two things at play's end to direct attention to another dimension. Just before he dies, Gogol's mistress misquotes the dirge from Webster's *The White Devil* to stress the resurrection rather than the burial. And Bucket arrives to arrest the doctor. When he announces his intention, the mistress, troupe, animals, and Mesmer point to Gogol's corpse, which the inspector then has removed. Thanking Mesmer, whom he calls Mr. Gogol, he departs satisfied that he has completed his assignment. The detective, whose forte in *Bleak House* is penetrating Lady Dedlock's disguises as Hortense the maid and Jenny the brickmaker's wife, does not suspect that in the house with the iron gates he is in the presence of a mystery because for him mysteries are rationally ordered and resolved.

In the contemporary transformation, the mystery of the Grail castle becomes the mystery of the imagination with roots in Gogol and branches in Mesmer that blossoms when they integrate. Since Mesmer cannot empathize with his host, cannot enter into him by identifying with him, Gogol enters into Mesmer. He incarnates the artist's spirit in the scientist's matter. That is, *Gogol* creates the imagination that Mesmer lacks during the performance of the play-within-a-play. The first time that Mesmer sees himself as the artist-host, he seizes Gogol—the images that the artist releases—to become Mesmer-Gogol. Calling for the music to begin, the integrated doctor-artist dances with his mistress, to whom he will presumably engage himself. He will stay on as king of the castle to create new ceremonies and rituals that reconcile antinomies in the mystery of death in life and life in death: the death of the body and the rebirth of the spirit in a new body.

Just as Gogol dies in the body so that his spirit can be reborn in Mesmer's body, the Grail story dies as a body of medieval images to be reborn in contemporary images. By recreating a narrative tradition in a dramatic experience, *Gogol* affirms theatre as the new body for nurturing into life the reborn spirit that is the imagination. Before he dies as Gogol, the host tells his guest the effect he hopes that the castle's staged scenes have on the spectators. "I hope they have opened a wound that won't close, a dark space in the center of the chest, in which darkness, if they look carefully, they can see the stars" (48). True to the medieval romance recreated in *Gogol*, the wound becomes the way to reunion for madman-artist and doctor-scientist, performers and audience, subconscious and conscious minds. In the demystified modern world, the Grail is the imagination's inexhaustibly renewing power to create a unified self that can participate in communal experiences. Its castle is the theatre of healing ceremonies and rituals, individual and collective.

The chapter has accomplished what it set out to do. Witnessing artists in the dominant culture duplicate the achievements of minority artists, we have learned what humanity can recover and how it recovers. In each play a character reconnects with himself/herself, enabling the character to recover a human community, creative ability, and sustaining traditions.

The faculty or power that connects is the interactive imagination, not imagination by itself, which is the fantasizing of chapter 4, and not history by itself, which is the eternal repetition of the past in the television and film studios of chapter 4. We must therefore look at a few plays that dramatize the interaction. The theatres of Tally, Howe, and Jenkin certainly do, but we want to look at the interaction in the everyday worlds of supermarket products and hometown festivities.

To be creative, characters in an Eric Overmyer play must match or reconcile their internal images with external objects. It is a good play with which to begin this section that closes the chapter because it corrects Hungry Mother's studio perspective. It gives respect to the world of common objects outside his studio. Beth Henley's two plays give respect to the personal self no matter how mean its situation.

Overmyer's *Native Speech* dramatizes the collapse of the old world. His *On the Verge* dramatizes the building of the new world. Since the author has characterized the latter as a "play about the imagination" and a "play *about* language,"[16] it is a play in which the imagination creates the world through language.

The play opens in 1888 with three women reaching the embarcadero for their journey into Terra Incognita. As they make a final check before moving inland, they speak in single-word images to describe the terrain features and their equipment (the actresses carry a few props): beach and cliff, machetes and umbrellas. The question they turn over as they talk is how to record what lies ahead. Not knowing what to expect, Fanny has brought a gross of fabricated postcards of generic scenes likely to be found in any location. Alex, for Alexandra, has brought a camera to capture images with the hope that they will remain intact in the box until the women return to civilization and have the film developed. Mary intends to bring back physical evidence, the only evidence acceptable to science. Immediately, however, as if it had been thrown on the ground to disprove Mary's assertion, Alex spots a metallic button with incomprehensible writing on it: "'Hec-kwhod-ont'?" (6). Physical evidence is not enough. Required to connect the letters comprehensibly is the power that comes from exploring Terra Incognita, the "last undiscovered, unexplored—bit" (1) of the globe. Overmyer's Terra Incognita is Jenkin's Grail castle. It is the unconscious, the realm that releases images that consciousness must seize and assimilate with objects from the sensory world in order for the explorer to progress into the future.

The power is the imagination, and it is essential to the creation of the self.

The process begins on a bare stage with the women's speculation about what they will encounter and intensifies as they move into the mysterious interior. The oldest, Mary, and the next in years, Fanny, have more control than Alex over the raw materials from which the imagination creates because they have processed more raw materials than she, which they reveal in the metaphor of assimilation. In anecdote and journal entry, the two relate their experiences with head hunters and cannibals. The native food, the rootstock manioc, Mary records in her journal as vile tasting; for a taste treat on a break, Fanny serves processed cream cheese on homemade date bread.

The play is rife with allusions to eating habits. Alphonse is the first human the ladies encounter in the interior. He embodies a colossal meal. A cannibal who devoured the German-speaking pilot whose dirigible crashed, he exemplifies the anthropological distinction between raw and cooked, savage and civilized. By eating the pilot, the jungle native has become, complete with accent and uniform, an Alsace-Lorraine native.

To create their new selves, the women must digest their experience. Alex's youth a disadvantage in limiting the raw materials that she processed before the adventure, it is an advantage in that she is more receptive to experience than the other two, who initially resist change. By wearing trousers, she is the first to reflect the play's feminist theme. She also is the first to experience verbal images so rushing at her that she regurgitates them before she can assimilate them. To the amazement of her companions as well as herself, she blurts out that there "are no cannibals in Tibet! No matter what the Red Chinese claim!" (20). No one of the three has the slightest inkling what a Red Chinese is.

Though she does not yet understand what is happening to her, Alex senses a connection while photographing an imaginary native. Since the image is native to the imagination, which is native to human beings, by connecting images she becomes imaginative. "Image. Native. Image-native," she muses. "Imaginative. I am a native of the image" (24). The two older ladies catch up in insight until Mary makes the connection between the imagination and the world. They have entered a "New World," she shares her realization with her companions. "Blossoming! Within and without!" (35).

As the women bushwhack jungles and scale mountains in Terra Incognita, they experience the sensation of speaking verbal images for which they have no percepts or referents. Yet as they penetrate the uncharted realm's mysterious interior, objects and concepts begin to intrude upon their consciousness because they are releasing images, which are native to the imagination. The deeper the penetration the more images released and the greater the understanding, so that by act 1's end, the three realize that not only have they been exploring geography, they have become intrepid time travelers approaching ever nearer to the future, beckoning to them through the released images. By connecting the images with objects and concepts, they are "absorbing the future" (36).

Making connections, the time travelers acquire language, answering the question raised at the embarcadero. In language they record their experience. When they find a second metallic button in act 1, "'I-Like-Ike'" (37), they connect it with the first button, "'Hec-kwhod-ont'?" In act 2 they reconnect the first comprehensibly so that the discovery reads, "I like Ike. Heck, who don't?" (59).

Exploring "within and without" (74), they stimulate their imaginations to essay new selves in new worlds. Fanny understands that she is free to remarry; Alex, that she can be a songwriter; and Mary, that she yearns to continue the adventure. When Mary exclaims in the closing speech that the future is boundless, she means that not only can she record the exploration, she can create it through the imagination's ability to create metaphors: to connect the image and the found object in a new relationship.

For the ego to create a new self in the new world, there must be social possibilities present, a fluidity of movement into the possibilities, and the imagination to essay a new self. The first two conditions are not present in Beth Henley's *Crimes of the Heart*, but the third is. The play takes place in a small southern town, a town that the heroines, three sisters, feel is repressive, even though one, Babe, is married to the most socially prominent man in the community. The townspeople are small minded and mean spirited. Furthermore, the circumstances of the women's lives stigmatize them. The father abandoned them, a betrayal that led to their mother's suicide. The oldest sister, Lenny, believes that her inability to have children makes her undesirable to men. The mother's suicide eventually landed the middle sister, Meg, in the psychiatric ward of a county hospital, and a boring marriage drove the youngest, Babe, into adultery and the shooting of her husband. Once the play opens, however, the situation improves because it worsens.

In this paradox is Henley's comic genius. Each sister is able to feel the other's pain but not by becoming the other so totally that she loses her identity, surrenders to the woe, and withdraws from life permanently. She retains enough of herself to see the absurdity in the other's situation. The same can be said about her personal situation in that she feels life's pain but retains enough detachment to see the absurdity in it. Act 3 images the paradox in successive scenes. Babe goes upstairs to hang herself as her mother did but runs back downstairs moments later, the broken rope around her neck, to answer the telephone. She then tries to suffocate herself in the oven, but as she has an insight into her mother's suicide, moves to extricate her head, only to hit it, stunning her so that she falls back in and has to be rescued by Meg.

In Henley's imaginative world, beneath the surface calm of the town and each individual in it lies the unexplored realm that is her equivalent to Jenkin's Grail castle and Overmyer's Terra Incognita. As the id, it is the source of psychic energy; as the unconscious, the wellspring of images for consciousness to assimilate, it is the source of creative energy. But it is dangerous as we know from Nelson's trilogy, where Charlie learns that reporters who crossed its boundary were burned by its current. Yet it must be activated if one is to discover himself/herself.

That is the paradox in Henley's comic genius and plays. The sisters' cousin who regards them as "trashy"[17] is repressive in the town and repressed in herself. Terra Incognita is unknown to her. The sisters, on the other hand, have at least tapped into theirs, releasing its potential for violence and self-destruction but also activating their imaginations to empathize with one another.

For Henley a heroine/hero is one who takes the risk and accepts the potential to create a new self. In the process of developing one's individuality, the heroine/hero is able to sympathetically identify with others. Babe's lawyer fits right into the family, for he has unleashed his own demons in his mission to bring Babe's husband to justice and win the case for his client, to whom he is attracted. By the power of their imaginations, to which they have fluid movement, they change their social possibilities. Interacting with one another as new selves, they create a new society.

Yet they do not assimilate their Terra Incognitas. Each character is only partly a new self and partly an old self. Neither is assimilated because in Henley's theatre the mine field beneath the surface is so explosive that it can erupt at any time. That is the play's closing image. The sisters reconnect with one another to celebrate Lenny's birthday with cake and party but without the assurance that calm will prevail. And an image does explode in the next play.

The repression in *The Miss Firecracker Contest* is only indirectly town sponsored, though the town, like that in *Crimes of the Heart*, is small and in Mississippi. The direct repression comes from within. It is a lack of self-esteem, inculcated by a family's or school's attitude toward the victim for not having the qualities of other members but reinforced through the years by the victim's attitude toward herself, an attitude for which she perceives daily confirmation in the world around her. After her mother died, her father left Carnelle Scott with her Aunt Ronelle, who reared her as inferior to her two cousins. To compensate, she concentrated on the one area where she felt that she could excel: with the males in the town with whom she gained a reputation for being Miss Hot Tamale.

Her attempt to overcome her past by essaying a new self makes Carnelle the heroine in a play with a cast of characters as comically crazy as the three sisters in the other play. If she can win the town's Miss Firecracker Contest, she sees herself, head held high, leaving town in a blaze of glory. She will have vindicated herself. Of course, she not only does not win—placing last—she is humiliated, tripping over her dress and being heckled by the hooligans, most of whom know her sexually.

In her disgrace, though, is her redemption. When her friends and relatives try to console her by pointing out the contest's insignificance, she verbally lashes them for not understanding her and even spits at them. She then makes a statement that separates the Henley heroine from the nonheroine. When the contest representative informs her that her role in the parade is to follow the float while carrying the flag, her cousin Delmount tells her that she does not have to humiliate herself any further. She brushes him aside. "Look, if you come in last, you follow that float. I took a chance and I came in last; so, by God, I'm gonna follow that float!"[18]

Taking a chance activates her imagination. Activating it, she initiates the creative process. When toward play's end she asks a former boyfriend, to whom she gave syphilis, what a person can expect from life, he says sarcastically, "There's always eternal grace" (134). His answer resonates in her, preparing the stage for the play's closing image.

Carnelle decides not to leave town but to join on the tent's roof two characters also taking a chance on life, cousin Delmount and her seamstress, now betrothed to him. The seamstress, Popeye, who visited the observatory the preceding day, remarks that the astronomer commented on space this way: "'If you can think of it, you've got it'" (136). Carnelle cannot verbalize her hope, but she does not have to. The play does visually.

The Miss Firecracker Contest closes with the three watching a display of exploding fireworks. The image, which is that of the exploding imagination, is the equivalent to the astronomer's comment. If the mind can imagine a possibility, it exists as a possibility to essay. Though Carnelle has not left town and still must contend with her reputation, she has a new sense of herself and her possibilities.

Knowing now that the imagination can heal the divisions within people by reuniting them with themselves and their human heritage, we are ready to investigate the healing process in the threefold self. The order changes, however. Instead of the personal self preceding the theatrical and national selves, the theatrical self comes first for the reason just given. To demonstrate that the imagination heals by creating a self that one essays while growing into it is to demonstrate the primacy of the role the actor performs in the theatre. We are back to Shattuck's argument about subjective processes and the histrionic sensibility as directions modern humans have taken ever since the notion of self replaced that of soul.

We turn next to the experimental theatre for what it tells us about the nature of the self. Then we will examine personal and national selves (and theatrical selves, because the three are interrelated) before concentrating on the healing process within American society.

6

Experimental Selves

The experimental theatre deforms the naturalistic theatre. Naturalism is both a historical movement and a mode of theatrical presentation. As a nineteenth-century movement, it conceives of human beings as physiological creatures, rather than metaphysical beings, who when studied scientifically, rather than imagined idealistically, are revealed to be determined by heredity and environment: by biological, psychological, socioeconomic, and cultural forces. As a mode of theatrical presentation, it champions a stage environment that actualizes the forces.[1] In this conception, since human beings are creatures of nature, they are perforce governed by the laws of nature. Thus the experimental theatre deforms these laws to alter the spectator's perception of the nature of people and their ability to create themselves.

Mabou Mines is a collective of artists who collaborate on original theatre works and new interpretations of existing texts. Conceived and directed by collective member Bill Raymond and Dale Worsley, with a text by Worsley that includes excerpts from the memoirs of Ulysses S. Grant and Julia Dent Grant, *Cold Harbor* has original music by Philip Glass, slide projections, and museum exhibits. The title refers to the site of Grant's attack in the 1864 Wilderness Campaign of the Civil War, when thousands of Union soldiers were slaughtered in a few hours.

The lights come up on a museum setting with two curators informally assembling materials for a Grant commemorative. Into the setting is wheeled an exhibit, glass front with wooden sides and back, containing the life-size figure of the Civil War general and eighteenth President. The exhibit is parked until the curators are ready for the museum staff to remove the figure from the case and place it in the commemorative's centerpiece, a tableau of dead figures. While the curators, testing equipment, project slides of Civil War carnage juxtaposed against halcyon scenes from episodes and sentiments in the general's life and times, Grant, played by Bill Raymond, comes to life. At first speaking slowly while whittling a spear of wood, he becomes increasingly animated until he breaks out of confinement to plead his defense against the carnage directly to the audience.

When Raymond alights from the exhibit case, he liberates the self from a naturalistic conception of it. The breakout is both image and metaphor, both Grant's refusal to surrender to a judgment on his life that is a synthesis of social-scientific documentation and the avant-garde theatre's refusal to allow the stage to become a laboratory for naturalistic drama, or drama based on the assumption that the natural and social sciences totally explain the human being. We can extend the metaphor to see in the transparent exhibit the naturalistic conception of people's interior as conterminous with their exterior. By shattering the exterior, Raymond reveals metaphysical people as opposed to physiological or psychological people. That is, if *Terra Nova* reveals the something in the nothingness of life, *Cold Harbor* reveals the something beneath the surface of the physical self. That something is the soul, which Raymond presents to the spectators in its passion, just as the work presents to them the soul of the new, experimental drama.

In conventional theatre the wheeling of the exhibit into the set would end the drama for Grant. Not so in *Cold Harbor*. Raymond's Grant achieves tragic stature, for while still in the case whittling, he sharpens ever more pointedly the knowledge he must take into eternity. It is the knowledge of Cold Harbor, with all the lives lost, itself a powerful metaphor for the death awaiting him, a death that offers no warmth despite his attempt to pull his coat around him as he finally accepts the inevitable and seats himself in the tableau of the dead.

Though the physical self must die, the chapter examines the various ways in which individual experimental theatres reveal the something beneath the physical self's surface: the metaphysical or imaginative self that coexists with the physiological or naturalistic self. For a change of pace, we will begin with an opera.

When Ruggiero Leoncavallo composed words and music for *I Pagliacci*, he contributed to the making of a school of opera comparable to naturalistic literature in which forces over which man has little or no control condition him. In *I Pagliacci* the characterization-role so adheres to the actor-performer that he becomes imprisoned in it. Canio, the head of a troupe of traveling players, suspects that his younger wife, Nedda, has a lover in the village in which the troupe has set up its stage. He does come upon them but not before the lover escapes, and since the time for the performance nears, he must conceal his broken heart under the clown's laughing face.

When he next appears, Canio is in costume for the role of Pagliaccio, opposite Nedda as Colombina, who entertains Arlecchino while he is absent. Hearing in Colombina's words the exact words he heard Nedda speak to her lover, he refuses to play the cuckold. "No! Pagliaccio non son," the betrayed husband rages at his wife, who tries to calm him by continuing the illusion that they are acting in a stage comedy. For Canio, make-believe has become reality. "Se il viso è pallido," he pulls at his whitened makeup to rip off the detestable role life makes him play. Yet only when he kills his partner and her lover, who is in the audience, is the "commedia . . . finita!"

Mud, the play examined in chapter 1, also is naturalistic in that Lloyd prevents Mae from rising above her socioeconomic state by killing her when she tries to leave him and Henry for a better life. Yet by designing stage directions that have the actors-performers freeze at the end of each scene, Fornes creates the possibility for a dual interpretation.

In an article exploring gestic language in Fornes's plays, Deborah R. Geis explains that though the original reason for the freeze-frame was an outdoor production without blackouts or curtains between scenes, productions should retain the cinematic style as a "reminder that the characters stand before us imprisoned in their bodies for the duration of each scene."[2] I want to support Geis's point while adding to it. I saw the play in a small performing space below street level on Manhattan's Lower East Side. When any one of the actors-performers was not in a scene, he/she sat on the side in full view of the audience and, with the audience, watched the character or characters freeze at scene's end until it was time to step back into the onstage characterization, there to freeze at scene's end. The double perspective is a reminder that whereas the character is imprisoned in the role, the actor-performer is free to step in and out of it. Mae was shot when she tried to leave; the actress did leave the stage.

The Ridiculous Theatrical Company takes the dual perspective to the heights and depths of the ridiculous. Under the guiding genius of playwright-director-actor Charles Ludlam, this experimental theatre developed a style that the founder defined in the playbill information as "ensemble playing which synthesizes wit, parody, vaudeville farce, melodrama and satire, giving reckless immediacy to classical stagecraft." The company's "reckless immediacy" risks collision between two poles of theatrical presentation: performing, or self-presenting, and acting, or role-playing. The challenge every company member faces is revealing both the performers and the characters they are playing without colliding and blurring them or, in a production in which they play more than one role, vacating one characterization for another without colliding and blurring them. They must be able to reveal and conceal. Though Ludlam died in the spring of 1987, the opening production of the 1987–88 season, his adaptation of Euripides' *Medea*, ensured that the style will remain the company's signature.

The background of the story is that having fallen passionately in love with Jason when he and the Argonauts came to her native Colchis, Medea aided him in his quest for the Golden Fleece and escape to Greece. As the classical tragedy opens, however, she is suffering the humiliation of betrayal, for Jason has left her and their two sons to marry the daughter of Creon, king of Corinth. Her situation is rendered desperate when Creon, aware of her jealous rage and fearing her powers as a sorceress, banishes her. By appealing to him, she delays the exile by one day, a day in which she plans to have revenge, the method to be partly determined by her ability to first secure a refuge to which she can fly following the murders.

Enter Aegeus, king of Athens and Medea's old friend. Played by Bill Vehr in the Ridiculous Theatrical Company's production, he was in his dotage, a king for whom sexual performance would at best be a dim memory. Yet as he explained, he had been to the oracle of Phoebus Apollo to inquire how children might be born to him. In the ensuing dialogue Ludlam's adaptation, while staying fairly close to Euripides' text, turned the company's leading lady, Black-Eyed Susan, loose for a ridiculous portrayal of Medea. Her smile incredulous, her eyes probing Aegeus's face for signs of intelligence, she asked him if he had a wife. "Perhaps that's his problem," she seemed to be saying to herself; "perhaps he's forgotten that procreation requires a woman."

In the company's form of farce, whirlwind events do not disintegrate a characterization. The actor vacates it for another characterization or another facet of a single characterization with mixed motives or split personality. After securing from Aegeus the promise of refuge in Athens, Susan darted back and forth across the stage, on the one side of which she was a mother appalled at the thought of sacrificing her children and on the other, a woman vowing to hurt the man who spurned her by murdering his children. And when Everett Quinton, who played Medea's nurse, returned from the palace in a crazily spinning circle to tell his mistress of the vengeance wreaked, he became the nurse reenacting the scene, Jason's princess devoured by the fire of Medea's magic, and finally the princess's father, who in attempting to release his daughter from the poisoned dress was dragged down into the corpse until, run down, Quinton himself was lying prostrate at Susan's feet.

Since versatility is a Theatre of the Ridiculous hallmark, it was not at all unusual that Susan and Quinton alternated in the roles of sorceress and nurse at alternate performances. Nor was it unusual that the chorus doubled as dragon-drawn chariot transporting Medea to Athens. Acrobatic stunts such as these establish the ridiculous acting style's outer limits, within which a more restrained technique focuses and illuminates. In *Medea* the image that fused the fifth-century drama and the twentieth-century adaptation was Susan's transformation in the pivotal scene with Vehr's Aegeus. Once he told her he was married, she asked him to relate the oracle's response to his inquiry. As he explained that he was not to "loosen the hanging foot of the wineskin" before returning home,[3] her smile changed from incredulity that he would petition the oracle for guidance on procreation to polite deference because she needed his protection. Yet while her lips were saying that the condition imposed on him seemed sensible, her eyes—rolling upward, inward, downward—were flashing the diametrically opposed insight that he had been duped into accepting an unintelligible answer to his petition.

When Susan peeped from within the characterization of Medea, she could not settle into Susan the performer. Neither could Quinton settle into the performer while becoming different characters. Whether adapting classical tragedy, Wagnerian opera, or film noir, the company's form of farce courts collisions because the players must maintain a balance between performer and actor while racing from characterization to characterization. The performer must be present to expose the illusion, but the actor cannot forgo the role to be simply a performer because all the while the production is exposing the illusion, it is maintaining it.

In *The Mystery of Irma Vep*, Ludlam and Quinton each played four roles. Ludlam was Lady Enid, servant Nicodemus, Egyptian guide Alcazar, and

Alcazar's daughter. Quinton was Lord Edgar, servant Jane, an intruder, and Irma Vep. The play's principal set is Lord Edgar's ancestral home at Mandacrest, to which he, widowed following the death of Lady Irma, has brought his new bride, Lady Enid. The production was a tour de force with the costume changes so rapid that at times the train of a gown would be trailing under a closing door as the actor, having shed it behind the set's wall, was entering in a new costume through an opening door.

Whether darting through doorways or motionless and talking, the two had to maintain the dual perspective. In act 3 a seated Lady Enid told a seated Jane that she wanted to speak to Nicodemus. While actor Quinton responded in the negative, the performer within the characterization of Jane tried to signal that the request was impossible and that his stage partner should not persist. In turn, while actor Ludlam accepted the response, the performer within the characterization of Lady Enid signaled with his eyes to the audience that he did not understand why he could not. After all, when not Lady Enid, he was Nicodemus!

Later in the same act, Irma the vampire stood over the body of the woman she had seized by the throat. Lady Enid reached up and ripped off the mask. "Edgar?" she asked, unable to believe her eyes looking at the face of Quinton as her husband Edgar. "No, Jane!"[4] Quinton protested. For the play to continue, he had to insist that his stage partner see him as the servant, which of course he was. In that scene, he had vacated the role of Edgar for the role of Jane disguised as Irma.

Ridiculous Theatrical Company actors do not desert their roles for other roles within the production. They cannot and be faithful to the spirit of ridiculous theatre. Ludlam's conception of theatre is an expression of the human being's oscillation between the poles of his sexual determinants. When one dominates, he is Lady Enid; when the other dominates, he is Nicodemus. But there is more to a self than sexual determinants. The multiplicity a production manifests in its multiplicity of styles, costumes, and allusions. The goal is not for the self to obliterate one set of determinants for another but to harmonize them until one set of impulses naturally becomes more dominant. As it does, the actor sets aside the costumes and mannerisms that express other roles for the costume and mannerisms that express the actualized role.

Experimental theatres such as the Ridiculous Theatrical Company and the others in this chapter expand the self contracted in naturalistic theatre. They do so not because they deny naturalism, the strength of which is that it is faithful to much of everyday experience, but because they affirm the coexistence of human beings' metaphysical and imaginative nature, discovered in chapter 5, which empowers them to respond to other impulses within their being. Human beings cannot live apart from the roles life makes them play, but they can choose to play different roles—four in *The Mystery of Irma Vep*. And while the actor is actualizing one, the costumes and mannerisms for the others wait behind the door for the actor to race back into with "reckless immediacy."[5]

The Wooster Group also establishes and undermines characterization, creating the illusion while destroying it. The group is a collective of experimental artists who mix live and video images. Group members appear onstage with television screens sometimes off and sometimes on with animated and still images. A performer can interact with the audience, another live performer, his/her own onscreen image, or another performer's onscreen image. And some of the screens play images that seem to have nothing whatsoever to do with the performance.

The technique of mixing discordant images and styles in a collage effect has almost infinite possibilities. A performer, for example, can vacate the character he/she is playing by leaving the stage and the character, which remains onstage in a still image or animated one if that portion of the performance was prerecorded. Separating himself/herself from the character, the actor reveals the performer in the character, especially if the actor then sits on the edge of the stage without participating in the action. The technique is disconcerting the first time theatregoers encounter it, yet once they are accustomed to it, it illuminates.

The group member also reveals the performer while he/she is in the character not by peeping at the audience but rather by performing. Since the reader can find lengthy analyses of the Wooster Group's works in an important book, from which I will quote momentarily, I will comment on two staged since the book's publication.

Brace Up! is the collective's deconstruction of Chekhov's *Three Sisters*. Guest performance-artist Beatrice Roth, a woman in her seventies who had left the traditional theatre when she found it no longer challenging, was cast as the youngest sister, Irina, a role she took but not by assuming the character as traditionally interpreted; she played it in a wheelchair. As narrator-master of ceremonies, Kate Valk created a character not in Chekhov's text. These two had an exchange that typifies the group's attitude toward staging the classics. When Roth arrived onstage, Valk asked her if she was in character—if she had done her histrionic warmups to prepare for the role she was to assume. Roth said that she was never in character, thereby avoiding Canio's imprisonment in Pagliaccio by refusing to play the role as written.

Willem Dafoe played the role of Andrei completely on video as he was not in New York when I saw the section of the work the group was performing at the time. Individual performers delivered monologues into microphones as if they were doing solo numbers in performance venues. With hangdog face and dry, self-mocking laugh, Ron Vawter was a Vershinin who philosophized at odds with his live image while across from him a screen held Jeff Webster's cheery image of a Tusenbach whose words were at odds with his video image.

The technique of juxtaposing discordant images reveals the tensions and contradictions between the performer's self and the character's self, between the performer and the other company members, and perhaps within the performer himself/herself. In one of the many interviews David Savran conducted for the book on the Wooster Group referred to above, artistic director Elizabeth LeCompte relates how a group member's doing an improvised action, whether gesture, dance, or language, becomes the "*sine qua non*, . . . the beginning, . . . the text." She explains, "I cannot stray from that text. As someone else would use the lines of a playwright, I use that action as the baseline."[6]

Replacing the characterization as preserved in the text, which is the traditional dramaturgical form for realizing the self, with the performer's conception is the first of five areas in which the group deconstructs the classics. At its worst, deconstruction is a pretext for putting one's ego onstage. At its best, it is the breaking down of the casing in which a drama is transmitted to reconstruct it in a contemporary conception. For the purist, deconstruction is a desecration because the text with stage directions preserves the author's original conception. For the deconstructionist, that argument is dubious given scholarship's demonstration of corrupt texts, but even granting it, a conception is valid only when it is original, and the author's is no longer original. The deconstructionist's, however, is. In order therefore for the drama to be vital, it must be liberated from the cerements in which it is encased. If the stage's sole function is to display preserved texts, the deconstructionist argues, it is a museum, and we know what Mabou Mines's *Cold Harbor* does to theatre as a museum.

Though the Wooster Group travels, it has a permanent home, one which the theatregoer would never mistake for a museum. In it the group deconstructs theatre's mise-en-scène, the second of the areas. When theatregoers arrive for the first time at the Performing Garage on Wooster Street in Manhattan's Soho district, they think that they misunderstood curtain time and are early. They must step over taped cables, dodge technicians setting up equipment, and maneuver into one of the chairs in the section or sections of the performance space set aside for the audience. They are not early, for no matter what time they arrive, the space will not be tidied up. A performance is a workshop experience, and although the lights go down at some point indicating that the performance is over for that evening, the work itself is open ended and ongoing. It is not unusual, for instance, for the stage manager to announce that that night the group will perform only a section of the work or that a role or two will be added or dropped.

The third area deconstructed, then, is theatre as product. Just as the performer, unlike the text, is always becoming, always creating himself/herself, so performance replaces production in the new theatre. An open-ended, ongoing work-in-progress replaces a completed work. Clarifying moments replace an aesthetic whole, and the moments continue to illuminate, unlike a product that, since it is finished, is dead: a museum exhibit.

The fourth area is dramaturgy, combined with the other three areas in the collective's deconstruction of *The Emperor Jones*. O'Neill's 1920 play is an expressionistic drama. In eight scenes it strips away not the bourgeois character of farce but the false self of an American black man who in attempting to escape his past as Pullman-car porter and convict has become the emperor of a West Indian island. When the play opens, Brutus Jones learns from a white man, a cockney trader named Smithers, that the natives are revolting. Knowing that he has subjugated them, because he considers himself superior to "low-flung, bush niggers,"[7] he has planned for this eventuality, or so he thinks as he leaves the palace for the escape route through the forest to the coast. Once in the forest, however, he progressively loses his way and his civilized state, for just as his clothing is flayed by the underbrush, so is his false self as he regresses from a man in control of himself and others through prison for murder and Pullman-car employment to slave ship bound for America and primitive worship in the Congo. He is finally killed by the revolting natives, who, tracking his progressive loss of control, have only to wait until he is helpless. For all his pretensions, he is one of them.

A production faithful to the text will have other characters such as Smithers

and natives. It will have other actors too, but they are not naturalistic characters; they are externalizations of Jones's subjective state: the fears and haunts,
for instance, that he encounters in the forest. And the scene involving the worship of the crocodile god does not mean that Jones began his life in the Congo
but that his race did. The fugitive from himself relives not only his personal
history but also his racial history.

In the fall of 1992, a notice posted on the exterior wall of the Performing
Garage announced that the two performers appearing in the work-in-progress
were Kate Valk and Willem Dafoe. Inside, a verbal notice just before the beginning announced that the two would perform only the first four scenes but
that the total work might be ready by the following spring.

To the surprise of no one familiar with the group, Valk played Jones and
Dafoe Smithers. An onstage screen provided the other images, with varying
degrees of psychological intensity. When entering the forest in scene 2, Jones
strikes a match to determine his position. Valk lay on the stage and put her arm
next to the screen on which was the image of a light so that by extending her
fingers, she appeared to be holding a match. When in scene 4 Jones sees haunts
of the chain gang to which he was shackled in prison, the screen carried images of shackled legs near a resting Valk, who sat up screaming in a nightmare
that projected haunting images onto a screen.

Offstage screens played video images of a form of Japanese theatre, perhaps
the same presentation used in *Brace Up!* which had a Japanese motif running
through it. Dressed in Japanese costuming, Valk and Dafoe spoke the lines the
playwright had written but in a performance space surrounded by television
screens, the assistant director with the script, and technicians. When they
spoke, they made no attempt to create a realistic discourse. In scene 1 when
Valk told Dafoe not to reach for the emperor's gun with the silver bullet,
Smithers was sitting on the edge of the raised performance space looking away
from the gun. When he answered her, he spoke into a handheld microphone.
She carried one throughout the evening, even into the depths of the forest.
When Dafoe joined her onstage, they stopped the plot continuity to dance a
stylized number.

Techniques such as making no attempt to conceal technicians with their
equipment and disrupting dramaturgy's narrative coherence and linear progression destroy the traditional illusion of a theatrical experience while creating a new theatrical experience. In a blackened face set against white neck,

hands, and legs, which she made visible in scene 2 when she checked Jones's aching feet, Valk was a white woman who had put on a black man's self—a false self. Yet once she began the action by exaggerating Negroid mannerisms as if in a minstrel show, she began the performance. And by performing, she and Dafoe created theatre.

Valk did something else that deserves the highest praise. She actualized both Jones's false self and the tragic stature of a man whose ego, which aspires to individuation beyond his reach, requires that he fabricate a self. The startling incongruity between the face and the body, the minstrel mannerisms and the terrifying cries that gradually replaced them, and the palace performance and the forest nightmare opened up the drama. At the center of *The Emperor Jones* is a discrepancy between being and becoming: between Jones's old self, the human heritage he cannot outrun, and the new, but false, self he puts on in the hope that it will become him, that it will fulfill his yearning to rule his life.

By deconstructing the four areas, the Wooster Group deconstructs the fifth and culminating area, a resolution that it does not reconstruct but shifts from theatre's old center in being to theatre's new center in becoming. In traditional theatre the spectators have an onstage frame of reference to guide their emotional engagement because the production stages the text, which is aesthetically shaped by the author's point of view. With the text deconstructed and the production deformed into a performance of discordant images and diverse styles, no one of which takes precedence over the others, the spectators have no onstage authoritative frame of reference to guide them. In traditional theatre the complete work resolves for the spectators the emotional conflict that the onstage conflict engenders within them. Discordant images and diverse styles also engender a conflict in the spectators, but an incomplete work-in-progress does not resolve the conflict for them. The spectator must contribute to the resolution if there is to be one.

Each Wooster Group piece, writes Savran in his book-length study,

> must be considered only partially composed when it is presented to the public, not because it is unfinished, but because it requires an audience to realize the multitude of possibilities on which it opens. As each spectator, according to his part, enters into a dialogue with the work, the act of interpretation becomes a performance, an intervention in the piece.[8]

By shifting from the text's authority to the spectator's participation, the collective creates theatre not only in which the performer and the spectator reform the theatre experience but also in which the performer and the spectator create themselves. The spectator has a histrionic sensibility too.

The passage by Savran also applies to the theatre of Richard Foreman. It is unfinished because its creator is not finished. Should spectators demand finality in their evening at the theatre, they have to impose their own onto the work. We will examine the play that Foreman considers his "best play," the one on which he would be willing "to be judged."[9] Since it takes its inspiration from a literary source that is the inspiration for a work by another playwright examined earlier, we can contrast Foreman's play and the original source and Foreman's play and the other contemporary work inspired by it.

The Cure was produced in 1986. As Foreman explains in *Unbalancing Acts,* a series of interviews with texts of five works, the play represented a new beginning for him. From the time of his founding of the Ontological-Hysteric Theater in the 1960s, his plays had become increasingly frenetic until with *Miss Universal Happiness* in 1985 he realized that he could go no further in that Dionysian direction. Beginning with *The Cure,* the plays would be "more meditative" (103). The foundation, however, does not change. "All of my plays," the playwright-director-designer introduces another work in the volume, "are about my attempt to stage my particular rhythm of perception, which is to say, admittedly, the plays are about *me*" (207).

As the name implies, Ontological-Hysteric is a theatre of being: Foreman's being. Actors impersonate impulses as they collide with one another or with objects to which they are attracted. From these collisions, consciousness is born, but the goal is not the impulses' integration. Foreman insists on the integrity of a multiplicity of impulses because our unconscious self, or multiple selves, and not our false, culturally assimilated, self is the source of our true identity. He concedes that, as in every person, one part of him desires wholeness, but that yearning "is open to question—is it a regression to a childish, and therefore undesirable, state?" (21).

The goal of his theatre is to alter perceptual fields so that the spectator, seeing with changed eyes, becomes conscious of new and different choices he can make. Foreman alters perceptual fields by frustrating the theatregoer's expectations. Since plays originate in the unconscious, they violate the conventions of naturalistic drama. In *Unbalancing Acts* he explains how he writes while in a semiconscious state so that he can record everything without revision. He also will redistribute lines among the cast after rehearsal has started if he thinks that the lines will work better spoken by other actors, who do not portray characters in a traditional sense but are impersonated impulses and ideas. The plays are not structured on character and situation confrontations. They dispense with narrative coherence and linear progression. Prerecorded voices mix with live voices. Lines of string section the stage to call attention to bodies and objects. During the first years of the Ontological-Hysteric Theater's existence, its founder even employed nonprofessional people to perform to further banish conventional theatrical artificialness from the stage.

These alienating strategies always made a synopsis of a Foreman play difficult. A synopsis of *The Cure* is almost impossible, though, because of three characteristics that distinguish it from earlier plays. The playwright has reduced the number of actors from twelve or so, eliminating the nine who functioned as a chorus commenting on the action, to three. He confines the action to the "internal world" (107) with the resulting loss of an objective referent such as that which might occur should an internal impulse collide with the world external to the self. The third has to do with a poetic quality, to which I will return below.

The absence of a story line should not deter us. In its place is a ceremony as marvelous as the one from which it draws its inspiration and as contemporary as the other recreation inspired by it, the recreation that we already have examined in Jenkin's *Gogol*.

In the introduction to the play, Foreman tells how he decided to set the action in a room where members of an occult society like the turn-of-the-century Golden Dawn Society would meet, but without eliminating meeting places for other groups. Whichever group meets there, the room should "*seem appropriate for some sort of religious ceremony.*" Since it has "*overtones of a funeral parlor,*" it is a place where life and death meet. The three speakers who inhabit the room—two men and one woman—speak throughout the play "*very slowly, as if in a dream*" (113–14).

One man enters and acknowledges a many-faceted jewel, following which he is joined by the woman and other man. The speakers of the lines are identified not by character names but by the names of the three actors in the original production. The three speak, change places with one another, interact as they move about the room, dance a variety of dance steps, quote passages on epistemology and aesthetics, and express aspirations and obstacles to self-realization. Recognizable performers in a Foreman work, they are multiple impulses or selves. The first man, David, seems more artistic; the second man, Jack, seems more oriented toward the world of everyday activities; and the woman, Kate, takes the role of the agent of transformation who has appeared in the Ontological-Hysteric Theater since its inception. She mediates between conflicting impulses to effect better interaction between them.

Were Foreman writing a play with the frenzied activity of the plays prior to *The Cure*, it would proceed. But he is trying for something different. Two of the three characteristics of the new direction already have been noted: reduced cast in an exclusively interior environment. The third characteristic is poetic quality, the quality that links his twentieth-century play with Wolfram von Eschenbach's *Parzival*, the thirteenth-century narrative poem that contains the marvelous Grail ceremony involving Parzival, Anfortas, and the Grail maiden.

Despite the visual quality of his work, and string sectioning alone frames his stage with painterly visions, Foreman thinks of himself as primarily a verbal artist. In fact, he calls visual art evil, as in the play *Film Is Evil: Radio Is Good*. It is evil because it implies that truth can be fixed on the surface, that it can be captured on film. The medium of film, he writes in the introduction to this 1987 play, "induces audiences to subliminally perceive matter and man bound together in the concreteness of a totally material, because filmable, world." And a few sentences later, he writes, "Film, by its very nature, works in our consciousness to limit our options" (150).

I do not mean to suggest that the problem appears with *The Cure* and subsequent plays like *Film Is Evil: Radio Is Good*. It always has been present in the plays. The frenzied activity of impulse collisions uncovers the metaphysical being within the physical being while verbal images released in a semiconscious state manifest the depths of the subconscious mind. The problem is avoiding coagulation once the spirit reaches the surface. Because it is more specific than poetry, prose concretizes more so than poetry, a quality that makes it ideal for realistic novels bound to life's surface realities but not for his theatre, which dramatizes life beneath the surface.

The Ridiculous Theatrical Company dramatizes the multiple selves a person is in the public world. The Wooster Group dramatizes the unitary self's liberation from its traditional anchoring so that it is always in the process of becoming multiple selves. The Ontological-Hysteric Theater takes the audience into Foreman's private world to dramatize the interaction among impulses, which are the multiple selves within the physical self.

Poetry is the medium for his theatre because it incarnates the spirit without deadening it into a congealed mass of a monolithic interpretation. "Fluid" (110) is one metaphor Foreman uses to describe the poetic quality he seeks to achieve in *The Cure*. Other metaphors are in the following sentence: "I would like to produce writing that is quite thin, transparent, so it functions as a talisman that lends itself to being worn through all kinds of life situations" (108).

In Western poetry there is a talisman of universal appeal that unites spirit and matter without the latter's depleting the former. We are ready to examine Foreman's recreation of the Grail ceremony in *The Cure*, bearing in mind that its presentation is consistent with a dramaturgy that violates plot continuity. The initial remarks of the three actors have to do with conveying truth. Art conveys it, but the immediate consideration then is selecting the medium of art that will convey the truth in the new direction of *The Cure*. Like a Wooster Group work-in-progress, every Foreman play is on one plane the experience by performers and audience of creating the play.[10] When David asks and Kate repeats "Beautiful childhood person. Do you know my real name?" (115 and 118), they are both questioning the form selected and selecting an example of the form that illuminates their choice.

I do not want to repeat a synopsis of *Parzival*, given in the *Gogol* section in the preceding chapter, yet some repetition is unavoidable. Not immediately, however, because whereas the staged scenes in *Gogol* begin with Parzival's arrival at the Grail castle, *The Cure* alludes to his adventures before he goes to the castle.

Wolfram von Eschenbach's poem opens years before Parzival's quest for the Holy Grail. Embittered by the death of her knight-husband, Parzival's mother rears her son in the forest so that he knows neither his name nor lineage. She also attempts to prevent his acceptance into knighthood apprenticeship by dressing him as a fool when he, seeing knights in the forest, declares his intention to become one. He himself complicates the question of his identity by slaying the Red Knight and donning his armor. In the early chapters of Wolfram's poem, when in the guise of the formidable Red Knight he knocks at a gate or door, he gains rapid entrance. Yet when the armor is removed and he steps forth in fool's garb, his audience is taken aback. Of course, by the time of his second Grail-castle adventure, he has matured tremendously. Among other discoveries, he learns that Anfortas, the stricken Grail, or Fisher, King, is his uncle as is his tutor, the hermit Trevrizent. The Grail maiden, Repanse de Schoye, is their sister and his aunt.

The Cure is sprinkled with such references as being called a "fool" (136), being robbed of one's clothing (136), wearing "armor" (137), and knocking on the door with an "iron fist" (140). Toward play's end, David turns to Jack and says, "I am NOT your uncle." Jack agrees with him in a scene in which he gains the name "Paul" (140). Both call Kate, who gains the name "Paula," the "rose maiden" (140–41). A Repanse de Schoye figure, she says, "I have had more visionary experiences than you can shake a stick at" (123).

Chapter 5 of the medieval poem narrates the young knight's first adventure in the Grail castle, where he witnesses a procession of maidens wearing garlands of flowers for headdress move through a great hall to the castle's lord, Anfortas, immobilized on a sling-bed. After they assemble a banquet table in front of him, Repanse de Schoye enters carrying the Grail. Even though the Grail possesses the miraculous power to supply unlimited food and drink for the golden bowls distributed to the company by chamberlains, Parzival fails to inquire about his host's health or the ceremony. Later he learns that had he asked "the Question," he would have released the stricken man from the state of living death.

The recreation in *The Cure* of the Grail-castle experience in *Parzival* begins when Jack, following David's quoting a passage on developing self-awareness, questions why he cannot express himself that way. Kate gives him a bowl and spoon and fills the bowl with cornflakes. The bowl itself is not golden, but the cornflakes are. She also tells him that the cereal is "not normal cornflakes" (122). She is right, for Jack instantaneously understands the difference between poetry and prose. While he to his amazement articulates the difference, she attaches cornflakes in a mysterious pattern to a blackboard that she lights. The three actors elaborate, with quotations, the distinction Foreman makes in his introduction. The more transparent poetry is, the more it is capable of expressing the mind's ambiguities and contradictions.

Since the onstage action in a Foreman play actualizes insights and concepts, the three now dance a variety of dance steps in unfettered movement to celebrate their discovery that poetry is not as delimiting a medium, or vehicle, as prose. But in a play containing other images such as automobiles, trolleys, and buses as vehicles for movement-expression, this scene is only the beginning of the Grail recreation. As the three dance, Jack attaches himself to a pillar. He is not rendered immobile, but his freedom to move is restricted. It is further restricted when he attaches himself to a chair in such a manner that although he can hobble with it tied to him, he is in Anfortas's predicament in a sling-bed. Jack has gained Anfortas's knowledge. Kate remains the agent of transformation, at one point running back and forth between the men, but by having eaten the cornflakes, Jack now chooses to express himself in questions, and the questions he asks have to do with rocks that mysteriously appear on the play's set. When David and Kate sit down to eat, they discover a rock and not cornflakes in each one's bowl.

Foreman's theatre is very playful. One reason is that the playwright enjoys punning. In *Unbalancing Acts* he explains that he subtitled a 1975 play *Her Fall-Starts* to pun on the way in which he incorporated into the play "false starts," or fragments rejected from other plays (92). It is conceivable that someone unfamiliar with medieval literature and the Grail romance might conclude from hearing a synopsis of *Parzival* that by talismanic stone Wolfram meant a miraculous rock rather than a miraculous precious stone. *The Cure* opens with an image of the Grail, but it would be a rare theatregoer who connects David's many-faceted jeweled ring with Wolfram's Grail castle.

Jack cannot fly with the rock because its weight holds him down. Neither can David and Kate eat their rocks. Yet even though a rock does not possess miraculous powers, it does serve a purpose. When Jack drops it to the floor, the noise signals an auditory experience, reinforced by his blindfolding himself while he speaks. This is one more strategy in Foreman's dramaturgy to disabuse the spectator of the premise of American culture that reality is essentially visual—that matter alone constitutes reality. The quotation that Jack speaks is the heart of the play and the recreation of Parzival's Grail quest in chapter 9 of Wolfram's poem.

From the hermit Trevrizent, Parzival learns the story of the Grail and that of Anfortas's wound. The Grail is a talismanic stone with the power to confer life on whoever looks at it because every Good Friday a dove descends from heaven to place a wafer on it, renewing its power to sustain life with food and drink. Anfortas's wound, the piercing of his scrotum by a poisoned lance, is punishment for pursuing unchaste love. In a state of living death on a sling-bed, he can only wait for his redeemer, a knight pure in heart who by asking "the Question" will liberate him from his suffering. It is during this part of the tale, chapter 9, that Parzival and the hermit discover their relationship. Trevrizent and Anfortas are the young knight's uncles; Repanse de Schoye is his aunt.

The quotation, from Joanna Field, that Jack speaks is a defense of Anfortas's experience in the world:

'I want, not knowledge, but experience of the laws of things; to suffer them, not only to observe them. To apprehend with regard to the things I come across—the necessities of their being, what immutable law makes them what they are, their physics and chemistry and actuality, to feel it. . . . Knowing is no good unless you feel the urgency of the thing. Maybe this is love; your being becomes part of it, giving yourself to it.'(128)

The passage, which does not distinguish between chaste and unchaste love as motivation for experiencing the world, explains why David later says to Jack, "I am NOT your uncle." The passage also prepares for a funny scene in which the three actors struggle not to heed "unwelcome ideas" (130), only to admit that they enter the mind insidiously through electrical sockets, toilets, mail, and so on. This scene is acted with first Kate and then David looking skyward for the magic word on the mountaintop that will guide them: presumably the Grail, which has writing on it.

Parzival and *The Cure* are two works of the imagination incarnating spirit. The contemporary work parts company from the medieval work on the requirements for guardianship of the incarnation. If Anfortas's experience incarnating his spirit disqualifies him, then from the point of view of *The Cure*, the Grail—the medieval incarnation—has a monolithic standard, making it a rock.

Parzival is one of Western literature's great love poems, but love sanctified. The spirit is incarnated in the body of marriage—Parzival is married to Condwiramurs—and fulfilled in the flesh—they are parents to two sons. Unlike Anfortas, the young knight remains chaste in his love, despite years of absence from his wife, which is why he succeeds to kingship of the castle. For sheer narrative power and sense of mystery, not only is his adventure in the castle memorable but so is his enthrallment by the drops of blood in the snow in which he sees Condwiramurs's image.

The questing knight's experience is modeled on the mystery of Christ's incarnation. Human love has its source in divine love, which sacrifices itself to incarnate its spirit in human matter. By asking his uncle on his second adventure in the castle, "'What ails you?'" Parzival, sacrificing himself to enter the stricken man by identifying with him, cures his uncle and himself. Anfortas becomes "whole and well again," and he becomes King of the Grail castle, to be reunited with his wife and family. Love, like the Grail, is inexhaustibly renewing.

Foreman is as much a religious writer as is Wolfram.[11] The difference is that for the contemporary American playwright the mystery is the self, which is in-exhaustibly renewing so long as one is alive and provided one does not prevent motion in his/her being, which is to say that he/she understands that impulses collide within the self and in the self's encounter with the world external to it. In the play's final scenes, the actors play with live and dead images: plastic fruit and painted fruit, fruit pits and fruit in bowls. And they ask questions, not the one question that Parzival must ask, but questions about experiencing life. Kate, for example, asks these questions:

> When you bite, do you engage the ear, more than the eye?
> When you bite, does it hurt?
> Does it hurt a fruit? And does the hurt fruit cry out? (139)

If the answers are "no," some part of the human's sensory apparatus has at-rophied. *The Cure* is meant to cure that sensory impotence. Hence the actors increasingly speak at varying decibels; to accompany varying movements; and in varying line lengths, some rhymed and some not.

Kate also asks whether the "pain of the cure *is* the cure" (139). Jack answers when he refuses to put on glasses, despite David's warning, in a line that con-tains a pun on Anfortas's wound, as the latter seizes a sword: "The point of that sword could scratch your very eyeballs" (142). Even though in the metaphors of another play film is evil and radio is good, Jack refuses to shield his sight because the cure is not in denying some senses for others. The cure is not in overcoming contradictory impulses by integrating them, but in accepting their existence. To pick up on the passage Jack quotes midway through the play, to be true to himself, he must "'suffer them.'" In Foreman's recreation of the *Parzival* ceremony, Anfortas does not want to be spared the pain of experience. If the consequence of experiencing his impulses and appetites is a sling-bed, he will hobble with it attached to him as best he can.

Yet just as images released from the subconscious mind can solidify on the surface into a monolithic prose, so the many impulses can solidify into a so-cially conditioned self unless consciousness resists the coagulation by insur-ing the flow of the currents of energy, or selves, within the being. Jack's attitude toward experience is but one attitude. David's is another. "I am NOT your uncle," he opposes him. And when Jack suggests that they travel, David de-clines the offer. Why should he? in effect he asks. Artist and recluse, he has all that he needs where he is. He too must be true to his impulses.

The conflict between ambiguous and contradictory impulses, reduced in number from *The Cure* on, prevents the self from becoming the exemplary glutton of Nelson's satire or the exemplary cannibal of Mamet's power plays, each of whom is a monolithic self. The drama in Foreman's theatre is the interaction among the impulses and between them and the external world. If every impulse were a desire for experience, all would be in Jack's predicament in a sling-chair. In fact, there is considerable evidence that temperamentally the playwright identifies more with the David figure, who opens the meditation by displaying the jewel and who opposes the idea that life is essentially experience.[12] Yet if all impulses were a desire for what stands under experience, no choices would ever be made.

Foreman's theatre is a work-in-progress that keeps all the currents flowing. His dramaturgy does not so much create a new self as uncover the old one covered over by socially conditioned experience. The spectators can recover theirs too but not by empathizing with the performers. Like Jenkin's strategies, Foreman's fracture the theatre experience. Unlike Jenkin's, Foreman's do not heal it. David and Jack do not become David-Jack as Jenkin's Mesmer and Gogol become Mesmer-Gogol.

For Jenkin the cure for the pain of individuality that isolates is empathy. His strategies engage the spectator in the unity of the theatrical experience because the imagination that enables the self to participate creatively in a communal response is the contemporary Grail's inexhaustibly renewing mystery.

In *Unbalancing Acts* Foreman writes about banishing empathy from the performance, discouraging "audience response that's so much a product of that feeling of togetherness exploited by normal theater" (73), and staging theatre for individuals only. The objective is to alter the perception of the spectators so that they discover that rather than overwhelming them, the multiplicity offers them choices. The aesthetic position yields the philosophical position. The alienating strategies disengage the spectators from the unity of the theatrical experience to engage their imagination in the competing currents of energy. In the Ontological-Hysteric Theater, the cure for the pain of individuality is not submersion in the group but accepting the pain and making it creative by opening oneself to the multiplicity of impulses flowing into being.

The Cure opens with a visual image of the medieval Grail as a many-faceted precious stone. It closes with a visual and verbal image of a contemporary Grail as a three-faceted fugue. With each of the three actors gripping a steering wheel, first Kate and in overlapping succession Jack and then David "*shout happily over the music*" lines that she alone spoke earlier: "In the manipulation of my car I am a total career. In the manipulation of my car I make a medium out of a traffic flow, for other automobiles are not so perceptually varied" (143). The interaction of these perceptually varied impulses, kept open and flowing so that they neither shut down one another nor congeal, creates a contemporary Grail as the inexhaustible mystery of the metaphysical, imaginative self that individually converts electrical impulses into creative choices, even though the risk is that the choices will solidify.

We have learned so far that in the experimental theatre, the self is not fixed and unitary. It is not finished forming so long as human beings continue to exercise their imagination to make choices about their life. The self is, in other words, an ongoing creation. Moreover, it actually contains many selves and not only during one's life but at any time in his/her life.

The self also contains naturalistic selves. They are aspects of the person conditioned by forces such as heredity and environment. All are present in the individual, although we have learned that any one part of the individual can function independently. One can live one's life without imagination, and one can exercise one's imagination unrelated to history.

Is it possible, however, to resolve these two sources of one's being so that one lives life to the fullest in time, or history, but timelessly, or imaginatively? That is the issue we address in the final play in this chapter. The play is John Jesurun's *White Water*, which seems to discover a cure for the quest for a healed, unified self. At least some of the players consider testing it.

In Jesurun's dramaturgy we find the same deforming devices found in the dramaturgies of the Wooster Group and Foreman. Live and prerecorded voices mix. Live actors interact with live actors and with talking heads on television screens. The action is recursive rather than linear, and the actors are impersonations of mental activities, or selves within the self, rather than developing characters.

Like Foreman, the playwright reveals in the narrative autobiography that prefaces the published text that he does not assign speakers to the lines while he is writing them. Later he does, but then he may switch lines between speakers. "The whole thing is one voice to me anyway," he explains, "with several people speaking it who sometimes are characters and sometimes are not, who switch their identities back and forth."[13] The whole thing that the play dramatizes is "someone's thinking processes, constantly whizzing around" (76). Since the action is interior, within the self, the contradictions and ambiguities within that self's thinking processes—the collisions within the whizzing around—generate the drama.

The reason for the whizzing around is the allegation of a supernatural intervention in nature. Different parts of the self respond naturalistically and metaphysically. Did the event happen? Can the allegation be disproved? If the sighting cannot be disproved, what is its significance?

Though dramatizing "someone's" thinking processes, which are not necessarily his, the playwright does locate the play's origin in himself. "*White Water* seems to have started in several different corners of my head simultaneously," begins Jesurun's tracing of the play's genesis in the narrative autobiography. He goes on to identify the occupants of the corners. The first is a television talk-show host, a questioner whom he imagines as a district attorney or lawyer. The second has to do with seeing visions, a "strange mysticism" (76) he associates with twelve- and thirteen-year-olds. The third is a hysteric.

To facilitate their interaction, he places them in a verbal boxing ring. With his background in film and television, he visualizes the ring as a television talk-show format, even including with the text the layout he used when he designed and directed his play. The set contains, among other items, a large table with chair in the center of the rectangular space. Two of the play's six characters appear in the opening scene: the host, Kirsten, and the producer, not named. Kirsten is seated at the table. The first occupant to be identified, she is the staged play's first focal point.

In the scene, she and the producer, a talking head on the monitor, evaluate the entertainment appeal of celebrities as guests for the talk show. When the lights come up on them, however, the discussion has been interrupted by Kirsten's revelation that the previous evening she saw something "floating up in the sky and then it went down into the gutter. A glowing ball." The host disagrees with the producer's suggestion that it was a soap bubble. "It shone from the inside," she explains, adding that even though it disappeared, she keeps "thinking about it" (79), a remark that irritates the producer, anxious to get on with the pressing business of selecting potential guests for upcoming shows.

Yet by scene's end they seem to have switched roles because the producer asks Kirsten if he can continue telling her what he saw the previous night. But Kirsten has had enough for one session. "No, that's it" (82), the host says. Then in the next scene, a boy, the occupant of the second corner, is interviewed as a potential guest for the show. His appeal is that he claims to have had a vision that appeared to him as a glowing light in the sky.

Under Jesurun's direction, three performers played the six interlocutors, each one doubling. His pairings are initially significant because they reveal how the playwright envisioned the interaction: producer and Mack, the boy who claims to have seen the vision; host Kirsten and lawyer Pegeen; and Doc and hysteric Cortez. The play's first scene opens with Kirsten's telling the producer about the vision she saw the previous night and ends with the producer's not being allowed to tell what he saw. The second scene opens with the questioning of the producer's other half, Mack, by two live actors, the host and a doctor, and two talking heads, the producer and Kirsten's other half, lawyer Pegeen. Mack claims to have seen a glowing light that, as the interview proceeds, becomes feminine; the boy experiences the light as feminine. The interview for a guest slot has become an inquiry into a matter that no longer can be repressed because in answer to a question, Mack says to the producer, "We've gone through this before" (84). The statement may mean that there was a passage of time between the first and second scenes during which interviews took place, but it also suggests that the producer and his other half, the boy, have been going through an interaction for some time in private that under mounting pressure has become public.

The play's pattern is that pressure on one part of the mind activates another part, initiating the whizzing around and the switching of identities. Each of the early scenes adds a new revelation and intensity. In the third scene, Mack, live, admits to the doctor's image on the monitor that the townspeople believe that the water at the site of the lady's visitations can miraculously cure anyone who drinks it. Calling himself "a lawyer and a priest" (93), the doctor's other half, hysteric Cortez, makes his first appearance in the next scene to try to prevent the studio from putting the boy on television.

Gender switches too in the whizzing around. I have been referring to the producer as masculine because when Jesurun directed the play, he chose two actors and one actress for the six roles, the two males to double as producer-Mack and Doc-Cortez. Yet the Spin Theater production of *White Water*, a production I will discuss below, cast a live performer in each of the six roles, balancing three males—Mack, Doc, and Cortez—with three females—Kirsten, Pegeen, and the producer. And even within Jesurun's text, gender is not fixed. In one scene Mack addresses the doctor as both "sir" and "ma'am" (91).

Nothing is fixed in this drama except the set. With his background, Jesurun conceives of it as an analogue to the mind, the locus in the self that receives and interprets channeled signals, sometimes deliberately and sometimes frenetically. In the set, the stage equivalent to Jenkin's Grail castle, Overmyer's Terra Incognita, and Foreman's ceremonial room, the action externalizes an internal conflict occasioned by an event to which the mind must respond. Whether the glowing light is real or imagined, fact or fantasy, is for the whole "someone" to determine, but since the mind is fragmented, one has to integrate the opposing processes within oneself, each of which responds in the manner unique to itself: through intuition or inference, for example, or with belief or skepticism. Because the conflict is externalized as theatre, it is presented as an inquiry with actors impersonating the processes, or selves within the self, in a quest for a reconciliation of the contradictions and ambiguities. Of course, the actors portray characters only some of the time. The other times they are images.

Long before writing *White Water*, Jesurun was fascinated by the possibilities television offers for interaction between live actors and video images. That fascination is evident in a layout that puts in each corner of the rectangular performance space a nineteen-inch television monitor on a pedestal three and a half feet high, which is approximately the height of a seated person. On one or more of the screens appears the image of the talking head with whom the live actor interfaces. By having three actors play six roles, Jesurun splits each into a divided self so that any couple or all six can be onstage at any time and without sacrificing the two qualities that must be present. The relationship between actor and image must be both natural and strange. It is natural that in the opening scene a talk-show host seated in a studio would conference with her producer via an in-house communication system. It is also strange for a live actor to engage in conversation with a talking head.

The two qualities are necessary for the action of an external drama that retains the contradictions and ambiguities of an internal drama. Although live acting suggests the capability of controlling speech to fit a changing situation and prerecorded speech on a monitor suggests a voice from a remote location, none of the actors impersonates only the conscious or subconscious mind. Kirsten, for instance, is live in the opening scene but an image in the scene in which Cortez arrives in the studio. It is the contrast in the interaction between different modes of expression, which manifest different modes of thinking, that is both natural and strange. The actor can be talking to a self external to him/her or to another part of his/her fragmented self. Furthermore, on a video monitor a talking head can be either sex or sexless so that in dialogue a live actor is delivering a soliloquy that juxtaposes next to a soliloquy coming from what looks like Mack's vision: a disembodied face in ambient light. The juxtaposition both supports and casts doubt on the twelve-year-old boy's story. He may have been in the presence of a being from another plane of existence; on the other hand, he may have been talking to his television set.

In a drama of intensifying pressure on a fragmented being, the contradictions and ambiguities compound as each part increasingly asserts itself in the face of the others' increasing assertions. In answer to a question about his parents, Mack says that he knows that they died in a car crash; in a later scene he has them on a second honeymoon in Tibet. The light he saw becomes a woman, although without feminine characteristics other than voice and face and not seen by anyone else, although crowds gather at the site, which has become a spring, claiming to be cured by its water: from 25 or 30 persons to 725 during the inquiry and of such devastating diseases and accidents as "cancer, broken legs, AIDS, terminal spinal meningitis" (96). In scene 4, Cortez arrives in the television studio to dissuade the producer and host from scheduling Mack on an upcoming show for fear that his story will cause mass hysteria in the viewing public. Before long he is hysterical himself, the maddest of the six roles. Scientists cannot agree on a chemical analysis of the spring water. Medical reports are suspect. Kirsten and the producer are accused of sending a crew to film an actress at the site.

The principal ambiguity, however, is Mack. Is he lying or telling the truth, imagining or perceiving? Jesurun does not say that the boy's vision of a healing intervention in nature represents humanity's regressive yearning for wholeness, but he does put the vision in the eyes of a twelve-year-old who cannot see breasts on the woman who visits him. Is it because that part of the mind that he impersonates has overcome the obstacles strewn on the quest for reconciliation and become pure and childlike again? Is it because that part of the mind, still immature, has not yet had the experience to reconcile carnal and spiritual love? Or is it because the numinous lady is real, or the distortion of a retinal disease? The play supplies no answers.

In the summer of 1991, Spin Theater staged *White Water* in a production that dispensed with all but one video monitor and had six performers, one for each role. The immediate effect was to lose the sense of strangeness created by the interaction of live performers and screen images. To compensate for the loss, directors Paul Schiff Berman and Deborah Lewittes dressed the cast in fantastic costumes. For the opening scene the producer, an actress in a woman's suit, hose, and heels, entered the studio across from Kirsten in a man's outfit of pants, shirt, tie, and vest. In the interview, Mack wore jeans and T-shirt and Pegeen wore a man's black tuxedo without shirt and tie while Cortez's cassock was paired with the doctor's Victorian frockcoat. As the inquiry progressed, Cortez changed into a toreador's costume with ruffled sleeves, Pegeen into a diaphanous white dress, and Kirsten into a red floor-length gown with bare back. Perhaps the most startling costume change, although it is in the text, was Mack's donning a cassock, which Cortez claimed came from the sacristy of his church.

With a cast of six in changing costumes, the directors could stage scenes that are static as juxtaposed soliloquies. The six entered and exited on different levels of a tiered stage, assumed poses and danced, and set and unset a dining room table. Acted scenes, as opposed to spoken scenes, became manic, such as the scene in which Cortez first tries to trick Mack into admitting that the glowing ball containing a woman was a basketball bouncing on the horizon and then tries to get him to admit that his vision is conditioned by his having seen the film *The Wizard of Oz*. Equally manic is the scene in which Pegeen and Mack relate to Cortez the first known cure at the spring, that of a dog hit by a car, buried, exhumed a week later, brought to the water, and stuck head down in the mud, who within a half hour was up and "running around for joy" (119).

The production also repeated swirling dance scenes and a deliberate dining room scene in which four of the cast took places at a table set for a meal, raised full glasses, and then froze, their eyes succumbing to uncertainty as their lips, caught in silly grins, silently debated, Is this miraculously healing water or mud? If they could drink, they could resolve the debate one way or the other. But they could only repeat the attempt, caught between the disposition to believe and doubt.

The scene, which images the mind's fragmentation, would have been repeated forever had the play not ended the only way it could, not in resolution but in retraction. For Mack the tension generated by the unrelenting inquiry becomes so severe that he ends his testimony by denying that he ever saw the lady. Yet paradoxically his denial is an affirmation. "The whole thing is a question mark," Jesurun writes in the autobiographical preface. "Questions are always more interesting than answers—nobody believes the answers anyway" (76–77).

The boy's denial is a convergence, a variation on the title of another Jesurun play, *Everything That Rises Must Converge.* In the text the only lights in the concluding scene are those of the three monitor images of Mack, Kirsten, and Cortez, each telling what he/she sees. The lights are reduced to two when Cortez's image goes out and then to one when Kirsten asks who is left in the room. Mack's answer, "Me" (142), accompanies the darkening of her talking head, leaving his the only face bathed in light. The play closes with his affirmation in a still point of light before that too goes out.

Is Mack's denial an admission of an earlier fabrication or a fabrication to neutralize the skeptical reaction to an earlier truth? The play does not resolve for the spectator what he saw, but the Spin Theater production gave him a vision to set his thinking processes whizzing around. Three spotlights held three live faces behind the scrim separating the stage and audience. After Cortez and Kirsten stepped back into darkness, the sole spotlight held Mack's disembodied face speaking, "Me," in a ball of light. The spectator saw what the boy had said he saw before his denial.

"In the end *White Water* focuses back on the audience . . ." (77), begins a sentence in the preface's concluding section. But there is light to guide the audience, for Mack's closing affirmation of himself, the twelve-year-old in every person, is an affirmation of the quest for the light. The image that stays after the lights go down is the image repeated throughout the production: the boy climbing ever so slowly, his body extended, a long flight of stairs leading to a light glowing in the upstage distance.

The final work in this chapter, *White Water,* confirms discoveries that this study made earlier and prepares the way for the final chapters. Jesurun does not resolve the questions the play raises because to resolve them is to choose one set of answers over another—to choose naturalistic humankind's determination over metaphysical humankind's hope, for instance. The sets express antinomies, which exist because human beings are naturalistic and metaphysical.

The divisions exist within the self, yet that does not mean that people cannot be whole. One's wholeness contains multiplicity, which expresses itself differently. One's unity contains contradictions and ambiguities. One is ambivalent as one responds to the different facets and impulses within oneself.

The resolution therefore lies within "me": the self which, containing multiplicity, can channel impulses into choices. In other words, whatever resolution occurs will come from within the questing self and not be imposed from without. It will not come from a numinous lady, an alien spacecraft, an unexplained sighting, or any authority.

The boy never reaches the light in the play. To reach it is to end the quest. In terms of the theatrical self, ending the quest means settling on a permanently fixed, unitary standard, which is death. In theatre as in life, Apollonian form opposes Dionysian fluidity, which is life, the flux which generates creativity.

In chapter 7 we will examine the works of two theatre artists for the presence or absence of resolution. The first artist creates a personal, psychological self. The second creates a personal, psychological self that becomes a national self. In chapter 8 we will examine various works for healing integration, for reconciling divisions. If the personal and theatrical selves can be whole and contain multiplicity, can the national self?

7

Reconciling Selves

Toward the end of Craig Lucas's *Blue Window*, one of the characters, Tom, who has been struggling all day to discover the song pressing on the perimeter of his consciousness, finally seizes it. According to the stage directions, the music he plays is the *"same song"*[1] another character, his partner Emily, sang earlier. Since the action froze while she sang it and since no one subsequently alludes to it, the song manifests the unconscious; it is everyone's unspoken desire. Unspoken until play's end, that is. As Tom plays the music, the other characters who, like Tom and Emily, have been struggling all day to express themselves to their partners reveal the desire welling from each one's unconscious. *"The music becomes rhapsodic"* (71) as the different voices entering contrapuntally from different locations interweave a shared feeling.

In the idiom of the song Emily sings, everyone wants the "'same thing'" (48–50). Everyone is searching for love. And although each one speaks the desire from his/her own perspective, together they express it in a common image. They want to float through a glass-window-television screen into the blue, hence the play's title.

Watching television, Emily gives a whimsical expression to the desire. "I wish everybody had a little window," she muses as Tom struggles to discover the song. "Right in front like a TV screen? . . . Like just a little window where you could see in and see what they were feeling and thinking about" (68). At first simply satisfying curiosity about another person, the image then affords entry into another, enabling the lover to know the partner better. Once able to know the other, he wants to experience the beloved so totally that he loses the sense of himself. He wants to enter—float in—the unconscious, from which loss of old self he will be reborn in a new, loving, self. As Alice says to her lesbian partner, Boo, as they talk of their trip to Italy reviving their love, "Come la nascita d'una bambina," which she translates, "Like a baby being born" (69).

But loving with that intensity—surrendering the self to another—involves risks that are not stated categorically in *Blue Window* but presented metaphorically in verbal images. Scene 2 is a party given by Libby for six guests, some of whom meet one another for the first time. At one point, Norbert, who teaches skydiving, explains that although it is difficult for anyone to jump through the blue window framed by the plane's door opened to the sky, he is having more than the normal amount of difficulty getting Libby to jump. After the party is over and five of the six guests have left, Libby explains to Norbert, who has stayed behind, why she resists being touched or held. Seven years earlier she was married. One day her husband asked her to leave the window where they were standing looking into the blue sky and come onto the terrace of their new apartment. As she leaned back looking up while he kissed her, the railing, unattached, gave way and they fell seven stories, he to his death and she to broken bones, months in traction, and a fear of human involvement.

Yet she knows that to return to life, she must jump into the blue, which is why she takes skydiving lessons, trying to overcome her fear. Perhaps she will. That she gives a party and then tells the numbing experience to Norbert is a sign that she is improving, for the image of the blue window ultimately is a portal to the imagination, the guide to the realm of "basic fears and basic inner mechanisms" (50) that all humans share. Through the imagination we enter into other people's lives; we empathize with them.

"'I think authors should be careful,'" Lucas said in a 1990 interview, "'not to tell what their work is about. Art is a process that involves the unconscious and the imagination. Audiences should be allowed to see for themselves.'"[2] *Blue Window*, however, is more heard than seen, even with the dramatization of voices in different locations blending at the end. The playwright also tries to make the play more visual by designing a set with a "*large, transparent canvas, framed like a window*" (7) upstage, tilted toward the audience so that the spectator looks through a window to enter imaginatively into the characters' lives. Nevertheless Libby's experience of the risks that love incurs remains a narrated story, a verbal rather than a visual experience.

Reckless is more visual than *Blue Window*, although its flaw is that it is too verbal. The night I saw the play, I sat next to two couples who, following the curtain call, remarked to one another how uplifting it was to see a show in which the playwright let his characters realize their full potential. Since aisle clearing took some time, because the audience had winter-weather garb to put on, I listened as they congratulated the heroine for overcoming her husband's taking out a contract on her life to become a doctor. They understood that scenes in the play are fantasy, but they were trying to make all the scenes fit, particularly the opening and closing ones.

Reckless opens with a woman, Rachel, in her nightgown standing at the window in the bedroom while her husband, Tom, in pajamas, stares at the screen of their television set. It is Christmas Eve, and she is euphoric, happy with her marriage and two boys and eagerly awaiting the opening of presents. But as she talks excitedly, two statements should alert the listener that the scene may not be what it appears to be. Noting the deepening snowfall, Rachel likens it to a good monster who carries people "away into a dream."[3] The other statement is that of a television announcer with a news item that an Albanian woman fled to Yugoslavia to give birth to a two-headed son. Following the announcement, Tom tells his wife that he has taken out a contract on her life. He regrets the act but cannot stop the professional killer, who is already in the house. Her only chance for survival is to flee while she can. She climbs through the window into the night.

The image connects with the controlling metaphor of Lucas's plays and extends it. Rachel is a Libby who by jumping through the window enters the portal of the imagination for her night journey. The problem is her verbalization of the reason for the journey.

In the contemporary American theatre, Jesurun and Foreman have created works that take the audience into an interior reality so shaped by a logic consistent within itself that the audience has no way of verifying what is happening on the exterior. Other playwrights such as Howe and Overmyer in *On the Verge* reconcile interior and exterior realities.

Lucas, however, has difficulty juxtaposing and meshing the two realms. Rachel's explanation should be a manifestation of her psychological state. It should be clear to the audience that the scene is within her dream, or journey, and not external to it.[4] The published text has an epigraph that was not in the playbill, but had it been, I do not know that it would have helped the theatregoer unfamiliar with the blue-window image. In the stanza quoted from a W. H. Auden poem, "Leap Before You Look," the speaker tells his bed partner to "leap" because their "dream of safety has to disappear" (6). To be vital, love must be tested and lovers must take risks. So must people in therapy.

Yet Rachel's passing reference to the dream state and an odd television announcement are not weighty enough to convey the dream state, with the result that the scene's mode of presentation is realistic. And once the opening scene establishes a realistic reason for Rachel's leap, a reason external to the leap, the play is stuck with it.

The flaw is not fatal. *Reckless* recovers and plays well so long as an oneiric logic drives it. Running away from an unfulfilled life, Rachel begins anew with a man and a woman also running away from their old selves. Dramatized in scene after scene, the dream, or night journey, represents a fulfillment. In the new family, the other woman, Pooty, is mother and sister. The man, Lloyd, is son, father, and husband because although he is married to Pooty, she is a paraplegic and therefore not a rival. When they need money, the three go on a television talk show—dressed as the solar system with Lloyd as the Sun, Pooty as Mother Earth, and Rachel as Venus—and win one hundred thousand dollars.

Where the play goes wrong again is in overdoing revelations. Scene 9 introduces the heroine in the office of a doctor to whom she relates what happened in the play's opening scene on Christmas Eve, following which the therapist asks her, "When did you have this dream?" (24). Apparently Rachel is a therapy patient encouraged to talk about herself by imagining a situation that will manifest whatever the repressed condition is that brought her to the office in the first place. She does not have to be a woman who abandoned her family but can be a woman abandoned by her family, through death perhaps. As another doctor says later, referring to patients, "Life's been reckless with these people" (50).

From here on, both the scenes in the dream, or imagined situation, and those in the doctors' offices take on a frenzied pace. Those close to Rachel in the dream die: husband Tom, Pooty, and Lloyd. The professional killer in the ski mask, who turns out to be one of her two sons, makes an attempt on her life but misses and kills someone else. Interspersed with these scenes are scenes in which she runs from office to office and doctor to doctor, played by the same actress in the same office. Since in each scene Rachel releases more of her repressed past, the dream logic penetrates scenes, supposedly realistic, intended to establish a context for the dream.

Instead of interpenetration leading to synthesis and clarity, the revelations strew the stage with cul-de-sacs and red herrings. One scene, for instance, appears to establish the death of Rachel's mother by a school bus. In a later scene another doctor tries to get the patient to believe that she can overcome adversity and become whatever she aspires to be. She, the doctor, offers herself as an example. She used to drive a school bus!

Despite the excessive verbalization, two scenes not yet discussed stand out. In scene 23 the doctor tries to get Rachel to repeat after her a declaration of her worth as a person. Although the patient is able to repeat the initial words, that she deserves to be loved, she cannot continue, overwhelmed by the weight of past experience, including the death of her mother under a school bus and the taking out of a contract on her life by the man she loved.

There is a pattern to *Reckless* even if all the strands are not interwoven. Like Libby in *Blue Window*, Rachel has retreated from life, but unlike the former, who finally tells her repressed story to a friend, the latter jumps through the window to act out her repressed story. Imagination has become an instrument of therapy, enabling the patient to create a situation in which she frees herself from the shackles of her old self. In acting out her pain, she discovers a cure.

Scene 27, the penultimate scene, ends with the doctor telling the patient to imagine "someone who makes people feel good about themselves and does all the things you ever wanted to do and has all the things you ever wanted to have" (53). Scene 28 is within the imagined situation, but the patient is getting better because the dream is getting better. The scene returns to the opening scene, at the Christmas season with snow outside the window, but Rachel is not now a fugitive from life but a doctor helping a young man in therapy because years earlier his mother abandoned the family on Christmas Eve.

In control of the situation, Rachel shapes the contents of the dream to fit the new self she essays to be. Becoming the young man's surrogate mother, she is a person who not only deserves to be loved but is capable of loving. Therapy's risk, the leaping through the window of the imagination to liberate the unconscious, has been successful. Rachel creates a new self—within the dream, to be sure—but by creating within a dream that she controls, she is moving toward reentry into the world from which she retreated before therapy and into a new self. Having accepted the past, she is moving toward a new future.

As Rachel comes to know Lloyd, to assure him that she does not hold against him his walking out on his family, she takes the position that the "past is irrelevant. It's something you wake up from." Lloyd disagrees. "The past is something you wake up to," he counters. "It's the nightmare you wake up to every day" (26). Both positions echo Dedalus's definition of history in Joyce's *Ulysses*. "History, Stephen said, is a nightmare from which I am trying to awake."[5]

Lucas's characters are grounded in history, but their leap of faith into redemptive love frees them from the nightmare of personal history. The song that closes *Blue Window* brings to the surface the characters' desire, which they seize when they blend each one's individual expression of it. Libby has not leaped yet, but by taking skydiving lessons, she is moving toward resolving her repressed past and her hope for a new future, which she expresses by adding her voice to the song.

Reckless moves closer to resolution. By imagining herself a surrogate mother in a therapy session, Rachel is becoming the woman she wants to be but up to now has felt herself so unworthy of being that in her night journey she is a fugitive from a husband and son who want to kill her. She is not simply fantasizing. Essaying a new self that she can grow into, she is resolving her divided self; she is integrating her inner need with an outer reality with which she is familiar.

Prelude to a Kiss is Lucas's most daring work, recasting the material of *Blue Window* and *Reckless* into a new perspective. In the note to the text in which he describes the original production, the playwright stresses the "imaginary leap required to make sense of the story" and the set that "suggested that things were more than they might seem." In the set's green wall was a "large window."[6] The lyrics to the Duke Ellington-Irving Gordon-Irving Mills song that frame the action and the title also connect the plays. The lyrics' *"song in blue"* (1) recalls Emily's song in *Blue Window* in which everyone is searching for love; the title recalls the kiss that plunged Libby and her husband into the blue.

Prelude begins as most love stories begin, with the meeting of boy and girl. These two marry within a few scenes. At the wedding, Rita, the bride, allows an uninvited guest, the Old Man, to kiss her. In the moment that their lips touch, they switch souls, a transmigration that Peter, the bridegroom, becomes aware of on the honeymoon as he gradually realizes that his wife is not the woman she was before the marriage.

Rita is the kooky one, but the trick of the play is that Peter is the focus. He does not need professional therapy, but he is the Libby-Rachel character abandoned by life who is trapped in the past. Rita is open to experience. A graphic designer, she works as a bartender until a situation develops in graphic design. To her question, when they first meet, about his aspirations, he replies that he has none. His professional situation is a metaphor for his psychological state: He stores the past. He manages the division of a scientific publishing company that puts the company's articles on microfiche for anyone who wants to retrieve the information.

Reconciling Selves

Peter is not open to experience. Surprised that Rita invites him to her apartment on their second meeting, that she talks dirty and is curious about sexual fantasies, that she was so politically engaged during a period of her life that she joined the Socialist Party and designed leaflets and posters, he inhabits a pre-1960 era, before sexual and political revolutions. And he consistently confuses socialism and communism. She has to correct him whenever the subject comes up; she was a "Socialist," not a "Communist" (11, 21–22).

The explanation for being outside of life, he, like Libby in *Blue Window*, reveals in his story. Starting with the separation of his parents when he was four, he was shuffled from relative to relative, sometimes because a grandparent became too ill to care for him, until he was old enough to rebel and flee to Europe. Unlike Rachel in *Reckless*, he does not climb through the window. Spellbound by the encounter with Rita, whom he admits is the "*Unknown*" (17) for him, he stands outside the building trying "to figure out which window was hers and what her life might be like . . ." (4).

But trapped in the past, Peter is unable to make the imaginary leap that Lucas stresses in the playwright's note. When Rita invites him to meet her parents, the pressing question for him is whether she told them his story. "Did you tell them about my family and everything?" (23), he asks.

He offers a more revealing insight on the honeymoon. Suspecting that something is wrong because Rita does not act or speak the way she did while they were dating, he says to her:

Do you ever think how we're each a whole, separate being beside one another. Each with a heart pumping inside and a soul and all our memories. How I can never, no matter how close we ever become, share your past, be with you as a nine-year-old, as a baby. (44)

Retelling his story makes his past a recurring nightmare. Denying empathy, as the quoted passage does, denies the ability to share anyone else's past, further insulating him in his own, recurring, one. Denying the imagination that enables lovers to leap locks him into himself throughout act 1. Act 2 dramatizes his release in a leap the impetus for which was initiated by the leap of his wife and the guest when they kissed.

In an offbeat variation of the boy-meets-girl, boy-loses-girl, boy-finds-girl theme, Rita leaves Peter after he tells her that he is wise to the switch and wants to know where his wife is. Toward play's end Peter brings his wife and the guest together but cannot force the reverse transmigration. Forcing them to kiss does not bring the desired result. Rita's soul remains in the Old Man's body and his in her body. Only when the two, ignoring Peter, talk to each other do they realize the play's truth. All that one has to do to experience life is to "want it. *Bad enough*" (90). Understanding their motivation for the switch at the reception, they switch back without kissing.

Depressed following his wife's death, the Old Man wandered away from his daughter's home, where he lives with her and her husband, and into the reception, attracted to the celebration. Seeing the "shine" (89) in Rita's eyes, flush from the excitement of the ceremony and the champagne, he wondered what it would be like to start life anew and as a woman who would someday be a mother. "Freaked" (89) by the day's activities, Rita, seeing the Old Man's eyes flashing back at her, wondered what it would be like to have lived a full life. In the moment they kissed, each one's soul leaped through the other's eyes, the windows of the soul.

Lucas's craftsmanship, wobbly in *Reckless*, is firm in *Prelude*. The explanation, lacking in *Reckless*, makes clear the motivation of the two who leap. And they do not deliver the explanation in monologues but fill it in as they understand their motivation, and they understand because after failing to force the reverse switch, each not only reaches within to examine the soul animating the body it temporarily inhabits but expresses it to the other soul to build a harmonic dialogue. Their interaction, synthesizing in the insight that to live all one has to do is "want it," is a miniature version of the concluding scene of *Blue Window* in which all the voices blend contrapuntally.

Yet although that scene is the penultimate scene, the theatregoer is not confused prior to the revelation of motivation because in a play in which Rita and the Old Man mirror each other, Lucas's craftsmanship has Peter the audience's mirror. A stranger to life, he is outside the action as is the audience; he therefore establishes the context lacking in *Reckless*. Speaking directly to the house throughout the play, as the others do not, he invites spectators to focus on him. The craftsmanship, building steadily, becomes artistry. His changing perception as he quests for Rita is his leap out of an old self and his creation of a new self.

Following the scene in which the newlywed husband tells his wife that he is wise to the switch and wants to know where his real wife is, Peter goes into the bar where Rita worked when single, and there he sees the Old Man with a drink. And he recognizes his wife in the body of the wedding reception's uninvited guest. The recognition is his discovery of love not as words in a wedding ceremony but as an emotional reality. In a passage quoted above, he told his bride that he could never be with her as a nine-year-old. That was his age when the grandfather with whom he was sent to live following his parents' separation had to be put in a nursing home. After leaving the bar, he and his companion go to the apartment. The companion is Rita in the Old Man's body, and they proceed to live together because the Old Man in Rita's body has gone to live with her parents. But they are not sexually intimate as lovers are. The relationship is that of a young man attentive to the needs of an older man who should be in a nursing home.

The past that Peter said could not be shared returns, yet it does not haunt. This time he is not an abandoned child; this time he breaks the recurrence by leaping. Confessing his love to Rita, he kisses the transmigrated soul on the wrinkled body's mouth. No longer outside of life, he experiences change.

Since Rita wants her body back and since Peter wants her back in her body so that they can fulfill their love, together they take the risk that lovers must take. They arrange a meeting with the Old Man in Rita's body in the penultimate scene, which with the final scene fulfills the play's artistry. When Peter steps to the side because he cannot force the reverse transmigration, he ceases to be a guide. Spectators no longer need his perception with which to witness the reverse switch. Those whose imaginations have been awakened by the action have their own magic windows.

The reverse transmigration is a birth. Not only do the wife and the guest synthesize when each says that all that questers of life have to do is want to transmigrate "*bad enough*," they also synthesize when each expresses the expectation to be actualized: "So much life inside" (89). To experience that life, the lover surrenders himself to the other, floats in the womblike state of unself-consciousness.

The reverse transmigration takes place because each desires to resume his life before the switch, but not as it was in the prison of the self. The return of the soul to the body is the bringing of life from the unconscious state to consciousness. The lover reenters himself, his consciousness, bringing with him his experience of the beloved; life that was other and separate is now shared because it has been intimately experienced. The reentry is a birth. As Rita says as her soul reenters her body, "Like a baby" (90).

The ultimate scene presents the play's couple directly to the eyes in the audience that see through magic windows. Together husband and wife give birth to the life each discovered in questing for the other. Discovering love, they discover that life is "never to be squandered . . ." or, we might add, abandoned. It is the "miracle of another human being" (92). The play ends with each, having taken the risk—the leap—that lovers must take, insisting that the other is the miracle, for love is the creation of a new, sharing, self.

Although the lover's return to the beloved is a reconciliation, in the theatre as in life, it is not necessarily a resolution of the differences that estranged the couple from each other or the person from life. In Lucas's theatre, reconciliation and resolution are not synonymous. Libby is reconciling with her past but has not yet resolved her problem. Rachel is further along in the recovery in that she has leaped through the window of the imagination, from which prism she can see her past self with which she is reconciling and the future self she resolves to be but is not yet. Only Peter has both experiences, but at first they are distinct.

The birth of the imagination in the bar scene saves him from disconnection from life, for it enables him to see himself as he would like to be, a rescuer of the abandoned: his wife and the Old Man, who are disconnected from their lives. Imagination connects him. He reconciles with his past by caring for the wizened man he could not care for when he was a boy. Following that reconciliation he reconciles with his wife, a commitment that is the play's resolution. He resolves to be a whole self but not solidified in himself, a condition that would trap him as he was. No longer abandoned, Peter shares life with Rita, who is no longer unknown but a real, living person for him.

Thus the design of Lucas's theatre is division, or opposition, to reconciliation to resolution. Imagination is the healing faculty in that it stimulates transmigration, a form of reversing roles or switching identities. It is a form of playacting in which the character undergoing therapy is put in touch with his/her repressed self. Essaying a new self, one can reconcile one's divided psyche and resolve to be the self capable of loving and worthy of being loved. By reconcile is meant bringing into agreement or harmony the division within the self. By resolve is meant not only ending the disagreement but also taking the reconciliation into life. The wholeness of the reconciliation does not expel the multiplicity within the character. Since human nature does not change, the multiplicity does not change. The change is in the character's resolve to move his/her integrated self forward.

The design of Sam Shepard's theatre follows a comparable pattern to reconciliation, but the similarity stops at that stage. And some of his plays do not reach even a momentary reconciliation.

Two would-be rock stars compete in *The Tooth of Crime* to be "numero uno,"[7] but although one wins, each is incomplete. Renegade Crow's forte is "style" (230), which is the imagination divorced from a ground such as history. Having risen to be leading contender, Hoss, the more human of the two who in performance becomes an *"ancient delta blues singer"* (238), has "turf" (242), which is the ground divorced from the imagination. Merging style and turf, infusing the imagination into the ground, would create a new self, a wholeness. But the combatants cannot, even though the irony is that they need each other. Hoss cannot win without the renegade's style, and Crow's victory is hollow without the leading contender's turf. Crow offers to trade style for turf, but Hoss cannot unless he can develop his own image. Style alone would leave him hollow.

The self's division is frequently imaged as twins in Shepard's theatre. Masculine imagination is the lawless aggressor, but it cannot defeat its opponent in *The Tooth of Crime*. Hoss kills himself. Neither can feminine ground, or body, force a victory, even when it is combined with lawless aggression. Masculine imagination and feminine body must interact to reconnect "uno" self, and in this play they do not reconcile.[8]

In *Angel City*, imagination insulated from reality infects while reality unleavened by imagination pollutes. Imagination is insulated in a film studio surrounded by the reality of the city's encroaching contamination. Yet although the play is set in a Hollywood studio, it is the civilized world that is at stake. As one of the two principal antagonists explains, the world has "no focus, no structure."[9] The vision is apocalyptic, reflecting the breakup of the old order. As the other principal antagonist admits, he is drawn to Hollywood because films have the power of replacing the dreams of people who lived under the old order. "Replacing their books. Replacing their families. Replacing religion, politics, art, conversation. Replacing their minds" (69). Imagination and external reality are the twin sources of inspiration in Shepard's theatre. In this play each is primarily represented by one of the two antagonists.

Hired by the film studio because of his reputation as a creator of magic, Rabbit Brown would seem to be the play's artist. He is not, however, the artist he fancies himself to be. An outsider in the industry of moving images, he left the natural world of northern California for the artificial environment of the smog-free studio, to which he traveled by buckboard, stopping at all the missions along the way, and he does not know what he is doing. For all his talk and magical bundles that he drags behind him, by the end of act 1 he has created nothing but confusion. Experienced with reality, he is ineffectual confronting the unexplored territory of the imagination.

Since Wheeler is the executive who hired Rabbit to bail out his financially troubled studio, he would seem to be the play's hard-nosed businessman whose decisions are based solely on the marketplace. His studio produces films to satisfy the public's need to escape reality for a few hours, and he justifies this mission by citing his ability to read the public's mind. Using his skin as evidence of the damage done by environmental imbalance, he explains that the ever-expanding megalopolis outside the studio, symbolized by automotive and smokestack smog and bulldozers leveling the traditional landscape for more condominium and office space, threatens to eat everyone alive. People will pay to get relief from the escalating danger, he argues, and a salable relief is a film that images the disaster that daily threatens to devour the audience. Yet he has sealed off the studio so that his "industry of imagination" (99) can flourish, and he has hired a man reputed to be skilled in magic, and not an accountant, to save a film, behind in its shooting schedule, in which the studio has invested heavily.

Rabbit's assignment is to invent a new conception of character able to vanquish the disaster. Only a new conception can provide a catharsis, given the disaster's terrifying proportions.

Even though he tries collaborating with other studio employees, lacking imagination Rabbit cannot invent a new conception. His conception is the conventional one that the experimental theatre has been rebelling against throughout the twentieth century. For Rabbit, the ultimate disaster is death because his characterization is naturalistic humankind whose identity is grounded in external reality. Time- and place-bound individuals more akin to persons than to images, they are conditioned by socioeconomic, political, psychological, and biological forces. Not immediately recognizable because mutable—living until dying—they become so in the setting, which accounts for their being who they are.

Neither can Wheeler by himself invent a new conception, but, the aggressive twin, he initiates the creative interaction by stalking Rabbit after the latter, admitting his lack of progress, protests that he was denied access to the film in which the new conception is supposed to appear. "LOOK INSIDE OF ME!" the studio founder, fanged with suppurating sores, obliges the reputed magician. "We're going down, Brown! We're coming face to face with something deadly" (103). The something "deadly" is Wheeler's imagination as revealed in his film, rushes of which he will allow the other man to see. He has a million movies churning in his blood, but they cannot get out. Trapped in the darkness within him, the images have poisoned his blood, and they cannot get out because in his studio he has sealed off external reality.

When Wheeler admits that his festering imagination and not environmental pollution is causing his skin to ulcerate, he is transformed from a snarling demon into a solicitous host, seating Rabbit in a swivel chair and encouraging him to relax and watch the images he summons from the dark. Played by two assistants, one male and one female, they enter from opposite sides of the platform, and while Wheeler shines a flashlight on them and narrates, they enact the drama. They are so antagonistic that they would "sooner die than attempt to coexist" (105). Their combat with sticks symbolizing swords covers many days until the female catches the male off guard and plunges her weapon into him. But the male does not fall. He inches himself along the stick until he reaches her, at which time they embrace and separate. Not dying and therefore not living in a naturalistic world, they await the next summoning.

The players incarnate archetypes, not characters. For Wheeler the ultimate disaster is life because his conception is metaphysical humankind whose identity is grounded in internal reality. Archetypes are primordial images transmitted in the unconscious, the storehouse of the human being's psychic heritage. Though ancient, the elemental images are accessible; unconditioned forces, they press against the surface of consciousness. They also are immediately recognizable when released because they are immutable, actualizing in ritual, not setting, the race's eternally recurring myths.

The ritual over, Wheeler asks Rabbit his opinion. "Terrible," he replies. "Corniest stuff I ever saw." The film lacks a disaster, he explains, echoing Wheeler's position when the latter first outlined the job description, implying that he is the studio executive. When he adds, "I thought you understood that" (108), he implies that Wheeler is the hired expert. They seem to have switched identities, each becoming the other.

All the while that each of the two antagonists is presenting his conception of character, neither of which can vanquish disaster, the play itself is creating a new conception. In the note to the actors prefacing *Angel City*, Shepard distinguishes between two conceptions of character:

> The term "character" could be thought of in a different way when working on this play. Instead of the idea of a "whole character" with logical motives behind his behavior which the actor submerges himself into, he should consider instead a fractured whole with bits and pieces of character flying off the central theme. (61–62)

In the traditional conception, a character with or without conflicting motives is a whole unto himself/herself. In the new conception, neither of the two antagonists is whole but together they are. The twin sources of inspiration for the creative process, imagination and ground, or objective reality, are polarized in Wheeler and Rabbit, who are two halves of a divided self.

Though his plays are not naturalistic in that characters make imaginative leaps into one another, Lucas's conception of humankind is naturalistic. Past events explain the behavior of Libby, Rachel, and Peter. Shepard's conception of humankind is not exclusively naturalistic.

From the beginning of his career as a playwright in the 1960s, the drama in a Shepard play arises from existence that is fractured into opposing antinomies: art and commerce, for instance, or private and public selves. Evolving through the years and plays, by the time of *Angel City* in 1976, the antinomies have become the twin halves of a person's dual nature, here split into two characters. Grounded in a real world, naturalistic humankind has a history. At the same time, metaphysical humankind has an imagination capable of transcending history.

Naturalistic humankind has a past and is interactive. The audience knows Hoss's and Rabbit's pasts revealed through dialogue and activities with advisors and co-workers. But by itself, not leavened by the imagination, humankind's naturalistic nature bogs down. Hoss is afraid to take risks; Rabbit is unable to invent. They become so dependent upon group support that they cannot function apart from society.

Metaphysical humankind has no past and is independent. The audience knows nothing about Crow, who is a renegade, or Wheeler, who seals off his studio and himself in his office. He releases archetypes, but their struggle is eternal myth, not temporal history. Left to itself, humankind's metaphysical nature becomes exemplary.

The tendency to be exemplary always is present in a culture that rewards "numero uno," the prize for which Hoss and Crow, the two would-be rock stars, compete in *The Tooth of Crime*. (This is the prize for which Charlie acknowledges the ringside audience's applause in the closing image of Nelson's *Conjuring an Event*.) Yet an aggrandizing culture alone cannot be blamed for Crow's behavior. Shepard locates the imagination in the metaphysical nature. Since the imagination has the power to fly above nature by imagining the supernatural and since it is the aggressive principle, when unharnessed from reality, it can appropriate. Crow appropriates Hoss's image. Unharnessed, it can become Icarian; soaring too far above the ground, it can turn its energy inward, consuming itself. By releasing his archetypes, Wheeler says in effect that he is the movie. He is the subject of the object he produces.

In the creative process, interaction brings the poles of the new conception of characterization together. Wheeler narrates the myth for Rabbit, who participates by consenting to watch the ritual and then evaluate it. The two collaborate. Imaginative Wheeler, who sealed the studio from the outside world, shares his project with an outsider, and realist Rabbit, who does not know how to use the stolen magic bundles that he drags behind him, enters the filmmaker's imagination. For the length of the presentation, the twins are reconciled.

With the rushes over, Rabbit turns the swivel chair to face the audience. He is fanged with suppurating sores. The two have switched roles. Rabbit is the studio executive while Wheeler is the expert fired for failing to produce.

Interaction momentarily reconnects the divided halves so that they reverse roles, but the reversal ends the similarity between the reconciliation stages in Lucas's and Shepard's theatres. Transmigration puts Lucas's divided self in touch with the repressed self, enabling the patient to move toward resolution and a new self. When Rita and the Old Man in *Prelude to a Kiss* reverse the transmigration, they bring back the experience of the other, assimilating to become whole. Almost immediately after reconciling, Shepard's divided self sunders into antagonists, though the interaction continues in their reversed roles.

The reconciliation in *Angel City* does not create a new self; it does not resolve the division into wholeness. And if neither twin assimilates any of the experience with the other, the repeated interaction is not growth, however small, toward integration but an eternal myth or the nightmare of history. Whether the continued interaction moves toward resolution is ambiguous.

After switching, Wheeler yells at Rabbit, "I'M NOT YOU, GODDAMMIT!

I'M ME!" (109). The protest suggests not knowledge of the other or assimilation of the experience but separation and theft of another's identity.

Yet Wheeler's opening, with Rabbit's approval, the Indian medicine bundle known as "'Looks-Within' place" to allow its green liquid to ooze out suggests the antagonists have learned that for the creative process to take place, imagination must infuse reality. The metaphysical nature must be incarnated in the naturalistic nature so that the whole man has irrational as well as logical motives, and archetypes must be delivered from the unconscious into the consciousness of characters to be formed into original, individual art actualized in contemporary images.

Ambiguous though the play's ending is, the twins' continued interaction creates in the studio images of contemporary battling warriors for an audience of their assistants who watch them *as though in the movies*" (111). That suggests that the process is more important than the resolution, for it is the process that creates images that effect a transformation in the participants of the process, including imaginatively engaged spectators.

Since the creative process of opposition to reconciliation through interaction continues to be the design of Shepard's theatre, we have to examine the possibility that gradually reconciliation moves to resolution and a new self. From the late 1970s through the mid-1980s, the playwright wrote five full-length plays that approach the disaster, the breakup of the old world that divides the self in the new world, through the divided American family. We will not examine all five, nor will we examine in equal degree the ones we do.

Curse of the Starving Class opens with the son, Wesley, picking up after the father, Weston, who in a rage shattered the door the night before because the mother, Ella, had made good her threat to lock him out the next time he got drunk. In the image of a physically shattered house is a spiritually shattered home. Not only do the father and mother not creatively interact, they do not communicate at all until the third of the play's three acts. They are not even together in the house until the end of act 2. He left when she called the police, not to return until the end of act 1 and then to pass into unconsciousness on the kitchen table in the next act. In the meantime she has left with a lawyer friend, not to return until the end of act 2.

Their physical absence withdraws the two principles that together unite a family. Weston has borrowed money to buy land, but by itself, divorced from his wife's nurturing, his masculine imagination bought arid land. Fed up with his dereliction, Ella is making arrangements through her lawyer friend, Taylor, to sell the property on which they live and move to Europe, but by itself, divorced from her husband's imagination, her feminine ground cannot fly. While she is negotiating with Taylor, in a drunken stupor Weston sells the property.

The parents' self-absorption splits the family. The son and daughter insist that they will not go to Europe with the mother should she sell the property. Wesley wants to stay and repair it while sister Emma resolves to leave on her own. When she attempts to, after stealing money and car keys from her mother's purse, she is killed in the car wired to explode by hoodlums come to the house to frighten Weston into paying his debts. Knowing that there is a contract out on him, he flees to Mexico.

Since the family is a metaphor for America in these five domestic plays, its disintegration is America's disintegration. Taylor speaks for the new order that has replaced the old order when he defends his role in encouraging Ella to sell the property:

> You may not realize it, but there's corporations behind me! Executive management! People of influence. People with ambition who realize the importance of investing in the future. . . . Everything's going forward! Everything's going ahead without you! The wheels are in motion. There's nothing you can do to turn it back. The only thing you can do is cooperate. To play ball. To become part of us. To invest in the future of this great land.[10]

It does not take Wesley long to figure out that the lawyer is the one who sold the worthless land to Weston. The son, who opposes the sale of the property, sees in him a scout for an invasion of zombies; for the bulldozing of the land, extended beyond Los Angeles in *Angel City* to national convulsion, disconnects man from life's landscape so that he becomes the walking dead. Alienation is a persistent theme in Shepard's nondramatic statements as well as in his plays.[11] And since America is a metaphor for the new world, its disconnection from the old world is the modern world's disconnection, its spinning off into the hurlyburly.

Weston, who experiences a rebirth in act 3, puts the blame for the alienation on an American Dream that fails to deliver its promise. To borrow against the future potential supposedly awaiting him, the dreamer has to incur debt. Yet when payment inevitably comes due and he cannot meet his obligation, he is driven deeper into debt. Weston, who borrowed money to buy worthless land, must sell the property on which the family lives. The sale, however, does not free him from the wrath of those to whom he is indebted. He becomes a fugitive, and Ella becomes a tenant in the house she once owned.

The American Dream championed by Taylor and criticized by Weston cannot deliver. It promises upward mobility through investment in the future, the spiritual ascent validated by acquisition of material possessions. Indeed, the very purchase of the possessions, since done on credit, supposedly validates the new, expanding, spirit in a new, expanding, self. But the proposition that the more matter one has the larger the spirit one has with its corollary, the less matter the smaller the spirit, is a perversion.

The play itself reveals the perversion. The four family members argue back and forth about whether or not they are in the starving class. They are but not because they are physically hungry. They crave a fulfillment the symbols of which they have been taught are material. Yet no matter how often one of them opens the refrigerator or how long he stares into the box, he invariably slams it shut in disgust because, empty or full, it fails to validate the new self with its expanding spirit. Their experience of the new self is just the opposite of the promise. Not even the frantic stuffing of the face with the symbols can satisfy the spiritual deprivation they suffer.

In the Dream of wholeness, one realizes his/her potential by using his/her imagination to discover real roles that he/she can grow into a new self. The divided dreamer betrays his/her human potential. Ella spends her time with Taylor, who is using her to get the property and who sneaks away when Wesley accuses him of selling worthless land to his father. Emma takes the perversion that separates spirit and matter, image and self, to its inevitable appropriation. Instead of transforming her reality, she plans to steal it. Like Icarus, she is melted in a ball of flames.

Weston is a dreamer who momentarily awakens from the perversion. Act 3 opens on him in the kitchen, no longer drunk and disheveled as he was when he came home but shaved and wearing clean clothes. The exterior transformation manifests the interior discovery made that morning when he walked around the property. At first he felt separate from the person touring, but as he began to merge with himself in the person of the owner, he resolved to stay home and repair the place that he had been ignoring for years. Returning to the house, he bathed and shaved, fixed breakfast, and washed a pile of dirty laundry.

By assuming responsibility for the property to which he connects himself, he assumes responsibility for himself. As he explains to Wesley, he spent years looking for fulfillment "out there somewhere" when "all the time it was right inside this house" (194). Removing the booze-soaked clothes in preparation for the bath was like peeling off a "stranger." Rejecting the false self of absentee landlord, he turns inward to be "reborn" (185).

He is reconciled to himself and his family. "And I felt like I knew every single one of you," he tells Wesley. He does not want to escape from them anymore because being "connected" (186) to them makes him feel good. To his son he recommends a bath. To his wife, who comes into the kitchen while he is cooking for Wesley, he recommends stretching out on the table as he did the previous day. "That table will deliver you" (189).

Though the original Dream delivers as the perverted Dream does not, it delivers wholeness. Since it does not foster the notion that one can create a new self unrelated to the past, it reunites Weston with his old self, which means that he must pay the obligations incurred by the old self. "Maybe you've changed, but you still owe them" (192), Wesley urges him to run while he can. Running, he leaves behind the Dream of wholeness for the perverted Dream because he runs away from nurturing reality. Divided between his allegiance to his family and his desire to stay alive, he allows his Icarian imagination to delude him into thinking that he can start a new life in Mexico. "Maybe" is his son's reaction. His daughter's is more emphatic. "He won't last a day down there" (194–95).

For one morning Weston reconciles his divided self by imagining the ground as a productive avocado farm. During that morning he says something that connects the five domestic plays. He realizes that the "family wasn't a social thing. It was an animal thing" connected by "blood" (186). *Curse of the Starving Class* is Shepard's most naturalistic play connecting the family members to one another by blood and to the animal kingdom from which they evolved. Much of the play's dialogue has to do with the concepts of heredity and environment. Emma's menstruation is a curse in that it determines her woman's role for her. Later Ella extends the curse to all biological transmission, over which males and females have no control. Everyone, including Weston, agrees that he inherited his father's poison for remaining apart from life. Wesley urinates on his sister's chicken-anatomy charts with a penis that reminds Ella of her father's penis. Emma's first attempt to flee the family is thwarted by the horse that drags her through the mud. When the bath that Weston recommends that he take does not give him a feeling of rebirth, Wesley smears his body with the blood from a lamb he butchers and then, freezing, puts on his father's clothes. Back in the house he tells his sister of the transformation that the clothes effected. "It seemed like a part of him was growing on me. I could feel him taking over me" (196).

Yet Shepard's characters practice a self-deception, called a lie of the mind in a later play. The self-deception in *Curse of the Starving Class* is that the culture's perverted Dream causes the family's suffering. It does not cause it; it aggravates the dichotomy in human nature that causes the suffering. The divisive Dream claims so many willing victims because it appeals not to an integrated multiplicity within the individual but to multiplicity's division into competing antinomies.

In this play the primary competing antinomies are the twin parenting principles. Ideally the father principle initiates interaction by infusing the mother principle. She then is responsible for nurturing the interaction. When the principles interact, they produce wholeness in the individual, the family, and the society. When they sunder, as they do in the play, they disintegrate the individual, family, and society.

Weston's masculine imagination is irresponsible. Ella's feminine reality is interactive but with someone other than her husband. As critics note, the mother is not a force in Shepard's theatre.[12] Neither is the father except in the memories of those he abandoned. He flees to Mexico or the desert. The mother, left behind to acquire, maintains the home and family, usually ineffectively.

Weston does not follow through on his resolve to stay home and repair the damage done. He cannot because he is unable to maintain the reconciliation achieved during the walk around the property. He can go in any direction he chooses, but he cannot go forward as a whole person unless his multiplicity-his divisions-his antinomies are held in some kind of harmonious mix. Of Shepard's plays studied to this point, resolution does not occur because the characters can reconcile for no longer than the moment.

Normally such a vision of man's inability to maintain a reconciliation would be called tragic. Shepard's vision, however, is not thought of as tragic because as soon as the characters switch identities and separate, they begin again the movement toward reconciliation. To this point the playwright's theatre is a recursive quest for reconciliation.

With the parents separated, the burden of reconciling the family, and perhaps healing it in resolution, falls on the shoulders of the offspring. Wild and domesticated describe the two brothers reunited in *True West*. The wild one is the older one, Lee, who, like the father, lives on the desert. The domesticated one is the younger Austin, who though he has a wife and children in northern California is living temporarily in the mother's house in suburban Los Angeles, to which Lee has come and, when the play opens at night, is in the kitchen disrupting his brother's concentration. Whereas Lee gets his money through dogfighting and stealing appliances, Austin works in the perverted Dream on projects that he hopes to sell as film scripts. He is trying to complete one such project for an approaching meeting with a Hollywood producer, Saul.

Tucker Orbison's analysis of the brothers' relationship as a divided self, with Austin as conscious ego and Lee as hidden psychic forces, explains why the older one is present without comment from the play's opening. He appears because Austin's anxiety to create a salable project induces an inner tension to manifest itself.[13] As in *Curse of the Starving Class*, the perverted Dream, or acquisitive society, does not cause the division but aggravates it into imbalance and antagonism. Once released, Lee stalks, not only disrupting Austin's concentration and interfering in his meeting with Saul, but convincing the latter that he, Lee, has a more authentic project than his brother's.

Incidentally, it makes sense that Lee is older. He is the metaphysical twin from whose subsurface nature the naturalistic twin developed a surface reality.

Lee has a more authentic project, but it is not salable in the form in which he gives it to the producer. We are in the antagonism of *Angel City*. Austin's project is a researched, period-piece love story. It is lifeless. Lee's project is a spontaneous, elemental chase story. It is deathless because the archetypes that he releases from his unconscious and that enact the race's past go on forever. If repressed back into the repository of the race's heritage, they wait there until the next summoning.

The only way for either brother's project to be made into a film is for the two of them, like Rabbit and Wheeler, to collaborate: Lee to talk and Austin to compose. Act 1 ends with their reconciliation as Lee verbalizes the chase images and Austin types, but the perverted Dream separates them in act 2. Saul's proposal that the brothers work together does not foster reconciliation; it sunders. By dropping Austin's project for Lee's more authentic one and offering to employ the younger brother to write the script, Saul reduces his role in the process to a demeaning one. For equality the divisive Dream substitutes a master-slave relationship based on salability. Lee's scene-5 closing line, "We're partners now,"[14] is malicious. He has the upper hand, and he knows it. Masculine Lee does not abandon his twin but becomes exemplary, denying feminine Austin his reality: the ability to interact.

Austin refuses the deal, however, and his refusal causes a reversal of roles comparable to the antagonists' role-reversal in *Angel City*. This one, in *True West*, is psychologically more credible, though, because Lee must generate his own script. He cannot. Not disciplined enough to compose, in a rage he smashes the typewriter. Austin can steal toasters and get drunk and relate as authentic a tale about their father as Lee can, but he cannot achieve the self-sufficiency that is the hallmark of the father and brother who have fled civilization's detritus for the desert's purity. Dependent on interaction, he pleads with his brother to take him with him.

When Lee, who resists domestication on any landscape, breaks his agreement to take Austin to the desert in return for his writing the script, the younger brother turns on him, throttling him with the telephone cord while pinning him to the floor. Austin will release his older brother on condition that he allow him to leave. Lee feigns unconsciousness until he is released, at which time he leaps to his feet and blocks Austin's exit. The lights go down on one of Shepard's most menacing images: the brothers squared off, each watchful of the other's next move.

Though the brothers do not write a script, they create one, as Wheeler and Rabbit do, in their persons. *True West* is the script that incarnates elemental archetypes in realistic characters in the cycle that is the structural design of Shepard's mature plays: opposition to reconciliation to separation. The antagonists' dialectical interaction is the past come to life in the contemporary West in the persons of stalking twins who are battling warriors.

Neither brother can assimilate the other to create an integrated self, but that fact does not prevent their creating art that pulses in ambiguity. The father has fled to the desert. The mother, who returns to her home toward play's end, flees rather than contend with her battling sons. The brothers continue the antagonism, but it is a division and an ambiguity in which they face each other under one roof.

Though *True West* has no resolution, the ending is an advance over the beginning so that the play is neither an eternal myth nor the nightmare of history. The offspring burdened with the responsibility of healing the division between the parenting principles inherit the same division. But they learn; they assimilate, however minute, contents of the antagonism. What they assimilate is the knowledge that the disaster that divided the psyche into twins can be used to effect a reconnection. Masculine imagination can initiate interaction, and feminine nature can nurture the interaction to reconciliation, and not only within the family but within the members of the family because a family is the individual magnified. In Shepard's new conception, every character contains both metaphysical and naturalistic natures, which interact as he/she interacts with other characters.

Evolving from play to play, antinomies accumulate meaning. In *Fool for Love*, the twin offspring of the parenting principles are the masculine and feminine principles-natures-selves within the divided human being. The exemplary self, which is metaphysical and imaginative, is masculine. The interactive self, which is naturalistic and grounded in objective reality such as history and society, is feminine.

Loner Eddie has come stalking his half sister May, who waits for him as she always does, this time in a motel on the edge of the Mojave Desert. Relentlessly they bring the past to life in the present, fulfilling the desire for and pursuit of wholeness as they collaborate to create love in their narratives and their persons. The reunion site is itself significant. Neither desert nor community, it is a reconciliation point midway between each antagonist's domain.

Their natures and not the culture cause the antagonism, although different standards in sexual behavior for the genders, for example, can aggravate the division. Their natures also cause the desire and pursuit. Eddie wants to bed May and then abandon her for the desert or another woman until the next pressing need for her. May wants to be bedded but not used. She wants to domesticate her half brother, a desire that he feels threatens his selfhood, just as she feels in his desire a threat to her resolve not to see him again until he changes his ways.

Two other characters are onstage. The Old Man is their father by different women. "It was the same love," he admits. "Just got split in two, that's all."[15] Existing in the minds of Eddie and May, he exists only in imagination, which is past and future, where he is sustained by the dream of love, the dream of wholeness. When he learns from his offspring that Eddie's mother committed suicide after he left her, he insists that he and May's mother "were completely whole" (55).

The other character is May's date, Martin. At the other extreme from the

Old Man, he exists only in reality, which is present. Lacking passion—he arrives to take social May to the movies because that is what a man is supposed to do—he is outside the experience of love.

Each of the three family members relates the family's story from his/her perspective. First the father, who roamed the West planting his seed in more than one womb; then Eddie; and finally May. Though they accuse one another of fabricating, of changing the version in the telling, the play does not dramatize history as such but the reconciliation of myth and history. *Fool for Love* actualizes the archetypes of myth in the history of an American family as lived by three of its members, two of whom in the telling incarnate the elemental images.

If their stories never changed, Eddie and May would be archetypes and not characters whose summoned appearance to enact their unchanging ritual would itself be a nightmare, the nightmare of eternity. Or if they were characters whose stories never changed, they would be trapped in the nightmare of history. Their stories change, just as their future can change, because in their interaction reconnecting archetypes with characters, they become creative. The interaction liberates them from the nightmare.

To Martin, Eddie tells the story of his first meeting with his half sister, a meeting that was the discovery of their love for each other. As he, shifting into present tense, focuses on the scene when his father's second wife comes to the door of her home and he, a boy standing on the porch, sees the girl standing in the doorway behind the embracing couple, the bathroom door in the motel room "*very slowly and silently swings open revealing* May, *standing in the doorframe backlit with yellow light in her red dress*" (50).

This scene epitomizes Shepard's theatre. As Eddie narrates, he pulls the bewildered Martin around the motel room in a circle of deepening intensity with the lights shifting to blues and greens of moonlight, the tense in the narrative shifting from past to present, and the monologue shifting from remembered experience to created one. The narration circles until it releases from the past's repository an image that fills the stage. For one moment the conscious and subconscious minds, past and present, imagination and history synthesize in an image.

A keeper of the past too, May completes the wholeness by first creating a narrative that complements her brother's, to the chagrin of the Old Man, who protests that he never knew that Eddie's mother committed suicide, and then creating an image with Eddie. Ignoring their father's objection, the two lovers embrace at centerstage and *"kiss each other tenderly"* (55) before an explosion of light illuminates the stage. Eddie leaves followed by May when she realizes that he is gone.

Wholeness is momentary; there is no resolution; the lovers do not create a new self. The Old Man achieves wholeness when he refers to his woman as "She's all mine. Forever" (57). But she is in his dreams or imagination. In life, imagination and reality have to interact. Yet since Eddie and May do interact, their embrace at centerstage indicates that Shepard's theatre is moving ever closer to wholeness in the individual, family, and society because the interaction and embrace of Eddie and May mirror the interaction and embrace of the two natures within each.

By the time of the last play to be examined, the antinomies have accumulated meaning from all the preceding plays. The masculine, exemplary self is the basis of the self in opposition to while also attracted to the feminine, interactive self that is the basis of society. By incarnating the clashing antinomies in two clashing families, Shepard extends the play's scope beyond that of the other four domestic plays, each of which is contained within one family. Interacting and not interacting in *A Lie of the Mind* are divided selves within divided families within a divided society.

When the play opens, Jake is telling his brother Frankie that he fears he beat to death his wife, Beth. After Frankie sees to it that Jake, who collapses, is safe with their mother and sister in southern California, he sets out to learn what he can about Beth because his brother has a history of violence and may actually have killed her. His quest takes him to her parents' home in Montana, to which her family brings her from the hospital. The union of brother and sister-in-law reconciles the two families, but it is only one of the many cycles of the structural design of opposition, reconciliation, and separation that the playwright builds into the play's architectonics.

By opening with images of a dominant man and a beaten woman in separate scenes, each within a family, *A Lie of the Mind* distributes the antinomies of self and society, which include the masculine and feminine archetypes, through two sets of parents and siblings. The larger cast allows for different interactions between the two families and within each family as it forms a constellation around the member who symbolizes it. Jake's masculinity is the image of his family, and Beth's femininity is the image of hers. The first two scenes have him, in the grip of his violent nature, smashing down the telephone while telling his brother that he fears he beat his wife to death, and her, awakening in the hospital with her brother standing beside her, her head swathed in bandages, inquiring about her husband in speech slurred by brain damage. In act 1's sixth scene, surrounded by her family she is in "*almost the identical position and attitude of sleep*"[16] that he surrounded by his family was in the previous scene.

Yet though act 1 ends with images of an imaginative Jake and a domesticated Beth, other interactions will develop within the various characters and between them. After imagining his nude wife, Jake takes from under his bed the box containing his father's ashes and blows them into the spotlight. The play gradually reveals his attitude toward his father and the role he played in his death. Beth persists in loving the man who beat her so badly that she could have suffered permanent brain damage. There are tensions between Jake and his brother and between his sister and mother, just as there are between Beth and her brother and between Beth's father and everyone else in his family.

Passages from the writings of Cesar Vallejo and H. L. Mencken, which preface the published text, establish the two natures of man: his essential being and his social conditioning. The former puts the contradictions within man's being. By quoting two contrasting paradoxes from Vallejo's writings, Shepard further emphasizes the division, with its opposition and attraction, within man himself. The latter, on the Western movement in American history, puts the clash between the two families in historical perspective. Jake's mother, Lorraine, and Beth's parents, Baylor and Meg, disavow the marriage of their offspring by pretending not to remember the other family. The reason goes beyond a dislike of the daughter-in-law or son-in-law. Beth comes from a family of ranchers rooted in Montana. Jake comes from a family of drifters who fit Mencken's description of the chronic nomads who halted on the push westward only because they were exhausted. Baylor refers to them as a "Bunch a' Okies" (29), which recalls the uprooted Joad family in *The Grapes of Wrath*. When Jake, recuperating in the room that used to be his in his mother's house in southern California, asks Lorraine where they lived before that time, she replies, "You-Name-It-U.S.A" (36).

Shepard's dramaturgy in the domestic plays envisions setting and action in which the twins—Lee and Austin in *True West*, for example—mirror each other. In *A Lie* the dramaturgy splits the stage and parallels and contrasts action and dialogue to mirror the schism in the human being, family, society that rends the fabric of American life.[17] The staging is epic in that it opposes and reconciles the divided self and society in a variation on the traditional Western that pits land and cattle barons against homesteaders, wild rovers against domesticated settlers who are realizing the American Dream of discovering roles to fill in the new world. Anyone who saw the original New York production with the Red Clay Ramblers knows that the play is American. In the text's music-notes section, Shepard recommends that at all subsequent productions the groups, whether bluegrass or not, play music "with an American backbone."

Jake's family is dominated by the archetype of wild masculine imagination; Beth's family, by the archetype of domesticated feminine reality. The son symbolizes his family because his father's abandoning them long before the time of the action puts him at the center of an old-world conception of the family. For Lorraine, Jake's depression is a blessing in that she can cook and care for her "boy" (23). He fills an emptiness in her life ever since her husband left her, and to keep him she will baby him, blame Beth for provoking the beating, and try to dissuade his sister Sally from returning to the house by arguing that she will so upset him that he will leave. When he does, she once again feels betrayed and left for dead because she feels useless without a man. Since her son was someone she could love who would love her in return without complications, she resists with all her might Sally's revelation about his role in the father's death, screaming at her daughter that it was she and not her brother who drove the man to his death in Mexico.

The daughter symbolizes her family because her father, contemptuous of "feebleminded women down here in civilization who can't take care a' themselves" (106), has withdrawn, to an unheated shack in the woods during deer-hunting season, but he has not abandoned them and his withdrawal does not devastate the women, who pursue a new-world conception of the family. Although Meg admits that a female needs a male in a way that he does not need her, she insists that the women in the family can take care of themselves. "We always have" (106), she neutralizes his invective. Beth herself is the play's outstanding example of a new-world woman who seeks self-fulfillment in a career outside of the home and dependence on the man.

The typical Shepard image, one that epitomizes the scene, occurs at the end of act 1 when Jake in one pool of light imagines a partially nude, invitingly soft Beth oiling her body in another pool of light. Jake tells his brother that he beat his wife when he became convinced that she was oiling her body not for him but for an actor appearing in a play with her. Frankie tries to explain that as an actress Beth must assume different roles, each requiring its special preparation, but Jake cannot understand. For him a man dictates the role his woman plays in their relationship. If she plays another role, she must be playing it for someone else and therefore desecrating their relationship.

Because he cannot imagine why a woman would want to change the old-world role that has served women through the ages (and centered men), he cannot understand that playacting is the great metaphor for the new-world experience in which wild imagination excites reality by discovering a new role for the person to play while domesticating reality nurtures imagination to discover a role that the person can essay until the new self fits. Since he cannot understand, he beats the imagination out of Beth until she can no longer remember him. She knows that she loves a man, but she cannot remember his name or visualize him. To recover from the damage, she must recover her imagination.

In Montana, trying to learn whether Beth is dead, Frankie is accidentally shot in the leg by Baylor, who brings him into the house, where he is forced to remain until the roads, snowbound by a blizzard, are passable. Partly because Baylor urges her to help Frankie as therapy for her own condition and partly on her own because she is recovering from the brain injury, Beth becomes increasingly importune until he has to hobble around the room to avoid her embrace. She wants him to marry her, a proposal he cannot accept because she is his brother's wife. If she were not married to Jake, he would be more receptive because he always has liked her. That point is made early in the play in conversation with Jake. The point is important. It means that Frankie's ability to imagine himself with Beth can easily be activated.

She is his stimulus to interact with her and within himself as she is interacting within herself. In place of the monologues that distinguish Shepard's early plays, she speaks simple, direct utterances that are among the most moving passages in his theatre. In act 2, when the wounded Frankie is brought into the house, she recognizes his face but cannot place him. As the scene ends she introduces Baylor not as her father who owns the ranch but as her father for whom love is dead because her mother is dead for him. She then introduces herself as one who knows love. "I know what love is. I can never forget. That. Never" (57). Once whole herself, she knows that love is the best healing medicine because it unlocks the prison of the self. As she regains her imagination, she resumes playacting while appealing to Frankie to join her: "Pretend to be.

Like you. Between us we can make a life" (75). She becomes the twin who stalks her hobbling brother-in-law, protesting that she belongs to Jake, to become whole with her. "You could pretend so much that you start thinking this is me. You could really fall in love with me. How would that be? In a love we never knew" (77).

The interaction between Frankie and Beth switches their roles as it does those of the antagonists in *Angel City* and *True West*. Invalid, he becomes the woman that she, in the masculine role, courts until he accepts her, at which time she becomes feminine again, laying her head on his chest. The playacting creates new selves for them individually and collectively. They will be husband and wife beginning a new family. For the first time in these plays, the reconciliation becomes a resolution. The lovers *"remain there in the embrace"* (129) holding through the remainder of the closing scene the image of wholeness that Eddie and May in *Fool for Love* hold only momentarily.

Encouraging her brother-in-law to playact, Beth assures him that together they can create a "whole new world" (114). The implication is that their resolution into wholeness will reconcile other divisions in their families and in society. Her prediction seems to come true. She and Frankie contribute to her parents' reconciliation. When Baylor kisses Meg at play's end, she swears it is the first time in twenty years; after kissing his wife, he tells her not to dawdle on her way to bed, where he will be waiting for her.

The play's ending is ambiguous, however. "In this, the longest of Shepard's family plays," writes Lynda Hart, "there is a longing for a resolution to some of the questions it engenders, but that resolution never comes."[18] Just as Baylor seems to be reclaiming his roles as husband and father in his family, he abrogates the latter by ignoring what is taking place around him while he fusses with the flag. Lorraine and Sally burn their house in southern California before returning to the old world, but beyond visiting relatives, their future is undecided. Jake is the outstanding question mark. He travels to Montana to see Beth, only to release her to his brother while declaring his love for her. In the mixture of resolution and nonresolution, another critic, Gregory W. Lanier, sees Shepard creating a new dramatic form: a fusion of comic reconciliation and tragic alienation.[19]

Ever since *Angel City*, we should have been able to predict that if a resolution were to come in Shepard's theatre, other interactions would have to start to keep the creative process alive, for as Rabbit and Wheeler demonstrate in the studio, their interaction creates images that engage an audience in the process. When at the end of act 3's second scene, Meg sees Beth lay her head against Frankie, she imagines their wedding uniting the families as her daughter's marriage to Jake did not. The play's closing lines are hers. In Montana she can see the fire from Lorraine's burning house in southern California, contained onstage in a bucket. To Meg the image looks "like a fire in the snow. How could that be?" she asks (131).

Imagination makes it be. Her vision does what Shepard's theatre does. It juxtaposes discordant images to startle the imagination, which is the aggressive principle, into stalking its twin. A lie of the mind may be a self-deception, but it is an act of the imagination that enables Beth, recovering from brain damage, to initiate interaction with the aggressive principle within herself and with Frankie to create a new self, just as he, unlike Jake, does by interacting with the feminine principle within himself and with her.

The masculine-feminine principles are not the sole antinomies in Shepard's characters. The dichotomy of naturalistic-metaphysical is a convenient rubric for his dramaturgy's fractured characterization, but the rubric includes multiple impulses, attitudes, and divisions. So long as it is active, the imagination stimulates interaction on many planes of experience. If Frankie and Beth continue to hold the embrace in what is their resolution, they are dead and the theatre that presents them becomes a museum of exhibits. Moreover, their holding the embrace does not detract from the desirability of resolution as a goal. Resolution does not have to be petrifaction. It can be creatively moving forward reconciled currents within the multiplicity.

Nevertheless the image of Frankie and Beth in stationary embrace is so disturbing that it symbolizes contemporary art's eschewing resolution as closure. As closure, resolution implies a permanence and a unitary standard that when combined militate against not only wholeness as a harmonious mix and the interaction that leads to reconciliation but also the ambiguities, contradictions, and ambivalence that characterize life. The image is also so rare in the contemporary American theatre that it should not alarm.

This chapter concentrated on reconciliation and the possibility of resolution in healing divisions within the personal self and the family. The next and final chapter before the conclusion concentrates on the same healing process in American society. This chapter ended with an epic play that images America in the twentieth century's fourth quarter. Plays in the next chapter image the national self on the eve of the twenty-first century.

8

On the Eve of the Millennium

The playwright today must dig at the roots of the sickness of today as he feels it—the death of the Old God and the failure of science and materialism to give any satisfying new One for the surviving primitive religious instinct to find a meaning for life in, and to comfort its fears of death with. It seems to me that anyone trying to do big work nowadays must have this big subject behind all the little subjects of his plays or novels, or he is simply scribbling around on the surface of things and has no more real status than a parlor entertainer.[1]

In the decades that playwrights have been digging since Eugene O'Neill wrote the quoted passage, they have not realized a new order to replace the old one, the breakup of which fractured mankind's existence, but they have uncovered a faculty capable of reconnecting people with themselves and the worlds they inhabit following the breakup. A play we have yet to look at, one that recreates an ancient drama in contemporary images, calls this faculty "God's gift."

John Guare's *Six Degrees of Separation* opens with a husband and wife running onstage *"in nightdress, very agitated."*[2] Within moments they remove their robes to stand before the audience *"smartly dressed for dinner"* (6). Rather than narrate what happened to cause their agitation, they will reenact the previous evening's events leading up to the loss of self-control. The transition is smooth. With composure regained, Flan (for Flanders) and Ouisa (for Louisa) Kittredge entertain a friend in their Fifth Avenue, New York, apartment until a doorman enters, supporting a young black man who, explaining that he was mugged in nearby Central Park, has come to them for help because he goes to Harvard with their son and daughter, who had told him about their parents. His wound bandaged, given a clean shirt, he proceeds to entertain the couple and their guest, preparing a meal and serving it to them with anecdotes about his father, actor Sidney Poitier, who following his birth left him and his mother for another woman. He has long since been reconciled with his father and stepmother.

The stranger, Paul, is so ingratiating, and his anecdotes are so captivating, that the theatregoers forget the reason for the reenactment. If they remember, they conclude that a mugging close to home caused the couple's agitation, until the scene erupts, that is. No printed text can communicate the power of the experience that occurs as the scene ends. The Kittredges persuade Paul to spend what few hours are left to the night with them, promising to wake him in time for his early morning appointment with his father. He retires and after Ouisa recreates her dream and Flan relates his, Ouisa walks into the darkened rear half of the stage to wake the young man. She stops outside the door to his room and calls his name, but since the only response she receives is a moaning from within, she opens the door and turns on the light, at which point the action becomes frenzied.

Two figures rise from the darkened bed into the blinding light: a naked Paul, who sits up, and a naked white man, who stands up and follows Ouisa, screaming for Flan as she retreats into the living room. When her husband orders the two men out of the house, the street hustler smuggled into the apartment during the night chases a terrified Ouisa around the room and physically threatens Flan before picking up his clothes and leaving, still naked, followed by an apologetic Paul, pulling on his clothes as he leaves. Very agitated, the couple face the audience and repeat the play's opening lines, signaling the end of the reenactment and the return to normalcy.

It is common knowledge that the inspiration for *Six Degrees* was Guare's learning about a young man arrested in 1983 for passing himself off as actor Poitier's son, but pursuing the facts about him and his confidence game yields no insight into Paul's life or behavior. The young man arrested in 1983 has a biography, reported in the mass media.[3] By withholding this biography from Paul, the playwright suggests another origin for the young man. The play's charming, articulate stranger is not what he appears to be when he enters the apartment, but he unmasks himself before the night is over. When Ouisa turns up the light in the bedroom, he reveals himself as wild and naked nature in a scene that is not faithful to the historical events that inspired the play but, I believe, is fashioned by Guare's imagination to invoke a classical tragedy.[4]

Guare's stranger is a contemporary Dionysus, the stranger in Euripides' *Bac-

chae, the god of antiquity who offers ecstatic release to those who accept him. The power that Paul actualizes, the power that he names as "God's gift," is the "imagination" (34), the contemporary equivalent to the supernatural power in the classical Dionysiac play.

"I am Dionysus, the son of Zeus," are the words that open the *Bacchae*, spoken to the audience by the god in the guise of an effeminate young man.[5] He has returned to Thebes, the land of his birth, because the city-state rejects his mother's claim that she and Zeus coupled. Hera tricked his mortal mother, Semele, into petitioning her lover that she be allowed to see him who in one of his guises had impregnated her. Forced to accede, Zeus appeared to her in his divine splendor, a visitation that consumed her, leaving her home a tomb before which smolders Zeus's flame. Yet the city-state, led by the dead woman's sisters, maintains that her lover was, like her, mortal and that she was consumed by fire for blaspheming the most exalted of deities so that by denying Semele's claim, Thebes denies his, Dionysus's, claim to divinity, making him an impostor. Hence, he explains as he continues to address the audience, he has returned to wreak vengeance on all who dishonor his mother and him. He already has driven the women population from their homes, frenzied, to the mountains to enact the ritual sacred to him. The next to be initiated into his mysteries is Pentheus, the young ruler of the city-state who excludes him from official worship and to whom the seductively smiling young man will shortly present himself as an initiate. "Therefore," vows the disguised Dionysus, "I shall *prove* to him and every man in Thebes that I am god indeed" (lines 47–48). The play is the exacting of this retribution, culminating in the manifestation of the deity's terrible, implacable nature.

Minutes after entering the Fifth Avenue apartment, Paul identifies himself as the son of an actor who will be directing a film version of the musical *Cats*. Looking at the audience, Ouisa says, "He named the greatest black star in movies. . . . Sidney Poitier!" The name divulged, Paul *"steps forward cheerily"* (22), for the only time in the play that he addresses the audience, and gives a capsule biography of the screen star. One can argue that since celebrities in a secular society replace the deities of religious cultures, Poitier is a contemporary Zeus, but the argument does not have to be made because Ouisa makes the correspondence for the audience. The Kittredges hope that their guest, Geoffrey, a wealthy South African, will supply the two million dollars art-dealer Flan needs to purchase a Cezanne for resale, at a handsome profit, to a

Japanese group. It is one reason they made reservations at an exclusive restaurant. Paul's bloodied arrival would seem to interfere in that it will distract from their efforts to interest their friend in the project. Yet Geoffrey, finding the young man's company enjoyable, votes to eat in so that they do not disrupt the rhythm of chatting and listening to anecdotes about his relationship with the man he calls "Dad," "Pop," "my father," and "my dad." The South African so enjoys the evening that when leaving he indicates that he will buy in for the needed two million, prompting Flan to declare, when he and his wife are alone, that "there is a God" and He is "Geoffrey." No, Ouisa corrects her husband; He is "Sidney" (44).

Jubilation aside, the Kittredges do not really accept Paul as the son of God any more than does Pentheus accept Dionysus as the son of Zeus. They accept the seductively smiling young man because he appears to be the cultured son of a famous person and he seems to know their children. But he is an impostor, and once he reveals himself in the bedroom, they demand that he leave. The opening of Guare's play is as comic as the opening of Euripides' play. The note is struck in the *Bacchae* by the incongruity of two old men, Teiresias and Cadmus, dressed in Dionysiac fawn skins, trying to put themselves in the proper psychological state for the ecstasy on the mountaintop to which they totter while holding onto each other. Equally incongruous is the idea that the distinguished actor-director Poitier would be in the city to direct a film version of a musical about cats. Guare wrings every laugh he can out of the incongruity by having Flan and Geoffrey ask Paul if they can be in the film but as humans. They want their contracts to stipulate that they will be cast as humans so as not to have to wear "cat suits" (37) as a prerequisite for participation in the filming.

A comic tone that darkens to somber is not the only similarity in the two plays. Each play begins with a stranger's assumption of an appearance that gains him access to a host-hostess: Dionysus as a seductively smiling initiate of the god and Paul as the seductively smiling son of a godlike actor. Each stranger identifies himself as the son, for even though Paul is not Poitier's son, he has so assumed the role that in his mind he is. Each also has his motivation for appearing where and when he does.

William Arrowsmith cautions against reducing Euripides' play to a contest between any two contrasted abstractions symbolized by the two antagonists—Pentheus as reason versus Dionysus as the irrational, for instance—because abstractions cannot convey the texture of the conflict or penetrate its depth to uncover the common ground where the antagonists ultimately meet.[6] Arthur Evans, who traces the god's lineage back to ancient Minoan civilization, summarizes the range of repressed forces and energies that Dionysus expresses:

> In his myths and rituals, Dionysos embodied both a feeling for the living continuities of nature and a concept of the human personality as an organism deeply rooted in the nonrational forces of the cosmos. Serving as the focus for the spiritual needs of Greece's underclasses, he became the god that the patriarchal establishment could neither accept nor eliminate. And so Dionysos represented the return of the repressed in several senses: return of the religious needs of the lower classes, return of the demands of the nonrational part of the self, and return of the Minoan feeling for the living unity of nature. And so in turn he threatened several repressors: the aristocracy of well-to-do male citizens, the domination of the intellect over emotion, the alienated ethos of the city-state. In each of these confrontations, he is personified by the character of Dionysos in Euripides' *Bakkhai*, just as the opposing tendencies are likewise personified by Pentheus.[7]

Guare's unmasking the impostor without disclosing his true identity is the masterstroke in his creation of a contemporary Dionysus because the mysterious stranger's motivation also follows from society's rejection of him. Denied an individual history, Paul remains a representative of all the repressed forces striving for acceptance into mainstream American life. Black, he represents racial and ethnic minorities, and homeless, he represents social and economic outcasts. Denied a personal history, he becomes mythic, his sudden appearance stimulating a collective imagination. Who, the families whose lives he disrupts ask and thereby cause the audience to ask, is the stranger who seems to know everything about them, who is both wild and elegant, and who wounds himself to gain entrance to a home only to rout it before the night is over? The Kittredge home is not the only one routed. With the reenactment over, their friends, Larkin and Kitty, stop by to tell them of their experience with Sidney Poitier's son. Notifying the police, the couples learn of another person the stranger beguiled, Dr. Fine, an obstetrician whose son went to prep school with their sons and daughter.

Despite the length to which Paul goes to gain confidence—as Ouisa reminds Flan toward play's end, "He stabbed himself to get in here" (117)—his motive is not that of the professional con artist. He does not swindle these families;

even Larkin and Kitty, who believed his explanation that the naked man he was chasing was a burglar, admit that nothing was taken from their home the night he spent with them. When he later contacts Ouisa, he alludes to blackmail, but the audience does not see him blackmailing anyone. During the telephone conversation, though, he provides an insight into his behavior. He did not like Larkin and Kitty and Dr. Fine because they left him "alone." The night he spent with her and her husband, however, was the happiest night of his life. "We all stayed together" (99), he says.

Just as Dionysus is motivated to claim his denied divinity by manifesting himself—his supernatural power—to his followers, so Paul is motivated to claim his denied humanity by manifesting himself—his natural power—to a group to which he can belong: a family, for example. The rites that he initiates therefore are those of a collective experience, and they are Dionysiac.

To appreciate how Paul manifests his power, we must turn to E. R. Dodds, an authority on Dionysiac religion, who singles out two rites central to the cult: the oreibasia and the omophagia.[8] The first is the nighttime dancing revels held on mountaintops, and the second is the eating of raw animal flesh. Fundamental to the rites is a group experience, what Philip Vellacott characterizes as "above all the excitement of group-emotion. . . ."[9]

The two rites occur offstage in the *Bacchae*, on Mount Cithaeron, with the herdsman and the messenger reporting them in their accounts of the Maenads' orgy and Pentheus's fate. But even before the reports, in the prologue Dionysus informs the audience that he has already initiated his ritual by driving the Theban women upland.

Paul too uses his power before initiating his rites. His natural power is his imagination, which he uses to create a guise that gains him access to a group. Once inside the home or family, he initiates the frenzied oreibasia, which the audience sees reenacted in the Kittredges' Fifth Avenue high-rise apartment at night.

The presence of a group makes the experience the first of the two rites. Paul's affair with the MIT student named Trent Conway, who for sexual favors traded information about parents of former prep-school classmates, is not an oreibasia. Larkin's and Kitty's experience is, though muted, because they are spectators rather than participants who relate how they were awakened by screams in the middle of the night and drawn into the hall to see the young man they had befriended chasing a naked blonde man.

A participant reports the play's most graphic description of a contemporary oreibasia. Rick and Elizabeth are a couple from Utah who have come to the city to be actors and who befriend Paul by taking him into their railroad loft. From the young man he borrows their savings, supposedly to get him to Maine and a reunion with his father, whom he identifies as Flan Kittredge, but instead spends the money on the two of them in a wild night that begins with their donning special dress for the occasion. "We went to a store that rented tuxedos and we dressed to the nines," Rick verbally recreates the event for the audience. "We went to the Rainbow Room. We danced. High over New York City. I swear. He stood up and held out my chair and we danced and there was a stir."

Rick resumes his narration at a point after the management requested that they leave:

> And we walked out and walked home and I knew Elizabeth was waiting for me and I would have to explain about the money and calm her down because we'll get it back but I forgot because we took a carriage ride in the park and he asked me if he could fuck me and I had never done anything like that and he did and it was fantastic. It was the greatest night I ever had and before we got home he kissed me on the mouth and he vanished. (91)

Above and beyond its shock value—more so than that of an encounter with a female streetwalker—the episode links the two plays. Researching the historical and cultural milieu of Euripides' play, Evans explores the connection between Dionysus's effeminacy and the transvestism associated with his rites to shed light on Pentheus's violent rejection of him. He is both attracted to and repelled by the god's homosexual invitation because he does not know himself, because he has repressed his real feelings and needs under the straitjacket of rational, masculine ruler. Evans goes on to relate the homosexual overture to a much larger invitation to sexual and religious initiation, just as he relates the god's homosexual ambiance to his much larger pansexuality. For Dionysus is not a particular mode of sexuality but the expression of the sheer joy of sex as a life force free of familial and societal goals.[10]

Six Degrees is not about homosexuality. Toward play's end Paul phones Ouisa. It is the first time that they talk to each other since the night he spent in their apartment. When she bitterly complains that by picking up the hustler he betrayed their hospitality, he interrupts, "I was so happy. I wanted to add sex to it. Don't you do that?" (108). Sex is a natural expression of his being;

its expression defeats the argument that swindling his host or hostess is his motivation for gaining access to the person. Once he works his way into someone's confidence, instead of maintaining the guise that gained him entrance, he betrays it by erupting sexually. He may calculate his way into someone's life by memorizing the person's biography, but once in, he sheds civilization's restraint. He becomes elemental: uninhibited and ecstatic in the oreibasia.

The episode also links the two rites. The oreibasia prepares the initiate for the omophagia, whether as possessed communicant or as devoured god. Following the herdsman's account in the *Bacchae*, Pentheus verbalizes an interest in seeing the mad women. Dionysus offers to escort him to the mountain on condition that he dress as a woman, a necessary disguise so that he can observe their revels without arousing suspicion. Though the condition is repugnant, the ruler agrees, and the god leads him, in linen dress over fawn skin, to the sacrifice. Since in the omophagia initiates rend an animal believing it to be the deity in his beast vehicle, their devouring of the flesh is the partaking of his power. By being the scapegoat victim in a rite that Dodds suggests may have involved the rending and eating of god in the shape of man in addition to his bestial form, Pentheus ironically becomes the god he denies.

Though no city-state ruler, Rick is a Pentheus, attracted to the young black man yet repelled by his experience with him, who did not know himself before he withdrew his and Elizabeth's money from the bank and went to the Rainbow Room with Paul. As the full force of the experience hits him, as he realizes what he did to Elizabeth and what he is—"I didn't come here to be *this*" (91)—the young man from Utah commits suicide.

Rick is not the play's only Pentheus character, and his suicide is not the play's omophagia. But he is typical of the play's characters, whose spiritual state we must address in order to appreciate the contemporary recreations of the two rites, the second of which assimilates contents of the first. The characters are unhappy people, members of families disintegrating into opposing camps of disappointed parents and disaffected children. To son Doug, Dr. Fine is a "cretin" and a "creep" for giving the house keys to a stranger. "No wonder mother left you!" (67), he hurls at him. Woody Kittredge speaks for all the offspring in telling his father that he hates him for giving his pink shirt to a stranger: "I hate it here. I hate this house. I hate you" (74). Even when the language is not abusive, it remains disrespectful. Ouisa refuses to take daughter Tess seriously when she phones to inform her mother that she is going to be married. "I know everyone you know," Ouisa snaps, "and you are not marrying any of them" (96).

The division separating persons from each other is symptomatic of the division within each person. Each character other than Paul identifies himself with something specific, be it profession, lifestyle, or object, the possession of which he feels distinguishes him from the herd. To the parents' request that their children contact former prep-school classmates to see if anyone has met a black man pretending to be Sidney Poitier's son, Doug Fine protests that he cannot because he has outgrown them. "How can you outgrow them?" asks Kitty. "You graduated a year ago!" (73). Ouisa, the play's most likable character, is not exempt as evidenced by her obsession with the two million dollars Flan needs to obtain the Cezanne. Since the possession of the something gives each character his identity, any threat to the possession threatens to disintegrate an attenuated self. Separated from elemental nature, the characters are incomplete; like Rick, they do not know their real feelings and needs. Alienated from themselves and removed from the mass of humanity, they have severed the bonds that form a community; they can no longer empathize with one another. Tess cannot understand why her father would want to appear in a film version of *Cats* any more than Flan can understand why she would want to mountain climb in Afghanistan.

The set reflects the division within each character's psyche. Above the stage revolves a canvas, on either side of which is a painting by the abstract artist, Wassily Kandinsky: On one side is a wild and vivid style; on the other, a geometric and somber style. The two represent two stages of his career. The earlier is the wild and vivid style from which he evolved to paint precise, geometrically arranged compositions. Revolving, it is the set's focal point. Once the play begins, it stops, at which time another part of the set, overshadowed by the revolving canvas, becomes the focal point. In a production note to the published text, Guare calls attention to the colors and shapes in the Kittredge apartment and the geometric interplay between them. The interplay between a bright red carpeted disc and a black rectangular back wall causes a "palpable tension" (xii).

Together the two-sided canvas and the palpable tension caused by the set's dynamic interplay symbolize the conflicting impulses within the play and within the characters. Once the play begins, the canvas stops revolving, opting for the geometric side. Flan and Ouisa are in control, for husband and wife appear onstage to tell the audience that they will reenact a scene in which they lose control.

To provide the wounded Paul and the audience with a context for the two-sided canvas aloft in their apartment, Flan gives the dates of Kandinsky's life, the name of the exhibition with which he is most associated, and a passage from his aesthetic. The passage is the third guiding principle of inner need, the impulse an artist feels to express his soul.[11] In art there is no conflict—or rather, there should be no conflict—between form and content, for the Russian's art and theoretical writings reflect his belief that form is the outward expression of a spiritual necessity within the artist. Though he is judged one of the twentieth century's great experimenters in nonrepresentational painting, he recognized that different artists express themselves differently in a spectrum from total realism to total abstraction. Thus for him the crucial consideration is not form itself but whether or not form expresses the content, or spirit, creating it.[12]

It is ironic that Paul's host, a dealer in images, should quote Kandinsky's aesthetic because he cannot recognize that the young man embodies the aesthetic, that his spiritual impulse shapes his form, or appearance: The image of Poitier's son expresses his need to be a member of a family. The explanation for Flan's blindness is his own need to create a successful self-image. He gave up a career as a lawyer for art presumably because he was attracted to the problems of form and color that Cezanne addressed and that he alludes to on occasion. Yet just as he turns the wild and vivid side of the Kandinsky canvas to the rear, so has he repressed that part of his nature to which wild bursts of color speak for that part which bids in geometric progression at art auctions. He is a middleman in a commodity transaction for works of the imagination that are not even purchased for aesthetic enjoyment but for investment value, so that when he reveals his feelings about art, they are the vibrations of envy for their friend's, Geoffrey's, investment success or delight in his own. "We are rich," he exuberates after the Cezanne sale goes through. "Tonight there's a Matisse we'll get and next month there's a Bonnard and after that—."

"These are the times I would take a knife and dig out your heart" (118), Ouisa interrupts, picking up his earlier smug remark that the fact that New Yorkers can be taken in by confidence games proves that they have hearts. The rending motif isolates Flan as Paul's antagonist and one of the play's Pentheus characters. More in control of himself than Rick is, he has the stranger apprehended and restrained. Since Paul does not topple his apartment building or escape police custody to lead him to the slaughter, he remains unscathed at play's end. His wife's words do not stab his heart; he will not allow them to because he will not penetrate beneath his self-image, as Rick does in his moment of illumination before committing suicide. He leaves for the Matisse auction unconcerned about Paul's fate, though knowing that he betrayed the young man when he phoned his wife by telling the police where he could be apprehended.

Opposed to Flan's restraint, which is needed to acquire the art that gives him his sense of self, is Paul's frenzy. He is so driven to belong that he stabs himself to gain entrance into others' lives, because he has no sense of self! When he first meets the Kittredges in their apartment, he introduces himself as Paul Poitier. On the telephone with Ouisa, he is "Paul Poitier-Kittredge. It's a hyphenated name" (109), he says.

In his terrible need to be accepted, he manifests his elemental nature to his Bacchae. One group, and there are two groups in Euripides' play, consists of his followers who devour him sexually. Trent Conway, the MIT student, is a devotee as are the street hustlers who follow him into the bedroom sanctuaries he secures by appearing wounded at the doors of hosts and hostesses. The other group devours him imaginatively.

In the *Bacchae* the omophagia takes place on Mount Cithaeron when Pentheus becomes Dionysus in the rite in which his mother, Agave, and the other women driven upland dismember and devour him. They partake of the deity's power in another sense too. They have to be possessed by Dionysus to participate in the rite. They are taken out of their civilized selves, the selves developed to function in the organized life of the city-state, and reunited with their elemental nature, for Dionysus integrates the follower with himself. "To resist Dionysus," writes Dodds, "is to repress the elemental in one's own nature. . . ."[13] The god also integrates the individual participant with the community of participants and with the totality of nature. In the Dionysiac excitement, induced by dancing or wine, the communicant in the group ritual possesses the god and is possessed by him. United with his elemental nature, his civilized self dissolves and he becomes one with the cosmos.

In his monologue, early in *Six Degrees* and comparable in length to the prologue in the *Bacchae*, Guare's stranger praises "God's gift to make the act of self-examination bearable" so that people can reconcile their "inner lives and the world outside that world—this world we share." The gift is the "imagination" (34), given to everyone, though dormant in most people.

The gift does not lie dormant in Paul. Having examined his inner life and discovered that in society's eyes he is invisible, he uses it as his one talent to create an appearance esteemed in the outer world that otherwise denies him, a world to which he aspires to belong. Once inside a home, he sheds his guise in the frenzied oreibasia to dispossess the host and hostess of their confining self-images by activating the gift in them. He releases elemental images that all the characters share beneath their ethnic differentiation. These are images that they have repressed in order to succeed in an exclusive, materialistic culture, images the repression of which have made them divided selves.

To the degree that he possesses their imaginations, they possess him. They devour him in their awakened imaginations and revive him in their recreated scenes with him. Until the scene in which Paul phones Ouisa, all scenes in which he appears are reenacted scenes or imagined scenes. When theatregoers see the young man with Trent Conway, they see a scene that Tess Kittredge dramatizes based on what her former prep-school classmate told her about his involvement with the stranger. Rick and Dr. Fine dramatize their experiences with him. When he is with Ouisa, she is recreating a scene or dreaming of him. Since he appears onstage only in another character's image of him, he lives only in those who devour him.

In contemporary terms the oreibasia is the ecstatic release of the unconscious; the omophagia is the ingesting by consciousness of the released contents. Of course the rites are potentially dangerous. As the stranger says about the god in the *Bacchae*, Dionysus can be "most terrible, and yet most gentle, to mankind" (line 861). Rick discovers a truth about himself that annihilates him. While others devour Guare's stranger imaginatively so that they can recreate or dramatize scenes with him, eventually they reject him. His collective experience panics characters already crumbling under the pressure to be successful individuals. Since the experience threatens to disintegrate their attenuated selves, they regurgitate him from their consciousness, just as earlier they evicted him from their homes. Only Ouisa assimilates Paul to create a new self.

Following the sacrificial rite on Mount Cithaeron, Agave, still possessed by Dionysus, enters carrying the trophy from what she thinks was the hunt for a lion whelp. Only during the scene does she recover her senses and realize to her horror that the head she holds in her hands is that of her son. Euripides' play closes with the epiphany of Dionysus in his glory above the palace to pass sentence on the House of Cadmus, Pentheus's grandfather, for denying his divinity. In removing the mask of the seductively smiling young man in the opening scene, the tragedy reverses the stranger's image. The son of Zeus and Semele is a merciless god.

Paul does not appear onstage apart from a character's reenacted scene with him until he phones Ouisa, initially to tell her that he did not know about Rick's suicide until he read the story in the paper. Though she has not seen him in person since the night she and Flan ordered him from their apartment, she collaborates in betraying the young man who by identifying himself as "Paul Poitier-Kittredge" imagines her as his mother. She arranges a meeting with him at a destination that Flan gives to the police. That collaboration makes her a contemporary Agave. But unlike her counterpart in the *Bacchae*, she is not banished from her homeland as a punishment for denying the stranger. Her punishment comes from within herself; it is the tormenting knowledge that she betrayed someone who wanted to be a part of her life. Her reward also comes from within; it is the power that the stranger actualizes in those who accept him. At play's end, to her husband she poses the question, "How do we *keep* the experience [with him]?" (118), and then answers it, not discursively but imaginatively. She reveals him present in her imagination.

The play enacts the ritual of Paul's possessing Ouisa's imagination until she keeps the experience with him. After they show the young man to his room in the opening scene, Flan and Ouisa retire, he to dream of paintings, she of Poitier, played by Paul, who appears onstage in her dramatized dream. In a later scene she sits up screaming because she visualizes him, again onstage in her dramatized dream, stabbing himself. It is Ouisa who acknowledges that in learning about hosts and hostesses to gain their confidence, the young man is a "Columbus," a "Magellan" sailing into a "new world" of human relationships. It is she who gives the play its title by understanding the boon that he brings with him on his explorations. Since everybody is separated from everybody else by only six people, a human community is possible if each person imagines every stranger as one of his six, as a "new door, opening up into other worlds" (81). By play's end Ouisa has opened wide her doors of perception and her heart to reverse her perception of the stranger that she and Flan evicted from their apartment.

The play's closing scene is as brilliantly conceived a stage image as the opening, frenzied, scene. It is the epiphany of Paul as a contemporary Dionysus not apart from Agave passing judgment on her but within Ouisa. Just before she leaves the apartment to go to the Matisse auction, she looks up at the black rectangular wall encased in a gilt picture frame. Agonizing over her inability to trace the young man through the labyrinthine structure of civilization's criminal-justice system and knowing that so long as he is denied a home in which to integrate himself he will continue to be a victim of his impulses, she has only moments before asked, "How do we *keep* the experience?"

Paul suddenly appears above her, not as a framed portrait but as a live image because her imagination is alive. In a stage direction that signifies epiphany, he "*glows*" in his symbolic fawn skin, the pink shirt set against the gilt-encased black wall. "The Kandinsky. It's painted on two sides" (120), he says and then disappears. As she smiles in understanding, the two-sided canvas begins to revolve. The repressed wild and vivid side is again visible because she revives it in the play's omophagia. Reconciling her need to be responsible to Paul with her realization that even if she and Flan could locate him he could not live with them, she provides a home for him in her consciousness.

This chapter and the following one are intended to parallel the book's opening two chapters but with differences. *We Keep Our Victims Ready* is a theatre work by a woman who rejects her victim status to reclaim female culture denied by the dominant culture. *Six Degrees of Separation* is a theatre work by a man in the dominant culture that dramatizes the plight of the outsider who wants to be accepted, is rejected, and is thereby forced to be a victim.

The book opened with performance art and will close with it, although merged with another dramaturgy. The 1990 Lincoln Center production of *Six Degrees* heralds the merger. Paul and the street hustler rushed naked from the rear of the apartment onto the thrust stage, bringing the oreibasia into the audience. Whether the imagination was so awakened that spectators were able to participate in the drama of reconciliation is for the individual theatregoer to say.

Only one of the cast, in the closing epiphany, accepts the young man's gift. That is his tragedy and triumph.

Unlike the god of antiquity who can force the recalcitrant to accept his supernatural power, Paul can only offer his natural gift in the oreibasia. To be himself, he has to rend the mask his use of the gift created to gain entrance to a home. With no other way to be accepted, his tragedy is that he has to sacrifice the one thing he desperately wants, a sense of self, because to belong to a family, he has to alter the participants' perception of him and themselves as members of a community beneath the masks life forces people to wear.

Since those who feel threatened and reject him deny his humanity, as society has always done to him, they deny their own humanity. They reject the gift that makes them human, that enables them to connect with and empathize with strangers. His triumph is that Ouisa assimilates him, integrating her divided self, which is a first step toward rebuilding a divided society.

That society has not healed its divisions was brought into America's homes on April 29, 1992, when television carried live coverage of the burning of central Los Angeles in reaction to the acquittal of the four police officers charged with the beating of a black man, Rodney G. King, almost fourteen months earlier. Footage of the King beating with footage of the beating of Reginald Denny, a white man pulled from his truck during the rioting, Anna Deavere Smith incorporates into *Twilight: Los Angeles, 1992*, her work-in-progress first produced by Los Angeles's Mark Taper Forum but presented at other venues since then. I saw it at Princeton's McCarter Theatre before it arrived in New York.

The footage played on the stage's rear wall during a speaker's presentation and twin panels suspended with the speaker's name aloft on the stage are the most visible props that Smith uses. Less noticeable are the slight costume changes she makes during the performance. Her donning of a necktie, for instance, signals a new speaker, but by the time it is on, she has become the new characterization, her behavioral patterns and speech patterns defining the character more readily than the prop does. Ruminative, she is King's Aunt Angela; in-your-face tough, an expert in the use of force; giddy, a woman shot while pregnant who smilingly recounts that the baby girl was delivered with the bullet in her elbow.

The African-American artist extends Finley's performance. As she imitates multicultural voices, she impersonates Eurocentric Americans, Hispanic Americans, and Korean Americans along with African-Americans. The playbill credits four dramaturgs—white, black, Latino, and Asian—with assisting her in rehearsing the various roles she assumes from the more than 175 persons she interviewed in gathering the material that eventually became the work-in-progress. For two of the characterizations, she learned Spanish and Korean.

Performed without intermission, *Twilight* is divided into five sections. The first section introduces Aunt Angela and two other persons. The second section, "War Zone," is the longest. In this section Smith impersonates Denny and others caught up in the actual rioting, for example, members of the Korean American family of Walter Park, who was shot in the head at point-blank range as he sat in his car. The third section, which consists of only one interviewee, gives the work-in-progress a direction. Speaking as Gladis Sibrian, Director of the Farabundo Marti National Liberation Front, Smith talks about the power of human beings to change the conditions under which they live. The power comes from within the person.

Sections four and five dramatize that power.

The three speakers of the penultimate section, "Justice," reveal their changing attitudes and perspectives. The first explains the events that allowed him to defend one of the four officers accused in the King beating. The second describes the jury-room conflicts and tensions that preceded the change that brought the jury into agreement in the second, federal, trial of the officers. The third, among the most moving of impersonations, is a Korean American woman who despite the loss of her store empathizes with African-Americans in their aspirations. But, she asks in tears, where is justice for Korean Americans?

The concluding section, "Coda," bears the subtitle "Limbo." Its lone speaker is Twilight Bey, an African-American organizer of a truce among Los Angeles's gangs. Smith as Bey identifies himself with the night, since he is black, but admits that just as the darkness of night gives way to the clarity of day so must he move beyond identifying himself solely in racial terms. With this illuminating insight, the performance ends.

In the program, Smith acknowledges Bey as one of the inspirations for the work's title. She then connects twilight and limbo as the time and the state of being in which the quester is on the verge of discovery and creativity, providing he responds to the "rustling." Although she does not explain the rustling, we should recognize it. Twilight-limbo is the stage that precedes the release of the images in Nelson's trilogy and Jenkin's castle, Overmyer's embarcadero and Guare's oreibasia that becomes the omophagia. The "race drama" is "no longer black and white," writes the creator of a work-in-progress that actualizes an America, not of a single division between a dominant and a minority culture, but of many divisions.

By interviewing and impersonating, by giving voices to Los Angeles's civil unrest, Smith's performance art makes the divisions immediate. Theatre also can narrow them. Monoethnic theatre has played a healing role within minority communities by bringing members together in the discovery of common experiences. Now, argues the performance artist in language that recalls statements by David Henry Hwang, theatre has a new role to play bringing together people from the larger society. Hwang would like to see the monoethnic theatre become multicultural, staging a "black play, an Asian play, a white play, whatever."[14] In the program Smith declares the need for the American theatre to build bridges to connect monoethnic communities into a larger community.

In Bey's spoken remarks and Smith's printed remarks, *Twilight* returns to Hwang's American Dream of wholeness. When we looked at it chapters ago, I detected a hope of assimilation in the future, even though I had to grant that the thrust of his argument stops at a plea for multiculturalism over ethnocentrism. So must I grant the same thrust to Smith's remarks, which respond to an "America which becomes more ethnically complex,"[15] even though I detect the same hope in her writing and in Bey's speaking.

In the last chapter, I made an alignment of history with naturalistic humankind and imagination with metaphysical humankind to supply depth to the meaning of reconciliation and resolution. Lucas's and Shepard's characters reconcile history and imagination but do not necessarily resolve them. I now want to make another alignment to supply greater depth to the two words. Multiculturalism aligns with reconciliation, and assimilation aligns with resolution.

In a chapter on the national self, Guare, Hwang, and Smith seem to be suggesting that if assimilation is to come, it will happen in the future. The immediate problem is reconciliation. Enclaved cultures must see the worth in other enclaved cultures and in so doing begin to interact harmoniously.

That hope shapes Smith's performance art, which dramatizes the possibility of change in American life. To estimate how pervasive the hope and the change are on the contemporary American stage, I conclude the chapter by examining three works by three authors for their attitudes toward reconciliation. We can think of the plays as proceeding from limbo as a transitional state between darkness and clarity, but I want to remind the reader that limbo in Dante's cosmology is inside the gate of hell. That geography becomes clear in the first play, by Mac Wellman. I also want to remind the reader that we are moving away from hell in this half of the book, the ascent half.

For most of its eight scenes, *Sincerity Forever* takes place in a car parked on the outskirts of Hillsbottom, U.S.A., on a summer's night and occupied by locals in their late teens to early twenties. Possessed by mystic furballs, which have infected the town, they admit that they do not understand the ideas their culture has taught them, ideas ranging from infinite regress to the divine plan for existence. They even question their identity. But they do not question their character. As they see themselves, demons may have poisoned their minds, but the furry creatures cannot penetrate their souls, for they still have their essential goodness. "But the most important thing is not what you know, but whether you're sincere or not," Molly assures Judy at the end of scene 1. "Sincerity forever"[16] is their motto.

The play's visual images are audacious. In each of five of the total of eight scenes, a pair of locals sit in the parked car and talk. No matter which two are seated, and one from one scene can pair with a different local in another scene, their dress is identical, for all wear Ku Klux Klan garb. When the two mystic furballs squat on the car's hood, they are whiskered and clawed. Christ, a character who likens the supposedly Christian community of Hillsbottom to hell, appears as an African-American woman.

Wellman's verbal images are bodacious. From spying upon the locals from the bushes, the furballs take possession of the car's hood in scene 4, there to disgorge invective at each other. "Fuck you, I am bigger than you . . . smarter than you, a better bowler. . ." (114). Though they never again physically command centerstage, they do verbally in that the Ku Kluxers repeat their invective in their speeches. Infected, the locals become members of the furballs' tribes of Belial and Abaddon.

The combination of audacious and bodacious images strips away the insincerity masquerading as sincerity. As their monologues and dialogue overlap, the Ku Kluxers repeat speeches other than those of the furballs. In scene 5 Lloyd and Tom repeat the speeches of Judy and George from scene 3, even to their declarations of crushes on each other. In scene 6 Judy and Molly repeat each other's speeches from scene 1. Since the characters' speeches are interchangeable, they have no identity. Verbally they are as indiscriminate as they are visually. Where they discriminate is manifested in their snobbery and their betrayal of trust and friendship, for as the furballs' possession of them intensifies, their speeches accelerate the repetition of earlier speeches and furball vituperation. The Ku Kluxers' sincerity is that of the intolerant and the prejudiced who disgorge invective at one another.

Christ's reappearance in the play dispossesses the demons. Christ first appears to warn Hillsbottom's residents of the furballs' spirit of negation. When they treat her with disrespect in scene 2, she leaves. When she returns, she assembles in scene 8 the Ku Kluxers in the space next to the car, where she delivers her ultimatum. And she can be as blistering as they. "WHAT THE FUCK DO I CARE ABOUT YOUR FUCKING SINCERITY! You can go shove your fucking sincerity up your tail pipe" (131).

Disabusing them of the notion that she has come to "reconcile" them, she berates them for caring only about themselves. God the Father, who created man in His infinite love, gave him the freedom to be himself. Yet "all you care about," she extends the semicircle to include the entire country, "is what you look like, what you look like in a mirror, a mirror some monster furball dreamt up for you to look at to make you blind. America, you got your eyes open so wide you can't see a fucking thing" (129). The mirror image consummates the combining of images. Possessed, the locals sound like furballs in their denigration of one another. Dispossessed, they look like one another and therefore reject anyone who does not look like them.[17]

In the Nevermore Theatre Project production, in scene 8 the actress playing Christ faced a semicircle of actors and actresses whose hooded backs were to the audience. Since she had banished the furballs, the Ku Kluxers were returned to normalcy, but their normalcy is stupidity; faceless conformity; and most satiric and chilling, insincerity masked as sanctimonious sincerity. They learn nothing from the furball poisoning or the cleansing in the clearing. "Who was that African-American babe?" (131), one of them asks about the departing Christ in the play's closing line.

Lack of imagination is the accusation Christ levels at the Ku Kluxers. They do not know themselves, which they would were they to use their imagination, because they are lost in "insane manias . . . of control, slaughter. . ." (131). Not knowing themselves, they cannot identify with the stranger; they cannot share her vision or her rage. They are hermetically sealed in a bigoted ethnocentrism's virulence.

Not absolutely denied, hope is all but abandoned in Hillsbottom. José Rivera's *Marisol*, on the other hand, ends with a paean to new possibilities. Before it gets there, though, it connects with other imaginative worlds encountered in this chapter.

When the Christ of *Sincerity Forever* departs the stage, she has a final word for America's suburban and rural dwellers: "Wake up to the hollow time that is, because that's where your parlous asses are, each and every one" (131). When ticket holders for *Marisol* entered the theater for the New York Shakespeare Festival production, they saw on the stage a curtain on which was written in black letters a poem for urban dwellers punctuated in red letters, "Wake up." Guare's mysterious stranger wakes up a household for an oreibasia, but he is dependent upon the awakened to partake of his proffered power in the omophagia. In the pivotal section of *Twilight: Los Angeles, 1992*, Smith as Gladis Sibrian in effect tells the spectators to wake up to the power already in them. The heroine of *Marisol* wakes up and to a revolution that fills the streets of heaven as well as of earth. But not immediately.

Rivera's play opens with the heroine, a Puerto Rican woman named Marisol, about to be attacked on a subway by a man with a golf club. Her guardian angel, a black woman, intervenes to save her as she has done numerous times in the past because her yuppie charge lives in parlous times. Torching a human being is everyday sport in the parks of the Puerto Rican woman's Bronx neighborhood. Gangs of skinheads roam the streets in search of prey. The crazed and the homeless haunt subways and abandoned buildings. Cries of the sick and the alienated, of criminal and victim, torture the night, piercing the chained and bolted doors behind which the defenseless toss in sleep troubled by the deepening realization that the unrest outside the doors is worsening.

O'Neill's old god is not dead yet in *Marisol*. He has become Finley's one male god to whose waning power two characters who are minorities in a double sense react. One is Hispanic American and one is African-American, and both are women. Though their reactions are different, they believe in communication between heaven and earth. In *Sincerity Forever* the infection that poisons the earth issues from the devilish furballs; in *Marisol* it issues from the dying god. In each case the playwright means the dominant culture of the region in which the play is set. That is, in *Marisol* the earth's disintegration into moral chaos is a manifestation of the enervated god's, or culture's, disintegrating power. He is soon to be deposed. As Angel confides in her charge in her troubled sleep, she is leading a revolution of angels against Him to "restore the vitality of the universe with His blood."[18] Marisol wants no part of the revolution, yet she cannot stop it, so that when the emissary from heaven leaves, she *"wakes up violently"* (33).

Rivera wants to reconnect heaven and earth separated by a sky which in Stevens's image in his poem "Sunday Morning" has become a "dividing and indifferent blue."[19] He begins with a culture within the dominant culture that still believes in communication between the two realms. That is why O'Neill's old god, though here worshiped as the vital center of a unified universe, is not dead yet as in other contemporary American plays. He is not dead yet in Marisol's minority American culture in which science, with its offspring technology, and materialism do not fill the void that they do in mainstream American culture. And that is why act 1's scene 4, in which Angel visits Marisol in her troubled sleep, plays so well onstage. The two representatives of the two realms believe in each other, for although the yuppie has sacrificed much of her native culture to assimilate, she retains her faith in divine intervention in human destiny.

Yet though the scene plays well, reconnecting for an audience for whom the connection has been broken, a secular audience for whom congress with the spiritual realm is unrealistic, is a formidable task. To counter, in an interview, that the connection is unrealistic, the playwright uses this scene to illustrate his argument that magical realism is inappropriate for his aesthetic if by that genre is meant the artificial imposition of magic onto reality. "'We all think magically when we sleep,'" he explains. "'In our dreams there are monsters and angels. Everybody has them. In my work, the internal psychology of the characters is just reflected onstage, which is not all that original either. It's the same thing Shakespeare did when he used a thunderstorm to reflect the fury of King Lear.'"[20]

Since the scene reflects yuppie Marisol's internal psychology, her attempt to stop her guardian from leaving for the imminent war in heaven reflects her anxiety that the urban nightmare manifests a deepening disorder in the culture for which she has sacrificed her native culture and her fear therefore of god's abandonment of her assimilated culture, a fear aggravated by the subway attacker's revelation that he has been abandoned by his guardian angel. The environment daily becomes more threatening whether or not Angel leaves, but when she does at scene 4's end, Marisol feels more helpless because she now feels alone in the environment. While she is forced to become more assertive to protect herself, in visions she sees the former guardian, each time more assertive until by act 1's end Marisol sees Angel, in military fatigues with an Uzi strapped to her back, shed her wings of peace. "War?" (38), the Puerto Rican woman asks.

In giving the heroine's internal psychology as a motivating force in one scene, Rivera has to be careful not to imply that every onstage occurrence is the projection of the heroine's internal psychology. Were that the case, she would be fantasizing, or imagining unrelated to external reality. He avoids the trap by having the emissary of a new order create arresting images hovering on a ladder between heaven and earth independent of her charge's perception or experience of her and by investing with objective reality the heroine's experiences of urban horror on the subway and urban friendship with co-worker June. Angel's attribution of the disorder to entropy also has to be taken as an objective explanation, apart from an internal dialogue within a divided self. The playwright's task of reconnecting spirit and matter remains formidable, however, for the emissary disconnects herself from earth's matter to storm heaven's throne.

To stage the archaic conflict in contemporary images, Rivera has act 1's urban nightmare become act 2's urban battlefield to reflect the revolution in the other realm. Individual scenes are powerful. The scene in which the man searches for his skin troubles the theatregoer's sleep after the performance. Other scenes invert everyday reality to signify the overthrow of the old order and the birth of the new. One of act 1's crazies is a man named Lenny, the brother of co-worker June, who evicts him from their apartment and is then clubbed by him in the street. In act 2 he delivers a stillborn baby.

The war is successful, but its operation is not, for the individual earthly battles do not make a heavenly war. Marisol has to verbalize her vision of it in mundane images of attacking and counterattacking angels. And the ending is summary. Killed on the streets, the Puerto Rican woman rises to report the revolution's progress in language that becomes a paean to the dawn of a "new history . . . possibilities . . . hope" (45). Joined by victorious Angel, who in the New York production put on the gold crown, they are bathed in the light of the millennium.

The play's strength is not its military revolution but its perceptual revolution. By disconnecting the heroine from her spiritual nature, Rivera forces her to look at her adopted culture as she has not. In the opening scene, for instance, when the man with the golf club enters the subway car, Marisol reacts as she always does in the presence of disruption. She burrows into the newspaper she is reading. Yet as she gradually accepts the reality that society's victims are minorities—the homeless and indigent, women and children—she realizes that the old god of her religious tradition is dead. The culture for which she sacrificed her native culture is that of Finley's one male god, who replaced her god. His time come, he too must die, to be replaced by a new god-culture with new myths. In an interview that coincided with the play's run in New York, Rivera was quoted as saying:

> 'This is the first play I've written with an eye on the next generation. We need to find new heroes and new myths for our society—the old ones just aren't working. The God we know now is a right-wing, white male, corporate God, in whose world racism, sexism and political injustice are rampant. As the millennium nears, I am amazed these things are still valid.'[21]

Clinging at play's opening to the myths that give her an identity in her adopted culture, the yuppie refuses to recognize that she has sacrificed her spirit for assimilation in a materialistic culture until her guardian disconnects herself. The act-1 disconnection is the impetus for the heroine's act-2 quest. The Ku Kluxers in *Sincerity Forever* do not understand the need for reconciliation. Marisol, whose guides are her imagination, her internal psychology, her belief in spirit's existence understands the need to reconnect spirit and matter, heaven and earth. But once killed, all that she can do is report that minority support on earth for the revolution tipped the scales to victory. She resolves her quest in heaven, discovering there a new, assimilated, self.

It remains for the final play to focus on reconciliation on earth. Like *Marisol*, Tony Kushner's *Angels in America, Part One: Millennium Approaches* begins with a disconnection. A rabbi praying over the coffin of a Jewish woman addresses her children and grandchildren (and the audience). "You can never make that crossing that she made," he commemorates her, for the great waves of immigration from Central and Eastern Europe are over. But, he goes on, "every day of your lives the miles that voyage between that place and this one you cross."[22] All people in America at century's end who want to realize themselves are voyagers between worlds. It is simply that the worlds have changed from what they were in the opening decades of the century.

Like the heroine of Rivera's play, the principal characters of Kushner's play initially resist the disconnection. But beyond the initial resistance, the playwrights' visions diverge. Social disorder makes the Puerto Rican woman aware of a cosmic disorder of which the earthly disorder is symptomatic. With the old god's power waning, she fixes her eyes on heaven, from which realm comes a new god to make a new connection. Disruptions in characters' relationships in *Angels* make them aware of a cosmic disorder, for the personal disruptions are symptomatic of the ruptures in society. Because their eyes fix on the fissures, or lesions, in their personal lives, they become aware of another world to which they must voyage before they can reconnect their lives. There is an angel from this realm, but her message is the antithesis of that of the heavenly messenger in *Marisol*.

Six of act 1's nine scenes involve two couples whose relationships become disconnected in act 2. When Joe Pitt tells his wife, Harper, that he has been offered a position in the Justice Department in Washington, she tells him that she does not want to go. She says that she wants to stay in Brooklyn and have a baby. But having a baby is impossible for them, for their arguments back and forth in scene after scene reveal that he is a closet gay and she is agoraphobic, addicted to Valium, and given to hallucinations. When Prior Walter tells his lover that he has AIDS, Louis promises not to leave him. But staying with the partner is as impossible for him as it is for Harper despite their initial resistance to leaving.

Harper can be said to speak for the four unhappy characters when midway through act 1 she foresees the irreversible widening of Antarctica's ozone layer, an obsessive image with her. "The world's coming to an end," she says (28). She can be said to speak for all of them again when midway through act 3, while imagining herself in Antarctica, she expresses a desire to make a "new world here" where she and her imaginary baby can "mend." A dead world to which she withdraws to "deep-freeze . . . feelings" (102–3), it is nevertheless a necessary stop on the journey to life, and coming as it does toward the end of part 1, her journey to the bottom of the planet prefigures Prior's journey to the top of the universe in part 2.

By focusing on four disconnecting partners imagining themselves backward and forward in time while struggling with their relationships in the present, Kushner frees the stage from naturalism's limitations. He calls the work a gay fantasia on national themes. In its musical sense, fantasia suggests a composition grandiose and supple; in its literary sense, it suggests a composition epic and intimate. The most intimate of scenes can open out through the imagination into a panoramic vision and then close in on anguished introspection. The fundamental dramaturgical principle, however, is interaction.

Act 1's second scene introduces the principle with two characters who, though not a couple, have an ongoing relationship throughout the play. The character Roy Cohn, based on the lawyer who came into national prominence during the McCarthy era, offers the Justice Department position to Joe. As they talk in Cohn's office amid a welter of ringing telephones, their voices overlap from time to time, suggesting an area of experience they share. Subsequent scenes reveal that both are gay, though they conceal their sexual orientation publicly. Scene 3 introduces the first of Harper's hallucinations, this one an interaction with an imaginary friend, a travel agent who accompanies her to the imaginary Antarctica in act 3. The hallucination brings another dimension, or plane, of existence into the quotidian world. After scene 4 introduces Prior and Louis, scene 5 splits the stage between two simultaneous realities: Harper and Joe at home and Louis at the cemetery, for he is a grandson of the dead Jewish woman in the opening scene. The next scene, 6, is the first interaction between the couples. In a men's room at the Brooklyn Federal Court of Appeals, chief clerk Joe comes upon word processor Louis, crying because Prior has AIDS. Before the scene is over, Louis, sensing that the other man is gay, reveals that he is.

From the above summary, we can conclude that the scenes are building for a dialectical interaction between the couples that will merge either the four or two of them, if only momentarily. They are building; such a scene does occur. But where it occurs testifies to Kushner's daring as a playwright. Although the scene does not rationally follow from the preceding scenes wherever it occurs, the longer he withholds it while building toward it, the more credence he attaches to it. Comparable scenes in Jenkin's theatre and Shepard's theatre occur later rather than earlier in their plays. Yet the first interpenetration scene in *Angels* is scene 7 of act 1.

Kushner describes the scene as a *"mutual dream scene"* (30). Though they have never met, Prior and Harper appear in each other's dream, he to inform her that part of her emotional problems stems from the fact that, unknown to her, she is married to a homosexual; and she to inform him that despite having AIDS, he is free of disease in the deepest part of himself. The interpenetration connects the two as characters who will negotiate the perilous journey between worlds. Their imaginations activated, they will undergo the perceptual change required to create new selves.

The scene exemplifies the magical realism that Rivera excludes as the explanation for the dream scene in his play in which Marisol and Angel converse. In the playwright's notes to the published edition, Kushner explains that he wants the audience to see both the realism and the magic. "The moments of magic," he writes, "are to be fully realized, as bits of wonderful *theatrical* illusion—which means it's OK if the wires show, and maybe it's good that they do, but the magic should at the same time be thoroughly amazing" (5). The scene is amazing. All the while that Harper argues that it should not be happening because the imagination cannot form an image of that for which it has no experience, the scene is happening. The directions for the scene indicate that it is *"bewildering"* (30).

In the playwright's aesthetic, interaction in the temporal, spatial world—the world of matter—builds to a climax that suspends disbelief because the interaction takes the mind, in Harper's words, to the "very threshold of revelation" (33). In this scene the revelation is the introduction of another reality, another plane of existence—the world of spirit, or images—into matter. Independent of each other, Harper and Prior travel from the world of matter to the world of spirit, but they do not leave matter behind them, nor do they remain independent of each other. The scene merges each one's perception of the spirit in the other's body.

The synthesis does not, however, resolve antinomies in a surrealist image. It begins a new interaction leading to another threshold and another synthesis. In scene 7, after Harper leaves Prior's dream, a feather falls into his consciousness while a voice above him calls to him to "Look up, look up, / prepare the way / . . ." (35). As the play continues to dramatize interactions, move back and forth between geographic locations, and shift perspectives, it continues to prepare the audience in realism and magic. Characters interact with other characters and with images. Appearing and disappearing ghosts of ancestors visit Prior and repeat the injunction from above; a book flips open to a large Aleph, which bursts into flames; the ghost of the executed Ethel Rosenberg visits the AIDS-infected Cohn.

The closing scene of part 1 is another magically realistic synthesis. In one half of a split scene, Joe, whom Harper has left, and Louis, who has left Prior, meet in a park and leave together for Louis's place. In the other half, the voice that Prior has been hearing ever since the mutual dream scene materializes as an angel who crashes through the ceiling of Prior's bedroom to announce to him that the "Great Work begins" (119). The messenger's arrival synthesizes Prior's disjointed emotional and auditory experiences but does not resolve the situation that sent her on the earthly mission. Rather, it sets in motion interactions that build to a new synthesis in part 2.

Kushner's aesthetic manifests his philosophy. In an interview granted to Don Shewey, the playwright discussed a variety of topics including spirituality and how he reconciles it with Marxist dialectical materialism. "'But I'm also enough of a Marxist and a humanist to believe that the material world is of tremendous consequence and there is nothing that overrides it or is free of it. If there is a spiritual dimension, it's in constant interaction with the material.'"[23]

By excluding magical realism while insisting on internal psychology as the motivation for the dream scene in *Marisol*, Rivera limits the scene's ambiguity. Other images, of an angel independent of the heroine, do not limit, but the playwright's explanation does. Kushner's explanation emphasizes the ambiguity as did the New York production. Of course the wires show, but they add to the ambiguity without detracting from the struggle, which is fierce whether Prior is wrestling with a heavenly emissary or within himself. The contest should be fierce; it is between life and death.

Angels in America, Part Two: Perestroika introduces dialectical materialism in its opening scene, which corresponds to the opening scene of part 1. The oldest living Bolshevik asks the question that dialectical materialism addresses: "Will the Past release us? . . . Can we change?"[24] He does not define history as the character in Lucas's *Reckless* does by repeating Stephen's definition from Joyce's *Ulysses*, quoted in the preceding chapter, of it as a nightmare. Yet Kushner did in the interview cited above when he referred to the question of change: "'But how else do we set ourselves free from the nightmare of history?'"[25] The Bolshevik insists upon the necessity for change but cannot provide direction because he is dependent upon a theory and no one has advanced a theory to replace Marxist theory discredited by the collapse of world communism and the dismantling of the Soviet Union. Hence when this opening scene of part 2 reverts to the closing tableau of part 1, with the messenger hovering over a cowering Prior, the implication is that her message is the direction.

The angel has an answer to the question of how to be free from the nightmare of history, but it is neither Kushner's nor Prior's answer. When part 1 ends, the audience concludes that Prior dies. He should die given his condition. Wracked in body by AIDS and in soul by Louis's abandonment of him, he is in heaven's opinion the perfect candidate for death. That is why the principalities selected him to be the prophet.

The second act of part 2 repeats the closing scene of part 1 and elaborates on it. Prior recreates for a former lover, the nurse and drag queen, Belize, what happened after the angel smashed his bedroom ceiling. The heavenly emissary explains that God's creation of human life set in motion forces such as change, history, time, and progress, which in their interaction cause quakes of such increasing magnitude that they threaten the foundation of heaven, a city much like San Francisco. On April 18, 1906, the day of the devastating San Francisco quake, God absconded, leaving them, the principalities, in charge, but since they are powerless to prevent the inevitable catastrophe, they decided to select one man to show humanity the way to end the threat. They selected Prior to be the prophet because given his belief in the power of the spirit, they assumed that he would choose to be free of matter, particularly his infected matter. Angel, who is death's emissary, offers him a resolution of his problems in "STASIS! / The END" (54).

Angels in America is a playful play in its dramatization of ideas; it incarnates them in action laced with wry humor. Prior does believe in the power of the spirit so much so that he rebels. His indomitable spirit—knocked to the floor, he still shakes off his visitor—begins to interact anew with his wracked body, initiating a dialectic of opposites to effect the very change that the angel expected him to end. His rebellion against death answers the Bolshevik's question because he is not acting on Marxist theory or any theory but on his desire to live.

Part 1 of *Angels* is the voyage from the collapsing old world; part 2 is the voyage to the healing new world. The pace picks up with increasing overlapping in dialogues, a diorama that comes to life, and characters who not only move in and out of other characters' dreams but their waking experiences as well. In one hospital scene, the ghost of Ethel Rosenberg comes from the shadows to lead Louis in a Kaddish over Cohn's corpse. Prior reconnects too after visiting heaven with the angel who, returning to claim him, takes him to the heavenly city, which looks like San Francisco after the 1906 quake and which he leaves despite the Council of Principalities' vision of earth's entropy and final destruction. He chooses more life.

By choosing to return to earth, where change is possible, Prior chooses to participate in the creating of a new self and society. Only on earth do the self and society interact. Hell is all self-interest with no community. In Mamet's plays, characters do not interact; they devour one another. The opposite state, heaven, is all community with souls but not selves. In Kushner's play, not even God wants to be there; He absconded. On earth, however, self and society are interdependent. And since they are, men and women can interact to create themselves and their society.

Regardless of the form the creation, or national self, takes, so long as it does not solidify into a fixed unitary standard, the term "postmodern" can be applied to it on analogy with the theatrical self. I introduced the term in the book's very first pages but avoided using it until now because the term is polysemous. One meaning of it refers to a period following the breakup of the modern age, a breakup that is characterized by acceptance of the fragmentation from the breakup as opposed to questing for a new unitary standard as the modern age supposedly did.

A Wooster Group deconstruction is postmodern because it juxtaposes discordant images and diverse styles that do not resolve themselves for the audience. Staging multiple impulses and multiple conventions, styles, and costumes, the Ontological-Hysteric Theater and Ridiculous Theatrical Company are postmodern. These three do not complete the list.[26]

Can the national self be whole while composed of multiple constituents? That composition is the nation's strength. That composition also is the strength of the contemporary American theatre, a multiplicity of individual theatres that the book has been examining for eight chapters. The vitality of an individual theatre is in the interaction that generates, reconciles, and on occasion resolves antinomies such as imagination and history, Dionysian flux and Apollonian form, and Prior's indomitable spirit and wracked body.

Prior returns to earth because he can reconcile himself to life's fragmentation. Paradoxically, by interacting with death, he allows it to contribute to life's healing. He tells Louis that their relationship as lovers is dead, yet the audience sees them together again, in the closing scene, as friends who share interests. In an amazing scene, Harper, who also makes the journey from the old to the new world, verbalizes her reconciliation with life in spectacular imagery. From an airplane window, she sees the souls of the dead rising from the earth to form a net that, by filling the hole in the ozone, repairs the damage to earth's protective rim that, in her despair in part 1, she felt was irreversible.

Because he accepts death, Prior becomes a prophet of more life that someday will heal the lesions in mankind and society. *Angels in America* closes with him, Louis, Belize, and Hannah in Central Park by the Bethesda Fountain. Though it is winter, he can imagine the water flowing from the statue of the winged angel in the summer. Waving to the audience, he becomes the earthly counterpart to the heavenly messenger in the closing scene of part 1, with the same words but a different message. The "Great Work" (148) he refers to is healing, which begins in interaction.

Kushner adds a final word to interaction in the afterword to the published two-volume text. With its emphasis on individual achievement and reward, America intensifies the tendency in every human being to be exemplary: to appropriate the world as subject and object. "We are all children of 'Song of Myself'" (152), he writes. Yet, he concludes, reversing Harper's image of the "net of souls" (144) back to the living earth, the "smallest divisible human unit is two people, not one; one is a fiction. From such nets of souls societies, the social world, human life springs. And also plays" (158).

Creating interaction, theatre stimulates the healing process. Whether on the national level the process heals divisions between enclaves by fostering respect for one another's culture or integrates multicultural enclaves into a culturally assimilated nation is a question the twenty-first century will answer. In either event the conclusion looks at theatre's role in the process. A statement Jesurun made about his play examined in chapter 6, here offered as a representative contemporary work, gives the reason. "In the end, *White Water* focuses back on the audience. . . ." Stimulating the spectator's imagination, theatre expands perception and participation in the creating.

Conclusion: Engaging the Spectator in the Creating

Within weeks of seeing Finley's performance of *We Keep Our Victims Ready*, with a woman friend I again became a member of a Living Theatre ritual. I had participated decades earlier, but it was not until the fall of 1990 that I rejoined the company founded in 1947 by Julian Beck and Judith Malina. In the 1960s *Paradise Now* brought notoriety and leadership in interactive theatre at home and abroad. In the 1980s the company, under the direction of Malina and Hanon Reznikov, returned from Europe to perform collective creations such as *The Body of God*.

Since *The Body of God* is a ritual, I could apply to it Beck's imperatives for engaging the audience. In his collection of thoughts about the Living Theatre's mission, the co-founder notes that for spectators one of theatre's attractions is the ability of actors to become the characters they play. He calls their accomplishment "heroic" because they "get out of the labyrinth of lower consciousness" to enter another consciousness. In effect he then asks, If performers can become members of another class by acting, why cannot spectators? Well, of course they can—by acting! There follow the Seven Imperatives of Contemporary Theatre[1] for awakening the histrionic sensibility of the spectators so that they can participate in the creation of the theatre ritual and therefore of the self and the society.

I could apply the imperatives, but I do not want to. Only weeks earlier I had watched a ritual. Now I was about to enter one, and I want to share my experience rather than conduct an analysis. The experience recapitulates the book's argument.

As the theatregoers entered the rectangular room on the ground floor of a run-down building in New York's Lower East Side, they were asked to take a sheet of cardboard and a paper bag. On the former they could sit; in the latter they could place whatever they were carrying in their hands. The objective was to have the participant divest himself/herself not only of possessions such as purse or book but of the old self, the self solidified in material possessions. Although I complied, my divestiture occurred later, as I suspect it did for most participants.

The Body of God is a ritual involving professional Living Theatre performers, homeless men and women from the area, and theatregoers. The first two groups were merged indistinguishably when the third group entered the room, which was darkened to simulate the night sky and empty of furnishings to simulate the street. Merging with the theatregoers who elected not to sit on the cardboard, they orchestrated movement to the first of several locations within the room. There individuals became performers, professional actors and homeless persons together or by themselves. They narrated stories of abandonment by society or enacted scenes from the struggle to survive on the street. When they finished, they merged with the reactivated movement to the next location.

Separated from the woman with whom I came and self-conscious sitting alone, I drifted to the rear of the crowd to observe. Others—they could have been orchestrators or gregarious theatregoers—would not leave me alone. They kept their eyes on me, moved toward me, extended their hands until I was with those leaving the cardboard to participate within the flow.

Simultaneous with drawing into the flow was the constant altering of perception. The movement was not a promenade around the room's perimeter but a voyage from performance station to performance station. As a result, the viewing perspective kept changing so that I never knew with whom I was holding hands or where I would be when the movement stopped. I might be next to a homeless person who was performing and thus seeing homelessness from within the abandonment. Moreover, with the performance finished, the performers merged with the flow. They dissolved in the crowd so to speak, changing the composition of the movement so that it was in constant flux, its goal to draw in everyone who felt or was deemed unworthy of membership.

My imagination had been stimulated. I interacted to the extent of holding hands with strangers and joining my voice to theirs in the communal chanting that ended the ritual. And I could empathize with homeless people more so than I could before entering the building.

Conclusion

By acting, I had left my old, withdrawn self for a new self more committed to taking the interior, perceptual revolution into the exterior world in which I live and work. For while moving in the constantly changing flux, I participated in creating a model of an integrated America. The evening my friend and I participated, the theatregoers, professional actors, and homeless residents of Manhattan were multicultural, with ages ranging from the twenties to the seventies. Individually we discovered new selves, and collectively, since *The Body of God* is a collective creation, we created a new society.

We did what this book set out to do. It has taken us from performance to performance to recognize the uniqueness of each but also their connection. With the theatre and the nation each searching for an identity in a time of transition or flux caused by the breakup of the old world of sustaining traditions and shared values, no one theatre is the standard, and neither is any one group in the ritual the standard. Together they are the contemporary American theatre and nation. In the sense in which the book defines "postmodern," in the discussion of *Angels in America*, as the rejection of an exclusive standard for the acceptance of multiplicity, the contemporary American theatre and nation are postmodern—but postmodern in quest of a new unity.

In two chapters in this book, I discussed Gurney's *The Perfect Party*, first as a metaphor for the American Dream and second as a fabrication of a false self. Each time I focused on the host's and the party reviewer's attitudes while asking the reader to wait until later for the wife's, the hostess's, attitude. Toward play's end, after the reviewer has criticized her host's conception of a perfect party, his wife, Sally, faults both of them for judgments based on a unitary standard of perfection. In their imposition of a monolithic standard, she sees the dominant culture's imperialism: the impulse to structure the world according to its exemplary vision of wholeness. The impulse is typical of all aspects of American life, she goes on, giving the American theatre as her first example. A theatre that excludes all but the ideal fabricates a false self.

Sally then gives her idea of a party. It will begin not with an imposed standard but with friends, none of whom will be pressured to perform or conform. "Everyone is bringing over various ethnic dishes . . ." (250), she concludes, in the spirit of conviviality that should engender interaction. Should a new society be created from the diversity, it will be fluid as opposed to fixed, but it will be real. That reality is the American Dream of wholeness.

This book makes no pretense of wholeness. It has left out many important theatre artists. But I hope that it has presented enough of their fellow artists' dishes for the reader to appreciate the new selves the American theatre has become in the twentieth-century's final quarter.

What the American theatre will become in the twenty-first century depends to some degree on people who normally would not be interested or at best would be occasional spectators becoming participants in creating. If this book has whetted their appetite for participation, it has been successful.

Notes

Index

Notes

Preface

1. Jerzy Grotowski, *Towards a Poor Theatre* (New York: Touchstone-Simon, 1968) 19.

1. Women's Theatre

1. Karen Finley, *We Keep Our Victims Ready* in *Shock Treatment* (San Francisco: City Lights, 1990) 132. Hereafter to be cited in the text.

2. Sue-Ellen Case, *Feminism and Theatre* (New York: Methuen, 1988) 29.

3. An excellent introduction to performance art is Richard Schechner, *Performance Theory*, rev. ed. (New York: Routledge, 1988). Chapter 3 is particularly relevant.

4. In response to the excitement Finley generated in sold-out performances that summer and fall, the *Village Voice Literary Supplement* (9 Oct. 1990: 19) published the text of "It's Only Art."

5. According to C. Carr ("Artful Dodging," *Village Voice* 15 June 1993: 30–31), the four artists eventually settled out of court with the NEA and finally received the grants denied them.

6. Mircea Eliade, *Myths, Dreams, and Mysteries*, trans. Philip Mairet (New York: Torchbooks-Harper, 1960) 61.

7. Marija Gimbutas, *The Language of the Goddess* (San Francisco: Harper, 1989) xix–xx.

8. *Out from Under: Texts by Women Performance Artists*, ed. Lenora Champagne (New York: Theatre Communications Group, 1990) 93–94 and 174.

9. Marlane Meyer, *Etta Jenks* in *WomensWork: Five New Plays from the Women's Project*, ed. Julia Miles (New York: Applause, 1989) 138. Hereafter to be cited in the text.

10. Gimbutas xvi.

11. For excarnation, see Gimbutas 151–57 and 211. For snake symbolism, see xix, 121, and 316–17.

12. See Theodor H. Gaster, ed., *The New Golden Bough: A New Abridgment of the Classic Work by Sir James George Frazer* (New York: Criterion, 1959) 356–66; Robert Graves, *The Greek Myths*, vol. 1 (New York: George Braziller, 1957) 92–96; and Pamela Berger, *Goddess Obscured: Transformation of the Grain Protectress from Goddess to Saint* (Boston: Beacon, 1986).

13. Wendy Wasserstein, *The Heidi Chronicles* in *The Heidi Chronicles and Other Plays* (1990; New York: Vintage-Random, 1991) 171. Hereafter to be cited in the text.

14. Perhaps the rocker scene as myth explains why Wasserstein adds a chronicling image to the published text. In the Playwrights Horizons production of the play that I saw, with Joan Allen as Heidi, the lights came down on mother singing to daughter in the apartment. A club edition of the play published shortly thereafter—*The Heidi Chronicles* (Garden City, NY: The Fireside Theatre, n.d.)—contains the text of that production. The text from which I quote adds an image as the audience exits: "*a slide of* Heidi *triumphantly holding Judy in front of a museum banner for a Georgia O'Keefe retrospective*" (249). With the myth having been revealed, mother and daughter can begin to act on the values realistically.

15. Sue-Ellen Case has collected seven of the group's performance texts in *Split Britches: Lesbian Practice/Feminist Performance* (New York: Routledge, 1996).

16. Maria Irene Fornes, *Mud* in *Maria Irene Fornes: Plays* (New York: PAJ, 1986) 15. Hereafter to be cited in the text.

2. Other Minority Theatres

1. Brian Friel, *Philadelphia, Here I Come!* in *Selected Plays: Brian Friel,* Irish Drama Selections 6 (Washington: Catholic U of America P, 1988) 97. Hereafter to be cited in the text.

2. David Henry Hwang, *FOB* in *FOB and Other Plays* (New York: Plume-NAL, 1990) 32. Hereafter to be cited in the text.

3. Hwang, Introduction, *FOB and Other Plays* x–xv.

4. Suzan-Lori Parks, quoted in the introduction to *Women on the Verge: Seven Avant-Garde American Plays*, ed. Rosette C. Lamont (New York: Applause, 1993) xxxi.

5. Suzan-Lori Parks, *The Death of the Last Black Man in the Whole Entire World* in *Women on the Verge* 241. Hereafter to be cited in the text.

6. August Wilson, *Joe Turner's Come and Gone* (New York: Plume-NAL, 1988). Hereafter to be cited in the text.

7. Kim Pereira's *August Wilson and the African-American Odyssey* (Urbana: U of Illinois P, 1995) is an invaluable guide through Wilson's multilayered texts. See in particular his discussion of the blood-letting scene (80–83).

8. A newspaper interview quotes Wilson as saying, "'I am more and more concerned with pointing out the differences between blacks and whites, as opposed to pointing out the similarities.'" He then goes on to itemize some of the cultural differences. See Mervyn Rothstein, "Round Five for a Theatrical Heavyweight," *New York Times* 15 Apr. 1990, sec. 2: 8.

9. August Wilson, *The Piano Lesson* (New York: Plume-NAL, 1990) 66. Hereafter to be cited in the text.

10. August Wilson, *Two Trains Running* (New York: Plume-NAL, 1993) 103. Hereafter to be cited in the text.

11. For the image of Hambone as the play's source and center, see Rothstein 8.

12. Jessica Hagedorn, narrative autobiography, *Tenement Lover* in *Between Worlds: Contemporary Asian-American Plays*, ed. Misha Berson (New York: Theatre Communications Group, 1990) 79.

3. Exemplary Selves in History

1. Roger Shattuck, *The Innocent Eye: On Modern Literature and the Arts* (New York: Farrar, 1984) 114.

2. André Bishop, introduction, *Plays from Playwrights Horizons* (New York: Broadway Play Publishing, 1987) vi.

3. Richard Nelson, *Conjuring an Event* in *An American Comedy and Other Plays*, ed. Bonnie Marranca and Gautam Dasgupta (New York: PAJ, 1984) 139. Hereafter to be cited in the text. I have retained Nelson's eccentric punctuation, even when a line is followed by ten exclamation points.

4. For a succinct analysis of the imagery of eating and digesting, see Erich Neumann, *The Origins and History of Consciousness*, trans. R. F. C. Hull, Bollingen Series XLII (1954; Princeton:/Bollingen Paperbacks-Princeton UP, 1973) 30 and 336.

5. Richard Nelson, *Jungle Coup* in *Plays from Playwrights Horizons* 240. Hereafter to be cited in the text.

6. I cannot tell whether the misspelling of Earhart is intentional or a typographical error. Lindbergh also is misspelled.

7. Richard Nelson, *The Vienna Notes* in *Word Plays: An Anthology of New American Drama*, ed. Bonnie Marranca and Gautam Dasgupta (New York: PAJ, 1980) 74. Hereafter to be cited in the text.

8. Richard Nelson, *Two Shakespearean Actors* (London: Faber and Faber, 1990) 102.

9. Quentin Anderson, *Making Americans: An Essay on Individualism and Money* (New York: Harcourt, 1992) 79.

10. A. R. Gurney, *The Dining Room* in *Plays from the Contemporary American Theater*, ed. Brooks McNamara (New York: Mentor-NAL, 1988) 297. Hereafter to be cited in the text.

11. A. R. Gurney, *The Middle Ages* (New York: Dramatists Play Service, 1978) 43. Hereafter to be cited in the text.

12. A. R. Gurney, *The Perfect Party* in *The Cocktail Hour and Two Other Plays* (New York: Plume-NAL, 1989) 191. Hereafter to be cited in the text.

13. Charles L. Mee Jr., *The Investigation of the Murder in El Salvador* in *Word Plays 4* (New York: PAJ, 1984) 94. Hereafter to be cited in the text.

14. Eric Overmyer, *Native Speech* in *Word Plays 3* (New York: PAJ, 1984) 156. Hereafter to be cited in the text.

15. Frank Rich, quoted on the cover of *The Colored Museum* (New York: Broadway Play Publishing, 1987).

16. George C. Wolfe, *The Colored Museum* 1. Hereafter to be cited in the text.

17. *The Divine Comedy of Dante Alighieri*, trans. with comment by John D. Sinclair, 3 vols. (1939–1946; New York: Oxford UP, 1961). Hereafter to be cited in the text.

18. Adrienne Rich, *On Lies, Secrets, and Silence: Selected Prose, 1966–1978* (New York: Norton, 1979) 35.

4. Exemplary Selves in Hell

1. David Rabe, *Hurlyburly*, rev. ed. (New York: Grove Weidenfeld, 1991) 200. Hereafter to be cited in the text.

2. David Mamet, *Glengarry Glen Ross* (New York: Grove, 1984) 16. Hereafter to be cited in the text.

3. Erich Neumann, *The Origins and History of Consciousness* 27–28.

4. David Mamet, *Speed-the-Plow* (New York: Grove, 1988) 56. Hereafter to be cited in the text.

5. Toby Silverman Zinman, "Jewish Aporia: The Rhythm of Talking in Mamet," *Theatre Journal* 44.2 (1992): 215.

6. David Mamet, *Oleanna* (New York: Vintage-Random, 1993) 48. Hereafter to be cited in the text.

5. Interactive Selves

1. Ted Tally, *Terra Nova* (London: Samuel French, 1981) x and 54. Hereafter to be cited in the text.

2. *Scott's Last Expedition: The Personal Journals of Captain R. F. Scott, R.N., C.V.O., on His Journey to the South Pole*, ed. Leonard Huxley (New York: Dodd, 1925) 476. Hereafter to be cited in the text.

3. Wilson kept his own journal. Although his entry for February 17, 1912, merely records Evans's death, his entry for the preceding day explains the petty officer's collapse that day as having "much to do with the fact that he has never been sick in his life and is now helpless with his hands frost-bitten." *Edward Wilson, Diary of the Terra Nova Expedition to the Antarctic: 1910–1912*, ed. H. G. R. King (New York: Humanities, 1972) 243.

4. Huxley, *Scott's Last Expedition* 499, n.26.

5. *Poems by Wallace Stevens*, selected by Samuel French Morse (New York: Vintage-Random, 1959) 23.

6. Tina Howe, *Painting Churches* in *Plays from the Contemporary American Theater* 395. Hereafter to be cited in the text.

7. Len Jenkin, *Gogol* in *Theatre of Wonders: Six Contemporary American Plays*, ed. Mac Wellman (Los Angeles: Sun & Moon, 1985) 5. Hereafter to be cited in the text.

8. David Magarshack, introduction, *Dead Souls*, trans. Magarshack (London: Penguin, 1961) 11.

9. Magarshack 7.

10. André M. Weitzenhoffer, "Mesmer, Franz Anton," *International Encyclopedia of the Social Sciences* (New York: Macmillan, 1968).

11. Charles Dickens, *Bleak House* (New York: Signet Classic-NAL, 1964) 165.

12. Wolfram von Eschenbach, *Parzival*, trans. A. T. Hatto (London: Penguin, 1980) 120. Hereafter to be cited in the text. Since this is a prose translation, the citations are to page numbers. A division Hatto calls "chapter," unlike other translators, who call it "book."

13. *Wolfram von Eschenbach: Parzival*, ed. Gottfried Weber (Darmstadt: Wissenschaftliche Buchgesellschaft, 1963) V.235,21–24.

14. *The Parzival of Wolfram von Eschenbach*, trans. Edwin H. Zeydel with Bayard Quincy Morgan, University of North Carolina Studies in the Germanic Languages and Literatures 5 (1951; New York: AMS, 1969) V.235,21–24.

15. See Peter Happé's introduction, *English Mystery Plays: A Selection*, ed. Happé (1975; London: Penguin, 1985) 24–27.

16. Eric Overmyer, *On the Verge* (New York: Broadway Play Publishing, 1986) 75. Hereafter to be cited in the text.

17. Beth Henley, *Crimes of the Heart* in *Plays from the Contemporary American Theater*, ed. Brooks McNamara (New York: Mentor-NAL, 1988) 284.

18. Beth Henley, *The Miss Firecracker Contest* in *Beth Henley: Four Plays* (Portsmouth, NH: Heinemann, 1992) 129. Hereafter to be cited in the text.

6. Experimental Selves

1. For the tenets of naturalistic theatre, see the extract from Èmile Zola's *Naturalism in the Theatre* in *The Theory of the Modern Stage: An Introduction to Modern Theatre and Drama*, ed. Eric Bentley (New York: Penguin, 1976) 351–72.

2. Deborah R. Geis, "Wordscapes of the Body: Performative Language as *Gestus* in Maria Irene Fornes's Plays," *Theatre Journal* 42.3 (1990): 299. Geis incorporates her argument about *Mud* in *Postmodern Theatric[k]s: Monologue in Contemporary American Drama* (Ann Arbor: U of Michigan P, 1993) 126–29.

3. Charles Ludlam, *Medea* in *The Complete Plays of Charles Ludlam* (New York: Perennial-Harper, 1989) 807.

4. Charles Ludlam, *The Mystery of Irma Vep* in *The Complete Plays of Charles Ludlam* 795.

5. *Ridiculous Theatre: Scourge of Human Folly*, edited by Steven Samuels (New York: Theatre Communications Group, 1992), is a compilation of Ludlam's nondramatic writings. For his position on polysexuality, his theatre's reinventing a multiplicity of discarded conventions, and the need for harmony, see pp. 54, 76, and 249.

6. David Savran, interview with Elizabeth LeCompte, *Breaking the Rules: The Wooster Group* (New York: Theatre Communications Group, 1988) 51.

7. Eugene O'Neill, *The Emperor Jones* in *Nine Plays by Eugene O'Neill* (New York: Modern Library, 1941) 7.

8. Savran, 55.

9. *Unbalancing Acts: Foundations for a Theater*, ed. Ken Jordan (New York: Pantheon-Random, 1992) 108. Hereafter to be cited in the text.

10. About an earlier Foreman play, the 1975 *Pandering to the Masses: A Misrepresentation*, Bonnie Marranca writes that it is a "consciousness-raising piece—a teaching play—whose goal is to make audience members aware of their moment-by-moment existence in the theatre." *The Theatre of Images*, ed. Marranca (New York: PAJ, 1977) 7.

11. In *Unbalancing Acts* Foreman asserts, "I have always felt that I'm a closet religious writer . . ." (5).

12. For a nondramatic statement of his theatre's objective to discover what stands under experience, see Foreman's "Manifesto III," in *Richard Foreman: Plays and Manifestos*, ed. Kate Davy (New York: New York UP, 1976) 186–92. David's dramatic counterpart is the character played by Will Patton in *What Did He See?* in *Unbalancing Acts* 271–305.

13. John Jesurun, *White Water* in *On New Ground: Contemporary Hispanic-American Plays*, ed. M. Elizabeth Osborn (New York: Theatre Communications Group, 1987) 76. Hereafter to be cited in the text.

7. Reconciling Selves

1. Craig Lucas, *Blue Window* (New York: Samuel French, 1985) 70. Hereafter to be cited in the text.

2. William Harris, "Mortality Is the Real Lead in Lucas Play," *New York Times* 11 Mar. 1990, sec. 2: 5+.

3. Craig Lucas, *Reckless* (New York: Dramatists Play Service, 1989) 7. Hereafter to be cited in the text.

4. I am sure that the fact that Lucas was an adopted infant abandoned by his mother has a bearing on the play, but it does not guarantee that Rachel abandoned her children or even has children. For a sketch of Lucas's life, see the Harris interview, note 2.

5. James Joyce, *Ulysses*, corrected and reset ed. (New York: Vintage-Random, 1966) 34.

6. Craig Lucas, *Prelude to a Kiss* (New York: Plume-NAL, 1991). Hereafter to be cited in the text.

7. Sam Shepard, *The Tooth of Crime* in *Sam Shepard: Seven Plays* (New York: Bantam, 1981) 210. Hereafter to be cited in the text.

8. The pilot's equation in "Icarus's Mother," E equals MC squared, which is the cornerstone of modern physics, expresses the interaction that is the creative process.

Imagination, or energy, and objective reality, or mass, must interconvert for the transformation that is art. Of the three sustained monologues in this one-act play, the middle one unites the two poles. In verbal and visual images, two women recreate for their audience their earlier interaction on the beach with the pilot above them.

9. Sam Shepard, *Angel City* in *Fool for Love and Other Plays* (New York: Bantam, 1984) 95. Hereafter to be cited in the text.

10. Sam Shepard, *Curse of the Starving Class* in *Sam Shepard: Seven Plays* 178–79. Hereafter to be cited in the text.

11. For Shepard's discussion of the traditional meaning of myth and its loss, see Carol Rosen, interview with Sam Shepard, "Silent Tongues: Sam Shepard's Explorations of Emotional Territory," *Village Voice* 4 Aug. 1992: 32–41.

12. See, for example, Doris Auerbach, "Who Was Icarus's Mother?: The Powerless Mother Figures in the Plays of Sam Shepard" in *Sam Shepard: A Casebook*, ed. Kimball King (New York: Garland, 1988) 53.

13. Tucker Orbison, "Mythic Levels in Shepard's *True West*," *Essays on Modern American Drama*, ed. Dorothy Parker (Toronto: U of Toronto P, 1987) 188–202. See also William Kleb, "Worse than Being Homeless: *True West* and the Divided Self," *American Dreams: The Imagination of Sam Shepard*, ed. Bonnie Marranca (New York: PAJ, 1981) 117–25.

14. Sam Shepard, *True West* in *Sam Shepard: Seven Plays* 32.

15. San Shepard, *Fool for Love* in *Fool for Love and Other Plays* 48. Hereafter to be cited in the text.

16. Sam Shepard, *A Lie of the Mind* (New York: Plume-NAL, 1987) 28. Hereafter to be cited in the text.

17. For a chart of the play's structural integrity, see Ron Mottram, "Exhaustion of the American Soul: Sam Shepard's *A Lie of the Mind*" in *Sam Shepard: A Casebook* 95–106.

18. Lynda Hart, *Sam Shepard's Metaphorical Stages*, Contributions in Drama and Theatre Studies 22 (Westport, Ct: Greenwood, 1987) 109.

19. Gregory W. Lanier, "Two Opposite Animals: Structural Pairing in Sam Shepard's *A Lie of the Mind*," *Modern Drama* 34.3 (1991): 410–21.

8. On the Eve of the Millennium

1. Eugene O'Neill, letter to George Jean Nathan, *Intimate Notebooks* (New York: Knopf, 1932); *O'Neill and His Plays: Four Decades of Criticism*, ed. Oscar Cargill, et al. (New York: New York UP, 1961) 115.

2. John Guare, *Six Degrees of Separation* (New York: Vintage-Random, 1990) 3. Hereafter to be cited in the text.

3. See Jeanie Kasindorf, "Six Degrees of Impersonation," *New York Magazine* 25 Mar. 1991: 40–46.

4. Kasindorf's article contains an interview with the young man, David Hampton, in which he contrasts what actually happened in the apartment that is the basis of the stage apartment with what happens in the play. Although he admits that he did phone a friend to spend the night with him, he denies any frenzy. "We were found in the bed the next morning sleeping back to back. There was none of this scene about somebody running around the house naked with their male organs dangling within public eyesight. It's totally farfetched" (44).

5. Euripides, *The Bacchae*, trans. William Arrowsmith (Chicago: U of Chicago P, 1960) vol. 4 of *The Complete Greek Tragedies*, ed. David Grene and Richmond Lattimore. Hereafter to be cited in the text.

6. William Arrowsmith, introduction, *The Bacchae*, trans. Arrowsmith 530–31.

7. Arthur Evans, *The God of Ecstasy: Sex Roles and the Madness of Dionysos* (New York: St. Martin's, 1988) 61.

8. E. R. Dodds, introduction, *Bacchae*, ed. E. R. Dodds, 2nd ed. (1960; Oxford: Clarendon, 1986) xi–xx. See also the appendix, "Maenadism," to his *The Greeks and the Irrational* (Berkeley: U of California P, 1951) 270–82.

9. Philip Vellacott, introduction, *Euripides: The Bacchae and Other Plays*, trans. Vellacott, 2nd ed. (London: Penguin, 1973) 31. See also Evans: "Hence the phrase *euhios daimon*, 'the God of Ecstasy,' connotes the sudden presence of a supernatural force that leads people into altered states of consciousness through group ritual" (57).

10. Evans 19–38.

11. See Wassily Kandinsky, *Concerning the Spiritual in Art*, trans. M. T. H. Sadler (1914; New York: Dover, 1977) 26 and 32.

12. See Wassily Kandinsky, "On the Question of Form," *The Blaue Reiter Almanac*, ed. Wassily Kandinsky and Franz Marc, new documentary edition by Klaus Lankheit (1974; New York: Da Capo, n.d.) 149–53.

13. Dodds, introduction, *Bacchae* xvi.

14. David Henry Hwang, narrative autobiography, *As the Crow Flies* in *Between Worlds* 95.

15. According to the program, the remarks "were adapted from a keynote address delivered at a Cultural Diversity Workshop convened by Theatre Communications Group in Los Angeles May 1, 1993." The program goes on to note that an earlier version of the excerpted remarks appeared in *American Theatre*.

16. Mac Wellman, *Sincerity Forever* in *Grove New American Theater*, ed. Michael Feingold (New York: Grove, 1993) 102. Hereafter to be cited in the text.

17. Both editor Feingold and Wellman himself in correspondence prefaced to the script put the play in the context of the controversy surrounding the National Endowment for the Arts' denial of grants to support the projects of artists whose political, sexual, or aesthetic orientations do not conform to the dominant culture. This is the issue that Finley made the opening section of her performance of *We Keep Our Victims Ready* in New York in 1990. See editor's note, *Sincerity Forever* in *Grove New American Theater* 85–96.

18. José Rivera, *Marisol* in *American Theatre* July–Aug. 1993: 33. Hereafter to be cited in the text.

19. *Poems by Wallace Stevens* 8.

20. Tad Simons, "José Rivera," *American Theatre* July-Aug. 1993: 46. These statements clarify his earlier position on magical realism in the narrative autobiography to *The House of Ramon Iglesia* in *On New Ground* 194.

21. Karen Fricker, "Another Playwright Confronts an Angel and the Apocalypse," *New York Times* 16 May 1993, sec. 2: 7.

22. Tony Kushner, *Angels in America, Part One: Millennium Approaches* (New York: Theatre Communications Group, 1993) 10–11. Hereafter to be cited in the text.

23. Don Shewey, interview with Tony Kushner, "Tony Kushner's Sexy Ethics," *Village Voice* 20 Apr. 1993: 32.

24. Tony Kushner, *Angels in America, Part Two: Perestroika* (New York: Theatre Communications Group, 1994) 13. Hereafter to be cited in the text.

25. Don Shewey, interview with Tony Kushner, "Tony Kushner's Sexy Ethics" 31.

26. For a frame of reference for the term "postmodernism" as it relates to performance in the arts, see Marvin Carlson, *Performance: A Critical Introduction* (New York: Routledge, 1996) 123–43. For a frame of reference for the term as it relates to theatre, see Jon Whitemore, *Directing Postmodern Theater: Shaping Signification in Performance* (Ann Arbor: U of Michigan P, 1994) 3–4. For a frame of reference for the term as it relates to cultural and intellectual history, see *From Modernism to Postmodernism: An Anthology*, ed. Lawrence E. Cahoone (Oxford: Blackwell, 1996) 1–3.

Conclusion

1. Julian Beck, *The Life of the Theatre: The Relation of the Artist to the Struggle of the People* (1972; New York: Limelight, 1986) 70–71.

Index

Abingdon Square (Fornes), 29
abstractions, 192–93
acting, 59–60, 90–91, 134–37; audience and, 219–22
action: exterior, 103–4, 110; imagination and, 129–30; interior, 104, 106–7, 109–10, 121, 143, 154, 161
African-American theatre (*see also* minorities; *individual plays*): diaspora, 36; heritage and, 41–43, 76–81, 141; new-world experience and, 72, 74, 80–81; song tradition, 36–41
America, family as metaphor for, 173–81, 184–85
American Dream, 63–66, 82–83, 173–79
American literature, self in, 61–62
American theatre, creation of, 221–22
Anderson, Quentin, 61
Angel City (Shepard), 187; archetypes and, 171–72, 174, 179, 182, 183
Angels in America, Part One: Millennium Approaches (Kushner), 211–15, 221
Angels in America, Part Two: Perestroika (Kushner), 215–18
antinomies, 113–14, 119, 157–58, 172; accumulation of meaning, 178, 181, 183
archetypes, 171–72, 174, 179, 182, 183
Arrowsmith, William, 192–93
assimilation: development of self and, 51–54; divided self and, 102, 121, 125–26; minorities and, 62, 68–69, 71, 80, 205, 209–11
Auden, W. H.: "Leap Before You Look," 161
audience (*see also* histrionic sensibility), 28, 157, 167–68, 209; appearance and, 59; dual perspective and, 5, 44; empathy and, 150; frame of reference, 141; images required by, 95–97; imagination of, 218; magical realism and, 214; myth and, 24–25; participation of, 3, 5, 122, 141–42, 150, 219–22; perception of, 21, 22, 142–43, 220; as reality check, 52–55, 56; rebirth and, 124; satire and, 57
Author's Confession (Gogol), 114

Bacchae (Euripides), 190–91, 194, 196, 199–201
Beck, Julian, 219
Beckett, Samuel: *Waiting for Godot,* 89, 108
Berman, Paul Schiff, 156
Bey, Twilight, 204, 205
Bishop, André, 48
Bleak House (Dickens), 116, 123–24
Blue Window (Lucas), 159–61, 163–66
body: government as, 6–8, 10; nature and, 5–10; as site of text, 2, 5
Body of God, The (Living Theatre), 219–22
Brace Up! (Wooster Group), 137–38, 140

Carlos, Laurie, 10–11
characterization, 133–38; archetypes and, 171–72, 174, 179, 182, 183; creation of self and, 173, 180, 182
Chekhov, Anton: *Three Sisters,* 137
Christianity, 37, 38, 74, 79; Christ figures, 69, 116–17, 120–23, 148
circle imagery, 17–18
Cold Harbor (Mabou Mines collective), 131–32, 138
collage effect, 137–38, 141
Colored Museum, The (Wolfe): heritage and, 76–81; new-world experience and, 72, 74, 80–81; satire in, 76–77, 80; visionary experience and, 73, 79–81

Index

comedy, 54, 66, 95, 127–28, 192

Commedia (Dante), 73–78, 106

community (*see also* interactive self; multiculturalism; old-world/new-world cultures), 11–12, 17–18, 41–44, 70; disunity and, 21, 22, 25, 124; reconnection and, 109; rites of, 193–95, 199, 203, 219–22

Conduct of Life, The (Fornes), 29

confiscation, 6, 14, 16–17, 38

Conjuring an Event (Nelson), 48–53, 61, 92, 101, 128, 173; modes of experience in, 48–49

conscious/unconscious minds: conjuring *vs.* reporting and, 48–52; impulses and, 142–44, 149–51; interaction of, 115, 120, 123–27; as source of plays, 142, 144

Contemporary Arts Center, 4

content *vs.* form, 19–22, 75–76, 85–86, 94, 95

cosmic disorder, 211–12

costuming, 17–18, 40, 136, 156, 202, 203, 206

creation of self (*see also* conscious/unconscious minds; fabrication of self): characterization and, 173, 180, 182; language and, 68–71; as ongoing, 151; psychological growth and, 50–51, 55; structure and, 53–54, 59

Crimes of the Heart (Henley), 127–28

Crossroads Theatre, 72

culture (*see also* dominant culture; multiculturalism; old-world/new-world cultures): context of, 34, 40–41, 47, 87, 127–28; decline of, 63–65; as requiring teaching, 17, 23

Cure, The (Foreman) (*see also* conscious/unconscious minds; Grail symbolism), 142–51

Curse of the Starving Class (Shepard), 174–79

Dafoe, Willem, 138, 140–41

Dante: *Commedia*, 73–78, 106

Dead Souls (Gogol), 114

death: deity and, 10, 208–11; excarnation, 14, 15; imagery of, 10, 30, 35–36; interaction with, 217–18; longing for, 88; pornography as, 15–16; rebirth and, 9–10, 14, 37–38, 124; spirituality and, 86, 94–96; of tradition, 110–12

Death of the Last Black Man in the Whole Entire World (Parks), 35

deconstruction, 138–41, 217, 221

deity: celebrities as, 191–92; Chinese, 32–34; death and, 10, 208–11; dominant culture as, 1, 6; goddess symbolism, 9, 14–15, 25–26, 30; minority culture and, 25–26, 32–33, 41, 208; old-world *vs.* new-world, 80–81; O'Neill's, 208, 209; science and materialism as, 85, 87–88; substitution of, 101; television as, 87–88; WASP, 64

dematerialization, 14–16

Dickens, Charles: *Bleak House,* 116, 123–24

Dining Room, The (Gurney), 62–64, 66

Dionysus, cult of, 190–95

divided self, 1, 21–22; conjuring/reporting and, 48–50; family as image of, 173–74, 177–85, 188, 196–97; interactive self and, 115, 117, 119, 122–23; structure and, 53–54

Dodds, E. R., 194, 196, 199

dominant culture (*see also* government): breakup of, 47; as deity, 1, 6; exemplary self and, 62; language and, 68; monolithic standard of, 221; woman's place in, 6

dramaturgy, 139–41, 184–85; alienating strategies, 150; interaction, 212, 214; plot continuity, 145

dream imagery, 161–62, 163, 209, 213–14

dual perspective, 5, 44, 133, 136

Eastern Standard (Greenberg), 83–84

Edwardians, The (Priestley), 110

Eliot, T. S.: *Waste Land, The,* 116, 121

emptiness, 92–96, 98, 100; humanity and, 107–10, 132

entrepreneurship, 42, 44

epiphanies, 28, 202

Etta Jenks (Meyer), 12–16, 65

Euripides, 134, 190–91

Eurocentrism, 6–8, 11

Evans, Arthur, 193, 195

Evans, Edgar, 103

Everything That Rises Must Converge (Jesurun), 157

Index

exemplary self (*see also* history; histrionic sensibility; interactive self), 61, 98; aggrandizing culture and, 172–73; connection and, 87–88, 112–13; imperial *vs.* hypertrophied, 52, 61; interactive scenes and, 69–70, 87–88; as masculine, 181; metaphor and, 71

existence, purpose of, 85–86

experience (*see also* community): impulses and, 148–50; modes of, 48–49

experimental theatre: Ontological-Hysteric Theater, 142–44, 150, 217; Ridiculous Theatrical Company, 133–37, 144, 217; Spin Theater, 153, 155–56, 157; Wooster Group, 137–40, 144, 145, 217

explosive energy, imagery of, 49, 51, 53–55

fabrication of self (*see also* creation of self), 82–84, 86, 92, 95, 101, 139, 141

facade, concept of, 86–88, 92

family: disintegration of, 196–97; as metaphor for America, 173–81, 184–85; parenting principle, 178–81

farce, 83, 134–35

femaleness/femininity: contemporary image of, 23–24; interaction and, 22, 178, 180–81, 183–85; three stages of, 15; traditional values, 19–20

feminist heritage, 17–20, 25–26, 87

feminist performance art, 5, 10–11

Field, Joanna, 147–48

Film Is Evil: Radio Is Good (Foreman), 144, 149

Finley, Karen: *Modern Prayers,* 3; *Shock Treatment,* 3; *We Keep Our Victims Ready,* 1–10, 16, 23, 202, 219

Fitzgerald, F. Scott: *Great Gatsby, The,* 83

FOB (Hwang), 32–36, 38, 62, 76, 83

Fool for Love (Shepard), 181–83, 187

For Colored Girls Who Have Considered Suicide When the Rainbow Is Enuf (Shange), 10, 11, 17–18, 30, 76–77, 79

Foreman, Richard, 142, 161, 228n10; as religious writer, 148–49, 228n11. Works: *Cure, The,* 142–51; *Film Is Evil: Radio Is Good,* 144, 149; *Miss Universal Happiness,* 142; *Unbalancing Acts,* 142, 147, 150, 228n11

form *vs.* content, 19–22, 75–76, 85–86, 94, 95

Fornes, Maria Irene: *Abingdon Square,* 29; *Conduct of Life, The,* 29; *Mud,* 26–30, 133

Friel, Brian: *Philadelphia, Here I Come,* 31–32

"Funnyhouse of a Negro" (Kennedy), 76

Geis, Deborah R., 133

gender identity, 136, 152, 155

Gimbutas, Marija, 9, 14

Glass, Philip, 131

Glengarry Glen Ross (Mamet), 89–93, 98

Gogol (Jenkin), 113–24, 145, 204; psychological dimension of, 123; quest theme in, 115–21

Gogol, Nikolai, 113–14

government (*see also* dominant culture): denial of expression, 4–6, 10; Eurocentrism and, 6–7; as external political body, 6–8, 10

Grail symbolism, 66, 117, 118, 145–51; imagination and, 113, 120–21, 123–24

Great Gatsby, The (Fitzgerald), 83

Greek myth, 12–14, 190–93

Greenberg, Richard: *Eastern Standard,* 83–84

Guare, John: *Six Degrees of Separation,* 189–203, 204, 208, 230n4

Gurney, A. R.: *Dining Room, The,* 62–64, 66; *Middle Ages, The,* 64–66, 83, 113, 123; *Perfect Party, The,* 66, 82–83, 221

Hairy Ape, The (O'Neill), 49

Hart, Lynda, 187

healing: imagination as, 163, 168; interactive self and, 113, 119–20, 122–23, 129–30, 217–18; love and, 186–87

Heidi Chronicles, The (Wasserstein), 11, 16–25, 42–43, 65, 87; feminist heritage in, 17–20, 25–26; prologues, 21–22, 23; published text, 224n14; structure, 17, 20–21; surrogate playwright in, 23–25

hell, imagery of, 93–94, 101; heritage and, 73–74, 77–79; imagination and, 121; life choices and, 75–76

Helms, Jesse, 3, 4, 6, 7

Index

Henley, Beth: *Crimes of the Heart,* 127–28; *Miss Firecracker Contest, The,* 129–30

heritage: African-American, 41–43, 76–81, 141; feminist, 17–20, 25–26, 87

history (*see also* exemplary self): freedom from, 163–65, 215–16; imagination and, 113; reconciling selves and, 163–65, 173–74, 177, 182, 205, 215–16

histrionic sensibility (*see also* audience; national self), 47, 51, 57, 59–60, 61, 130, 142, 219

Homeric Hymn II (To Demeter), 12–14

Howe, Tina: *Painting Churches,* 110–13

humanity, 107–10, 124

Hurlyburly (Rabe), 84–89, 91

Huxley, Leonard: *Scott's Last Expedition,* 105–6

Hwang, David Henry, 205; *FOB,* 32–36, 38, 62, 76, 83

Iceman Cometh, The (O'Neill), 86

idealism, 96–98

identity (*see also* creation of self; self): false, 83, 139, 141; gender, 136, 152, 155; minority, 33–34, 38, 42; possession and, 197, 199–201; switching of, 151, 153

imagination: action and, 129–30; apprehension and, 49, 54–56, 58–59; of audience, 218; Grail imagery and, 113, 120–21, 123–24; healing and, 163, 168; history and, 113; interactive self and, 112–13, 120–26, 128; language and, 125–27; as masculine, 169, 178, 180–81, 183–85, 188; new world and, 126–27; as power, 194, 199, 201; reality and, 169–74; reconciliation and, 168, 207; recreation and, 200, 228–29n8; window imagery and, 160, 161

impulses, consciousness and, 142–44, 149–51

individuality, 18–19, 150–51

ingestion metaphor, 50–51, 92–94, 101, 126

Innocent Eye, The (Shattuck), 47, 48, 55, 59, 130

interactive self (*see also* community; exemplary self), 61–62, 98; divided self and, 115, 117, 119, 122–23; emptiness and, 107–10, 132; as feminine, 180–81; healing and, 113, 119–20, 122–23, 129–30, 217–18; imagination and, 112–13, 120–26, 128

interactive theatre, 219–22

Investigation of the Murder in El Salvador, The (Mee), 67–68

I Pagliacci (Leoncavallo), 132–33

irrationality, 57–58

Jenkin, Len: *Gogol,* 113–24, 145, 204; *Limbo Tales,* 116

Jesurun, John, 161, 218; *Everything That Rises Must Converge,* 157; *White Water,* 151–57, 218

Joyce, James: *Stephen Hero,* 28; *Ulysses,* 163, 215

Jungle Coup (Nelson), 48, 52–57, 61, 69–70, 82, 95

Kandinsky, Wassily, 197–98

Kennedy, Adrienne: "Funnyhouse of a Negro," 76

Kushner, Tony: *Angels in America, Part One: Millennium Approaches,* 211–15, 221; *Angels in America, Part Two: Perestroika,* 215–16

language, 68–71; dialogue, 112; imagination and, 125–27; Jewish aporia device, 98; listener and, 88–91

Lanier, Gregory W., 187

"Leap Before You Look" (Auden), 161

LeCompte, Elizabeth, 138

Leoncavallo, Ruggiero: *I Pagliacci,* 132–33

Lesbians Who Kill (Split Britches Company), 26

Lewittes, Deborah, 156

Lie of the Mind, A (Shepard), 183–88

Limbo Tales (Jenkin), 116

Living Theatre, 219–22

Long Day's Journey into Night (O'Neill), 49

Lopez, Eduardo Ivan: *Silent Thunder, A,* 45

love, 148; risk and, 96–97, 160–61, 165–68

Lucas, Craig, 228n4; *Blue Window,* 159–61, 163–66; *Prelude to a Kiss,* 164–68, 173; *Reckless,* 161–65, 215

Ludlam, Charles: *Medea,* 134–35; *Mystery of Irma Vep, The,* 135–36

Index

Mabou Mines, 131–32, 138

Malina, Judith, 219

Mamet, David, 150, 216; *Glengarry Glen Ross,* 89–93, 98; *Oleanna,* 98–101, 108; *Speed-the-Plow,* 95–98, 101

Mapplethorpe, Robert, 4

Margolin, Deborah, 26

Marisol (Rivera), 207–11, 215

Marxism, 215

masculinity: deity and, 6–8; imagination and, 169, 178, 180–81, 183–85, 188; two environments of, 28–29

McIntyre, Dennis: *National Anthems,* 84

Medea (Euripides/Ludlam), 134–35

Mee, Charles L., Jr.: *Investigation of the Murder in El Salvador, The,* 67–68

Mencken, H. L., 184

Mesmer, Franz Anton, 114–15

"Message to the Public" (Scott), 102–5

metaphor, 70–71

metaphysical nature, 132, 137, 144, 151–52, 157, 205; twin imagery and, 174, 179, 181

Meyer, Marlane: *Etta Jenks,* 12–16, 65

Middle Ages, The (Gurney), 64–66, 83, 113, 123

minorities (*see also* African-American theatre): ascendancy of, 68–69, 71; assimilation and, 62, 68–69, 71, 80, 205, 209–11; bodies as excluded, 6–7, 10; Chinese plays, 32–35; death imagery and, 10; deity and, 25–26, 32–33, 41, 208; Eurocentric myth and, 6–7; heritage and, 41–43, 76–81, 141; identity, 33–34, 38, 42; Irish plays, 31–32; Japanese theatre, 140; old-world/new-world cultures and, 31–35, 45–47; as victims, 6–8, 202, 210

mise-en-scène, 139

Miss Firecracker Contest, The (Henley), 129–30

Miss Lonelyhearts (West), 69–70

Miss Universal Happiness (Foreman), 142

Modern Prayers (Finley), 3

monologues, 3, 37–39, 41, 91–92, 186

moral choice, 105, 108–9

motherhood, 24–25, 78

Mud (Fornes), 26–30, 133

multiculturalism (*see also* community; culture; old-world/new-world cultures), 7–9, 34–35, 205, 221

multiplicity of self, 1, 150–54, 157–58; impulses and, 136, 142, 144; national self and, 217; reconciliation and, 168; women's theatre and, 7–9, 11–12, 17–18

museum imagery, 4–5, 72–73, 110, 131–32

mystery, 122–24, 148–49

Mystery of Irma Vep, The (Ludlam), 135–36

myth: audience and, 24–25; Eurocentric, 6–7; government and, 6–8, 10; Greek, 12–14, 190–93

National Anthems (McIntyre), 84

National Endowment for the Arts (NEA), 1, 2, 230n17

national self (*see also* history; histrionic sensibility), 5, 52, 61, 130, 203, 216–17

Native Speech (Overmyer), 68–71, 125–27, 161, 204

naturalism, 131–33, 136–37, 157, 170, 172, 174, 205

NEA. *See* National Endowment for the Arts

Nelson, Richard, 59, 150, 204. Works: *Conjuring an Event,* 48–53, 53, 61, 92, 101, 128, 173; *Jungle Coup,* 48, 52–57, 61, 69–70, 82, 95; *Two Shakespearean Actors,* 61; *Vienna Notes, The,* 48, 57–61

Neumann, Erich, 93

Nevermore Theatre, 207

obscenity, 2–6, 8–9

old-world/new-world cultures (*see also* community; multiculturalism), 175, 185–86, 216; African-American, 72–74; deity and, 80–81; feminism and, 25–26, 64–66; imagination and, 126–27; minority theatres and, 31–35, 45–47

Oleanna (Mamet), 98–101, 108

omophagia, 194, 196, 198–200, 202

O'Neill, Eugene, 49, 86, 189; deity of, 208, 209. Works: *Emperor Jones, The,* 139–41; *Hairy Ape, The,* 49; *Iceman Cometh, The,* 86; *Long Day's Journey into Night,* 49

On the Verge (Overmyer), 125–27, 161

Index

Ontological-Hysteric Theater, 142–44, 150, 217
oral tradition, 44
Orbison, Tucker, 179
oreibasia, 194–96, 200, 202
Overmyer, Eric: *Native Speech,* 68–71, 125–27, 161, 204; *On the Verge,* 125–27, 161

Painting Churches (Howe), 110–13
panic theme, 53, 55–56, 59–60
Paradise Now (Living Theatre), 219
Park, Walter, 204
Parks, Suzan-Lori: *Death of the Last Black Man,* 35
Parzival, (Wolfram von Eschenbach), 113, 116–24, 144–48
perceptual fields, 142–43
Perfect Party, The (Gurney), 66, 82–83, 221
performance art, 10–11, 26, 202, 204–5; body as site of, 2–3, 5
performing *vs.* acting, 134–36
perpetual motion, 85–87
Persephone myth, 12–14
personal self (*see also* creation of self; self; subjective processes), 9, 31, 47, 60, 130
Philadelphia, Here I Come (Friel), 31–32
Piano Lesson, The (Wilson), 38–41, 62–63
Playwrights Horizons, 48
poetic quality, 144–46
pornography, 12–16, 65
postmodernism, 138–41, 217, 221
power: empowerment, 1–2, 8; imagination as, 194, 199, 201; relationships, 99–101
Prelude to a Kiss (Lucas), 164–68, 173
Priestley, J. B.: *Edwardians, The,* 110
psychological growth, 50–51, 55, 123
psychology, internal, 209–10
puns, 147, 149

quest theme (*see also* old-world/new-world cultures), 24, 30, 45–46, 115–21, 148–49, 157–58
Quinton, Everett, 135–36

Rabe, David: *Hurlyburly,* 84–89, 91
Raymond, Bill, 131, 132

reality: external, 55; as feminine, 178, 180–81, 183–85; imagination and, 169–74; visual, 144, 147, 149
rebirth, 9–10, 14, 37–38, 124
Reckless (Lucas), 161–65, 215
reconciling selves, 24–25, 211; history and, 163–65, 173–74, 177, 182, 205, 215–16; imagination and, 168, 207; interior and exterior, 161; multiplicity of self and, 168; opposition to, 173–74, 178–80, 187–88; risk and, 160–61; therapy imagery and, 162–64; twin imagery and, 169–70, 173–74
Redwood Curtain (Wilson), 45
religious right, 2–4
reporting, 48–52, 82–83
revolution, 53–55, 67–68, 210–11
Reznikov, Hanon, 219
Rich, Adrienne, 80
Ridiculous Theatrical Company, 133–37, 144, 217
Rivera, José: on internal psychology, 209; *Marisol,* 207–11, 215; on millennium, 211
role reversal, 173–74, 180, 187
Roth, Beatrice, 137–38

satire, 52, 56, 57, 61, 76–77, 80
Savran, David, 141
Scott, Robert Falcon, 102–5
Scott's Last Expedition (Huxley), 105–6
self (*see also* creation of self; divided self; fabrication of self; identity; multiplicity of self; *individual attributes of self*): in American literature, 61–62; conscious *vs.* unconscious, 48–52; education and, 27–28; expansion of, 136–37; maturing of, 21–22; modes of experience and, 48–49; as object, 82; public *vs.* private, 31–32; reunion with, 9–10; structure and, 53–55, 59; thinking *vs.* feeling, 58–60
self-absorption, 88–89
self-discovery, 23, 29–30, 109–10, 112–13
self-esteem, 85–86
Serrano, Andres, 4
set, 91–92, 110, 131–32, 152–54, 197–98, 206
Seven Imperatives of Contemporary Theatre, 219

Index

Shange, Ntozake: *For Colored Girls Who Have Considered Suicide When the Rainbow Is Enuf,* 10, 11, 17–18, 30, 76–77, 79

Shattuck, Roger: *Innocent Eye, The,* 47, 48, 55, 59, 130

Shaw, Peggy, 26

Shepard, Sam, 228–29n8; on characterization, 172; narrative technique, 182–83. Works: *Angel City,* 169–73, 187; *Curse of the Starving Class,* 174–79; *Fool for Love,* 181–83, 187; *Lie of the Mind, A,* 183–88; *Tooth of Crime, The,* 22, 169, 173; *True West,* 179–81, 187

Shewey, Don, 215

Shock Treatment (Finley), 3

Sibrian, Gladis, 204

Silent Thunder, A (Lopez), 45

Sincerity Forever (Wellman), 206–8, 211

Six Degrees of Separation (Guare), 189–203, 204, 208; Dionysus myth and, 190–93; historical basis for, 190, 230n4; Lincoln Center production, 202; motivation in, 193–94

Smith, Anna Deavere: *Twilight: Los Angeles, 1992,* 203–5, 208

"Snow Man, The" (Stevens), 107

Song of Myself (Whitman), 51, 52, 218

soul, 47, 60, 132

Speed-the-Plow (Mamet), 95–98, 101

Spin Theater, 153, 155–57

spirituality: art and, 198; death and, 86, 94–96; growth and, 95–96, 108–9, 117; illness and, 113–15, 119–20; of woman, 14–15

Split Britches, 26

Split Britches Company, 26

spokesman character, 41–44

Stephen Hero (Joyce), 28

Stevens, Wallace, 107, 208–9

subjective processes, 47, 48, 55, 58, 95, 130, 151–52

"Sunday Morning" (Stevens), 208–9

Tally, Ted: *Terra Nova,* 102–10, 112, 121, 132

television imagery, 85, 89, 95, 125; deity and, 87–88; interaction with live performers, 152–55; window imagery and, 159–61

Templeton, Fiona, 11

Terra Nova (Tally), 112, 121, 132; exterior action, 103–4, 110; historical events in, 102–3; interior action, 104, 106, 107, 109–10; structure of, 106

text, 2–3, 5; deconstruction of, 138–41

theatre as product, 139

theatre of being, 142

theatrical self (*see also* conscious/unconscious minds; creation of self; histrionic sensibility), 130, 217

Three Sisters (Chekhov), 137

Tooth of Crime, The (Shepard), 22, 169, 173

tradition, death of, 110–12

tragedy, 52, 56

transformation, agent of, 144, 146–47

True West (Shepard), 179–81, 187

Twilight: Los Angeles, 1992 (Smith), 203–5, 208

twins, imagery of, 169–70, 173–74, 178, 184–85, 188

Two Shakespearean Actors (Nelson), 61

Two Trains Running (Wilson), 41–45, 47

Ulysses (Joyce), 163, 215

Unbalancing Acts (Foreman), 142, 147, 150, 228n11

Valk, Kate, 137–38, 140–41

Vallejo, Cesar, 184

Vawter, Ron, 138

Vehr, Bill, 134, 135

Vellacott, Philip, 194

victims: empowerment and, 1–2, 8; minorities as, 6–8, 202, 210; purging of, 9–10

video, use of, 137, 138, 140

Vienna Notes, The (Nelson), 48, 57–61

visionary experiences, 73, 79–81, 152–53, 155

Waiting for Godot (Beckett), 89, 108

Wasserstein, Wendy: *Heidi Chronicles, The,* 11, 16–25, 42–43, 65, 87

Waste Land, The (Eliot), 116, 121

Weaver, Lois, 26

Webster, Jeff, 123, 138

Index

We Keep Our Victims Ready (Finley), 1–10, 16, 23, 202, 219; art as subject in, 3–5; "It's Only Art," 3; "I Was Not Expected To Be Talented," 3

Wellman, Mac: *Sincerity Forever,* 206–8, 211

West, Nathaniel: *Miss Lonelyhearts,* 69–70

White Devil, The (Webster), 123

White Water (Jesurun), 151–57, 218

Whitman, Walt: *Song of Myself,* 51, 52, 218

Wildmon, Donald, 3, 4

Wilson, August, 224n8; monologues and, 37–39, 41. Works: *Joe Turner's Come and Gone,* 35–38, 39, 44, 72–73; *Piano Lesson, The,* 38–41, 62–63; *Two Trains Running,* 41–45, 47

Wilson, Edward, 103, 226n3

Wilson, Lanford: *Redwood Curtain,* 45

window imagery, 159–65

Wolfe, George C.: career of, 71–72; *Colored Museum, The,* 71–81

Wolfram von Eschenbach: *Parzival,* 113, 116–24, 144–48

Wooster Group, 137–40, 144, 145, 217; *Brace Up!,* 137–38, 140

Worsley, Dale, 131

Zinman, Toby Silverman, 98, 100

Robert J. Andreach received his Ph.D. from New York University and has taught at a number of universities. After a stint as a theatre reviewer, he returned to full-time teaching at the U.S. Military Academy Preparatory School in New Jersey. He is the author of *Studies in Structure* and *The Slain and Resurrected God* as well as numerous articles in scholarly journals.

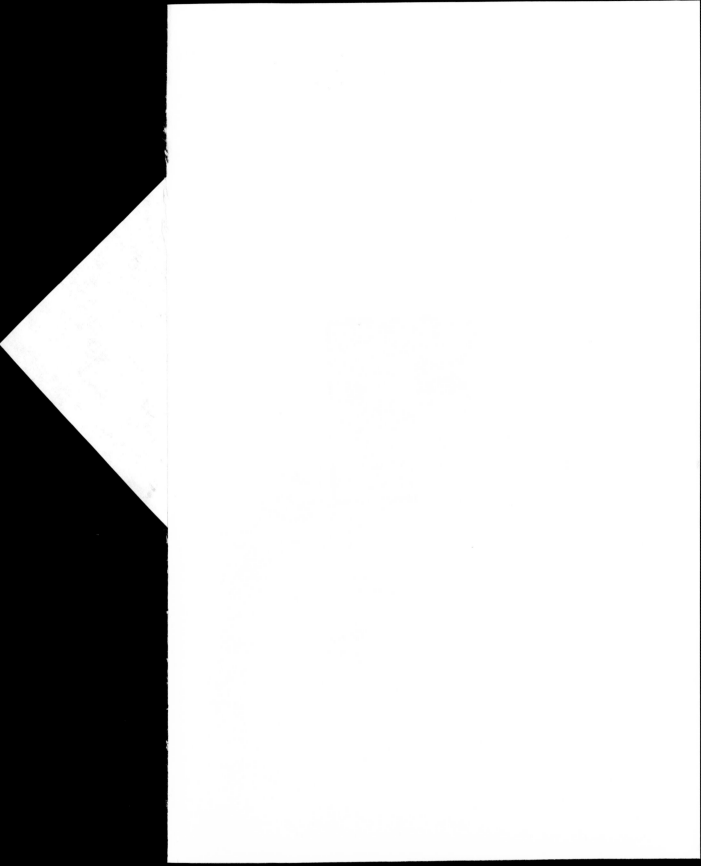

DATE D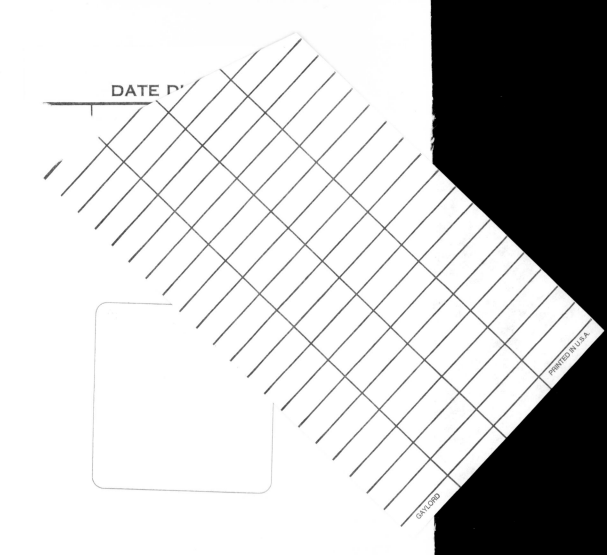